Buildings that Changed the World

Klaus Reichold

Bernhard Graf

Buildings that Changed the World

Prestel

Munich · London · New York

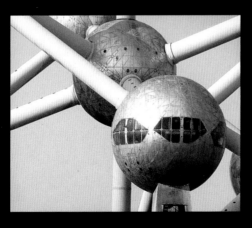

Foreword

The ancient Greek writer and chronicler Herodotus is not only famous as the "father of history." As the first known tourist he is also considered the founding father of travel literature. Herodotus traveled throughout Asia and Africa before settling in Italy where he died sometime between 425 and 420 B.C. Thanks to his descriptive talent, colorful, richly anecdotal narratives about the countries and peoples of the known world can now be enjoyed for posterity. For example, he penned an account of his visit to the Cheops pyramid in Giza in which he describes his amazement at the pains taken by the Egyptians to build such a huge structure: "If 1,600 silver talents were paid just to feed the enormous crowd of construction workers with radishes, onions, and garlic, what gigantic sums of money must have been spent on building materials?"

Herodotus was neither the first nor the last traveler to be moved by the majesty of the pyramids. They must have been incredibly astonishing to those who followed the progress of their construction as well. Today, more than 4,500 years later, nothing much has changed: year after year hundreds of thousands of tourists come to Giza to marvel at one of the seven wonders of the world.

In *Buildings that Changed the World* the Cheops pyramid is an example of one of the earliest structures selected. The reader will discover a wide range of highly diverse buildings: fortresses, castles, palaces, Roman baths and bridges, churches, and temples—even plans for entire cities, and complexes, monuments, towers, and statues. Architecture is only marginally the subject of this book. For it is not only impressive architecture alone which has fascinated man throughout the ages as if with a special type of magic. It is the stories surrounding these edifices and the events which took place in them that lend these buildings their enduring mythical auras.

It is believed that in ancient times Stonehenge was a stage for enigmatic rituals celebrating cosmic powers. In a similar way, legend surrounds the world-famous fortified monastery at Mont-Saint-Michel, which is said to have been constructed following the miraculous appearance of the archangel Michael. And according to ancient tradition, the ruined city Teotihuacán in Mexico was the birthplace of the gods. An irresistible mixture of myth and historical fact accounts for the special *spiritus loci* of these great cult places, a spirit which can only be felt when actually *in them*—the reason all of

these places still attract thousands of visitors today. For a Muslim, the pilgrimage to Mecca is the most momentous event of his life. In the Kaaba he is captivated by a shrine where, according to Islamic belief, Allah appeared to the people. A Christian might well experience something similar when standing at the spot in the Church of the Nativity in Bethlehem where "the word became flesh."

There are places where world history has been made: the ancient Greek stadium at Olympia, where every four years games were held in honor of Zeus, the father of all the gods; the cliff fortress Masada, where Romans finally exhausted the heroic resistance of the Jews; the Palatine Chapel in Aachen, where kings were crowned; St Paul's Cathedral in London where pomp and circumstance have always played a role. All of these structures continue to fascinate us. Today their walls still reverberate with the voices of those who suffered, wept, celebrated, or died there. Thus, this book conjures up the echo of times long gone by while simultaneously tracing developments: what would the world look like today without the functionalism of the Bauhaus and Le Corbusier's architectural variations, without skyscrapers in the style of the Empire State Building or visionary designs like those seen in the two Guggenheim Museums? Which buildings or structures have provided "the stuff of history" and why? And why have bitter disputes always erupted whenever major new building projects are announced?

First and foremost this book delves into cultural-historic details associated with the buildings and structures depicted. It chronicles the events which took place within their walls and the people who influenced the structures in some way—perhaps because they commissioned or oversaw their construction, criticized or simply admired the results.

This journey will take readers through 5,000 years of the history of mankind, and to all continents. Hopefully the words of the nineteenth-century English writer Leigh Hunt will ring true for all of you. Hunt wrote "Almost nothing gives us as much pleasure as the art of making connections between a place and all sorts of interesting or amusing stories. To be sure, one masters this art all the better the more knowledge one gains." It is the aim of this book to accompany you on this journey.

The Authors

Petrified Dancers
The Enigma of Stonehenge

England; three building phases between 3100 and 1100 B.C.

"A feeling of silent dread took hold of us in this bleak wilderness at the sight of a work whose creators we do not know, and which stood before us like a vision from another world."

Johanna Schopenhauer, the mother of the philosopher Arthur Schopenhauer, upon returning from a trip to England, 1858

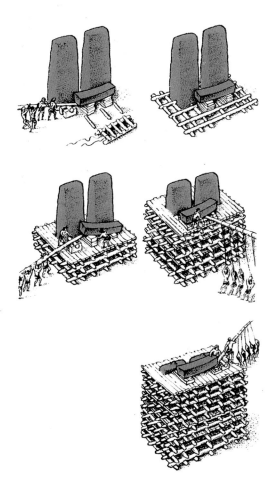

A team effort—positioning a lintel onto its supports

A mysterious shroud lies over the Druids, the priests of the Celts, who were considered to have been magicians, healers, and astrologists. In the nineteenth century, they were believed to be the builders of the magical stone circle known as Stonehenge. From a distance, this structure seems lost in the boundless, gently rolling plains. As you approach it, however, it rises up like a giant and dominates the land-scape. The Druids, it was said, erected the mighty blocks of stone around 100 B.C. in order to create "a monument to pagan Britain." Today it is an accepted fact that Stonehenge had nothing to do with Celtic priests. It is now known that the Druids did not hold their cere-monies in temples but in forest clearings, and before the time of the Celts, the pillars of Stonehenge—an ancient word originally meaning "hanging stones"—had already been exposed to the elements on this plain in southern England for thousands of years.

Who created this ceremonial ground, this mythical focus of energy? It must have been our neolithic ancestors who, around 3100 B.C., erected the first structures on this mysterious spot. They dug a circular ditch, piled up an earth-work, and made holes along a ring inside it, in which cremated human bones have since been found: the ashes of human sacrifices? Did the victims serve the purpose of making contact with the underworld? Or was Stonehenge origi-nally a burial ground, a gateway to the beyond, the scene of ritual round-dances in honor of the dead?

At Stonehenge, mystery also shrouds the ring of stones itself, which was erected in a second building phase around 2000 B.C. Was this center-stage for an archaic stone cult? Was a mother-goddess, like the one pictured on one of the pillars, worshipped here? Or did the arrangement of stones function as a type of observatory? The holes which surround the circle could be interpreted as simplified repre-sentations of the paths of the sun and moon. The circle of stones itself is also arranged ac-cording to astronomical observations: the entrance marks precisely the point at which the sun rises on the day of the summer solstice. Stonehenge—enigmatic center of astronomical knowledge, where planet constellations could be studied in order to reach conclusions about

Stonehenge was once believed to be "a monument to pagan Britain"

Was this circle of stones a neolithic observatory?

solar eclipses and the workings of the world? Or was Stonehenge the scene of a sun cult such as that familiar to us from the Greek myth of Apollo?

In any case, we know that the people who lived at the time when Stonehenge was created had grown rich through farming and trade in metals with Ireland and the Continent; over three hundred prehistoric burial mounds have been discovered near Stonehenge—more than in any other region of Britain. Back then, the center of what today is known as Salisbury Plain could have been an important trading center for bronze axes, halberds, or gold jewelry. Perhaps the massive ring of stones at Stonehenge was meant to demonstrate the power, wealth, and cultural progress of the ruling class at that time. The construction work must have demanded a prodigious amount of effort: besides the fact that some of the stone had to be transported by sea and river, at the construction site the builders had the task of erecting thirty pillars, each weighing around twenty-five tons. They were joined by lintels weighing about seven tons. Finally, at the center of the resulting circle, they erected five enormous trilithons each consisting of a pair of huge uprights, weighing up to forty-five tons, capped by a massive lintel.

Tales of old claim that the pillars of the outer ring of stones are petrified dancers who had profaned the sabbath. But this eerie legend did not prevent people a hundred years ago from borrowing hammers from the blacksmith in nearby Amesbury to chip pieces off them to take home as souvenirs.

The Measure of the Earth
The Secrets of the Cheops Pyramid

Egypt; 2551–2528 B.C.

"Inscribed on the pyramid in Egyptian characters are details of how much had been spent on radishes, onions and garlic to feed the workers. If I remember correctly, the sum mentioned by the guide was equivalent to 1,600 silver talents. What enormous sums of money must have been spent on the iron needed for the work!"

Herodotus, Greek historian and traveler in ancient Egypt, *The Construction of the Cheops Pyramid*, 5th century B.C.

"These towering pyramids have been looking down on us already for four thousand years" (Napoleon, during his campaign in Egypt, 1798)

The three pyramids of Giza have been described as "prodigiously soaring monuments to death," as "mighty bastions of deceased pharaohs," as "ladders up to heaven" and "residences of eternity." The mightiest of them all is the Cheops Pyramid, also known as the Great Pyramid. It covers an area of over 13 acres, still reaches a height of 445 feet today, and consists of approximately 2.3 million blocks of granite, each of which weighs an average of 2.75 tons. Of the seven wonders of the ancient world, the Cheops Pyramid is the only one still in existence. A series of narrow passageways and corridors in the interior leads to the Grand Gallery, which opens up unheralded and in breathtaking manner to a clear height of almost 30 feet. From here a large step leads to a vestibule that provides access to the King's Chamber, the heart of this mighty structure. On one of the narrow sides of the chamber, exactly on the central axis of the pyramid, stands the granite sarcophagus in which the wise Pharaoh Cheops was laid to rest in the year 2528 B.C. after ruling for 23 years. If one may believe ancient legend or *The Tales of 1001 Nights*, at that time the Cheops Pyramid was a gigantic treasure house full of precious objects, unbreakable glass, and iron swords that did not rust. Cheops, it was said, was buried with all his riches. The walls and ceilings of the pyramid's various chambers—including a subterranean grotto hewn in the rock as a representation of the cavernous underworld—were allegedly covered with depictions of the planets and the sciences. Today, the frescoes and treasures have gone, and the sarcophagus is empty. The first grave robbers must have plundered these chambers in ancient times. The mummy, which apparently still lay in the sarcophagus around 820 B.C., may have been dismembered and sold in small quantities to European apothecaries; for the powder obtained by crushing mummies was a coveted medicine in those days. Not everyone, however, saw in the Cheops Pyramid the tomb of an Egyptian pharaoh. According to an Arab folk legend, it was the abode of Thoth, the god of writing and chirography and patron of the sciences, who had erected the pyramid to hide literature and wisdom from the uninitiated and to save them from the Flood. The Crusaders regarded the Cheops Pyramid as a grain store that had belonged to Joseph, the son of Jacob in the Bible. Others believed it to be a refuge in times of distress. The dimensions of the pyramid, from which, it was thought, the circumference and specific gravity of the earth, the orbital periods of the planets and the precise duration of the female menstrual cycle could

be calculated, were also believed to contain secret auguries. As late as the 19th century, the English scholar John Taylor stated that the Cheops Pyramid had been built to record the dimensions of the earth. Based on this, Charles Piazzi Smyth, the Astronomer Royal of Scotland and professor of astronomy at the University of Edinburgh, claimed that the English inch was derived from a unit of measurement he called the "Pyramid inch," which Noah had used to

In the grave robbers' footsteps:
the Great Gallery inside the Cheops pyramid

build the ark and Moses the tabernacle. Modern science views the Cheops Pyramid in a less idealized way. If one considers its immense mass and visualizes its former limestone skin glistening in the sunlight, it may be seen as a symbol both of the primeval mound and of Aten, the Egyptian god of the sun and creation. Originally, however, it had probably not been planned as a pharaoh's tomb at all, but as a job-creating measure for starving peasants during the annual floods when the Nile overflowed its banks. The 20,000–25,000 men who helped raise the Cheops Pyramid are thought to have been employed on three-month contracts.

Saved from the Sand and the Sea
The Cliff Temple of Abu Simbel

Egypt; 13th century B.C.

"It took us a lot of time and effort to make the entrance wider, because our ship's crew failed to turn up to assist in the excavation work. But once we had finally managed to break through, we stepped inside.
It was clear at first glance that this was a vast complex. Our astonishment grew as we realized that here was one of the most splendid temples in the world, richly decorated with wonderful inlaid work, paintings, and colossi."

Based on Giovanni Battista Belzoni's report on the excavation of the Great Temple of Abu Simbel, 1817

Even inside the temple almost everything was buried under sand

He was actually Swiss: Johann Ludwig Burckhardt, the son of a well-to-do business-man, a native of Basel. But on his travels through Egypt, which he undertook on behalf of a scientific organization, he called himself "Sheik Ibrahim." Burckhardt was particularly interested in antiquities from the age of the Pharaohs. He could hardly have hoped to find anything completely unknown when he made a sensational discovery on March 22, 1814, near what is now the border between Egypt and Sudan. On the west bank of the Nile, 175 miles south of Aswan, he chanced upon a towering rock face covered by sand drifts many feet deep. And then it happened: "Quite by chance, just as I happened to look to the south, my eye was caught by four immense statues carved into the cliff, but which were not yet buried by the sand."

Burckhardt had stumbled upon the great cliff temple of Abu Simbel, an awesome monument

Homage to the gods of the sun and of creation—a baboon frieze from the main temple

from the history of humanity which the Italian adventurer Giovanni Battista Belzoni began to excavate in the blazing heat three years later by order of the English consul general in Egypt.

The region around Abu Simbel, now known as Nubia, was already a barren, sun-scorched land 3,300 years ago, at the time when King Ramses II had the two temples constructed to mark the thirtieth anniversary of his ascent to the throne. The people in the region needed to import grain, fruit, and vegetables from the fertile Nile valley, and so, in exchange, they allowed the Pharaohs to exploit the mineral deposits in their area. The Egyptian rulers agreed to trade and came to consider Nubia as part of

their realm. Abu Simbel was meant to demonstrate that claim.

The large temple was dedicated to the most revered Egyptian gods of the sun and of creation, a divine triumvirate believed to be reincarnated in the person of the Pharaoh himself. For this reason, four sixty-feet-high colossi of the godly Ramses decorate the temple facade, which was chiselled out of the side of the cliff. Inside, a series of fourteen rooms penetrate almost two hundred feet back into the rock, among them a hypostyle hall and the sanctuary—enormous cave-like rooms which took workers years to carve out of the solid rock. It seems to have been one of Ramses' special ambitions to create monuments to himself and his loved ones, taking advantage of all the technical possibilities of his time. Some five hundred feet from the large temple he had a second cliff shrine built for his favorite wife Nefertari: this time dedicated to the goddess

Hathor. Although far more modest in its dimensions than the large temple, it nonetheless displays magnificent statues on the facade, rising thirty feet into the sky, portraying Ramses as the father of the gods together with his favorite wife as the goddess of the heavens.

After their discovery by Johann Ludwig Burckhardt, the temples were visited by occasional travelers to the Middle East before ever-increasing crowds of tourists arrived. Abu Simbel became a construction site once again from 1963 to 1968 when its monuments were threatened by the rising water level of Lake Nasser, following the construction of the Aswan Dam. Builders embarked on one of the most spectacular and daring undertakings in engineering history: the two temples were sawed out of the rock in their entirety before being dismantled into several thousand pieces and reassembled two hundred feet higher up. The temples are now covered by a gigantic dome made of cement, rock, rubble, and sand—an artificial mountain which looks deceivingly real. Only the structure's rear wall of cement, seen on the inside, reminds the visitor of the dramatic undertaking to rescue this immensely important complex.

The four colossi of Ramses. Abu Simbel was constructed as a symbol of Egyptian reign over Nubia and to mark the 30th anniversary of Ramses' ascent to the throne

The reassembled temple is now protected by a concrete dome

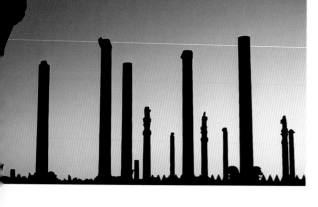

They Drank from Cups of Gold
Persepolis and the New Year's Festival

Located in present-day Iran; begun c. 520 B.C.

"Darius, the great king, King of Kings, king of all lands, son of Hystaspes, the Achæmenid. Here speaks Darius, the King: This is the kingdom I possess from the land of the Scythians beyond Sogdiana to Ethiopia, from India to Sardis, the kingdom that Ahura-Mazda presented me, the greatest of the gods. May Ahura-Mazda protect me and my kingdom."

Inscription on the foundation stone in the Throne and Audience Hall at Persepolis, c. 500 B.C.

The ambitious conqueror of Persepolis, Alexander the Great

Life in Persepolis was good. All sources agree that even the houses of common citizens "were equipped with every comfort, with beautiful furniture and decorative objects, with great quantities of silver and not a little gold."

The city, in the once fertile valley of Mervdascht, about one hundred miles east of the Persian Gulf, was once believed to have been "the richest city under the sun." But Alexander the Great, the youthful king of the Macedonians who dreamt of conquering not only the Near East but the Far East as well, was unimpressed. He called Persepolis the "most detestable city in all of Asia."

His aversion had its reasons. Persepolis was the place where Persian kings were crowned and buried, making it the most impressive of the four major cities of Persia, which was the arch enemy of the Greeks. The city was symbolic of the power of the kingdom, which stretched from present-day Turkey to India, and which stood very much in the path of Alexander's ambitious plans.

For this reason Alexander showed Persepolis no mercy when he conquered the city in 330 B.C. He plundered it and then set the torch to the city himself as an act of revenge for the Persian destruction of the Acropolis in Athens. The residential areas and their buildings were totally destroyed. But the impressive ruins of the palace still attest to the city's former grandeur.

The ruins cover an area of around 400 by 250 yards. The palace was built on a forty-five-feet-high, man-made elevation nestled against a hillside. A double staircase leads to the palace, ending in an imposing square entrance measuring twenty-five yards on each side. The unfinished entrance is all that remains of the "Gate of the People." Beyond it, raised platforms contain the remains of the palace of Darius and Xerxes, the treasury of the Harem of Xerxes, and the Hall of

a Hundred Columns, which may have been the gathering place of the army. The most impressive building is the Throne and Audience Hall, reportedly the "most majestic room in the world."

The well-preserved bas-reliefs on the parapets attest to the long forgotten ceremonies that took place here during important celebrations such as the New Year's festival. Men from Susa are shown bringing the King their tribute of weapons and tame lions. Babylonians are proffering valuable vessels and precious fabrics, along with their magnificent water buffaloes. Representatives from Lydia are leading horses to the King. There is a procession of subjects who have come bearing gifts, their tents, decorated with pennants, lining the walls of the city. They file past the king and attest to the wealth of a country that could exact tribute from delegations from Armenia, Cappadocia, Sicily, Egypt, Ethiopia, and India. The festivities depicted probably ended in a banquet for the delegates as the anonymous author described in the Old Testament Book of Esther, around 300 B.C.: "In the third year of his reign, he made a feast unto all his princes and his servants; the power of Persia and Media, the nobles and the princes of the provinces being before him: when he showed the riches of his glorious kingdom and the honor of his excellent majesty many days, even and hundred and fourscore days. And when these days were expired, the king made a feast unto all the people that were present....There were white, green and blue hangings fastened with cords of fine linen and purple to silver rings and pillars of marble: the best were of gold and silver, upon a pavement of red, and blue, and white and black marble. And they gave them drink in vessels of gold (the vessels being diverse one from another), and royal wine in abundance according to the state of the king."

The Palace of 100 Columns

The Throne and Audience Hall. Bas-reliefs on the parapets depict a procession of subjects bearing gifts to their king for the celebration of a New Year's festival

Crowned with the Branch of the Holy Tree
Olympia and the Games of Old

Greece; 6th century B.C.; destroyed 423 A.D.

"Although Cleombrotos gave up boxing, as a husband he receives blows almost worse than those dealt by Ajax and Chiron. His belligerent old wife can thrash like an Olympic champion, and he is filled with terror more than when he was in the stadium."

Gaius Lucilius, *The Boxer*, 2nd century B.C.

One of the sporting events depicted on an ancient vase

Excluded from participation in the Olympic games, women were only allowed to watch the races held in the stadium. For married women, even those were forbidden. And when the mother of a participant once disguised herself in order to circulate among the trainers and lost her outer garment in the frenzy following her son's victory, only the good reputation of her family spared her from severe punishment. Instead, the authorities ordered that, in the future, not only the athletes, but also the trainers, were to attend the games naked.

In Greece, the cult of the body and the admiration of masculine strength and skill not only has a long tradition but also a mythological paragon. According to legend, mighty Zeus himself had to wrestle his ancestors, the old Titans. Only after he had flung them into Tartarus, the deepest abyss of the underworld, could he begin his heavenly reign as the despotic patriarch of the gods. In order to honor him and symbolize his fighting spirit, the Greeks organized the Olympic games, the most important of numerous sporting events in ancient Hellas. They were held every four years at the time of the full moon and in the period after the summer solstice, sometime between July 27 and September 27. The location was Olympia, in the fertile Alphaeus valley of western Peloponnesus, the shrine of the cult of Zeus.

A sacred grove had already existed for centuries on the slopes of the Cronus Hill— among poplars, oaks, plane trees, and wild olive trees—before the cult of Zeus was founded on that spot around 1000 B.C. The first recorded games, which consisted only of races through the stadium to the altar of Zeus, took place there in 776 B.C. The winner was a man by the name of Coroibos who came from the region near Olympia. Gradually other sports were included in the games: long-distance races and demonstrations of skill with weapons, discus and spear-throwing, wrestling and boxing, horse races and chariot races, competitions for young boys, and the much-feared and often deadly *pancratium*, the so-called "universal competition," a combination of free-style wrestling and boxing. Parades and sacrifices in honor of Zeus followed the athletic contests.

During the golden age of Olympia, the crowds must have been overwhelming. Tens of thousands of spectators, including traders and performers, prostitutes and pickpockets, as well as writers and philosophers, singers and sculptors, came to the event which lasted a maximum of six days. It is said that the writer Herodotus read aloud from his books at Olympia, and in 488 or 484 B.C. the Athenian general Themistocles brought along a splendid tent which he showed off by hosting a banquet.

Informed by "holy heralds" about the dates of the games, delegations travelled to Olympia from all Greek states, even from distant colonies such as modern-day Marseilles, to take part in a truly pan-Hellenic festival uniting all of Greece. The champion was the center of attention. The simple wreath of olive branches which he wore as his trophy had no material value, but it was considered the greatest treasure that a mortal could aspire to possess. Accordingly, the winner was celebrated as a god for some time and was permitted to place a statue of himself in the shrine to the Olympian Zeus. When he returned to his native town, he was, as a rule, granted free board for the rest of his life, or generous gifts of money were lavished upon him as symbols of the community's pride. In addition he was often greeted with a triumphal procession for which even part of the town walls was torn down. People were convinced that a town which possessed such fine men had no need for fortification. And yet some cautioning voices could be heard: the dramatist Euripides, for example, believed that intellectual exercise might possibly be more important for the well-being of the state "than the strengthening of the arms and legs of athletes."

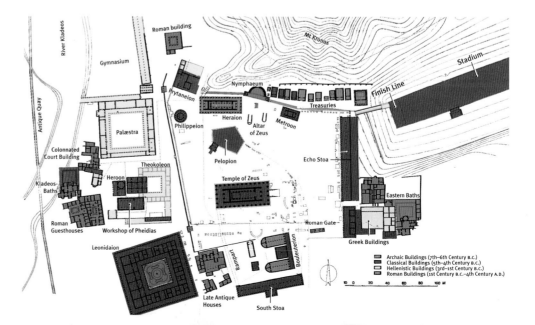

A model of Olympia prior to its destruction. The games
served to honor Zeus and to symbolize his fighting spirit

Thousands of spectators would have viewed the
competition from the lawned banks of the stadium

The stadium entrance

On Persian Rubble and Divine Splendor
The Acropolis in Athens

Greece; 448–443 B.C.
Architects: Ictinus and Callicrates

"No building project ever reaped as much criticism as the Acropolis. It was said that it had brought shame and infamy upon Athens. Other Greek cities, who had contributed to the financing of the construction work with their tax money, felt betrayed. The money should have been used to cover the costs of war, not to gild Athens, dress it up with temples, and drape it in jewels like a vain woman."

Plutarch, *The Biography of Pericles*, 105–115 A.D.

Just a short time before, the ruins were still lying in smoke and ashes: in August of the year 480 B.C. the Persians had once again invaded Athens, and pillaged, burned, and murdered. Yet not much later, after the Greeks, led by Athens, dealt the Persians two crushing defeats, all danger seemed to have been banned forever. The Athenians celebrated their victory in triumph and founded the Delian League, a naval alliance of numerous Greek cities, to secure their mutual protection in the case of future invasions. In exchange for heavy taxes paid by all citizens of the alliance, the Athenians pledged to defend any ally under military threat.

Wishing to reflect Athens' predominance in the league, the city fathers ordered the construction of impressive buildings. They were to rise above the rubble left by the Persians on the Acropolis—the former hill fortress where the kings of Athens once resided at a spot which, since time immemorial, had been dedicated to the goddess Athena. But many voices of protest rose in the face of this plan: the building project was not motivated by sincere religious devoutness, they said, but more by blasphemous dreams of worldly glory. Besides, what would the allies say? Wouldn't they feel that their taxes were being squandered on a gigantic monument to Athenian self-adoration instead of being more meaningfully invested in arming the fleet? Pericles, the "inventor of democracy" and one of the most important political thinkers in world history, who largely determined the fate of his native Athens during that period, appeased the people by explain-

ing: "the money does not belong to those who pay, but to those who receive it—as long as they honor their side of the agreement." Disregarding the fact that in the end no monies collected for the alliance were used to finance the project, it seems that Pericles' argument was finally able to convince the skeptics. The majority of enfranchised citizens were of the opinion that the new structures of the Acropolis should "be more magnificent than anything ever seen before." And so it was that, during a period of four decades, a monument was created which was truly splendid enough to honor the power of Athens, an exemplary architectural ensemble that would inspire builders throughout the ages. The crowning achievement of the Acropolis is the mighty Parthenon, which the Romantics would praise as "the most perfect structure of antiquity" for its unique harmony of proportions, and which was once ablaze with colorful frescoes, sculptures, bronze garlands, and golden shields.

The Parthenon owes its name to the goddess Athena. According to ancient belief, Zeus's daughter remained eternally chaste ("parthenos" in Greek), dedicating her life to serving her most beloved subjects. And that was how the citizens of Athens saw themselves. In the central *cella* of the Parthenon, they erected an "almost monstrous," thirty-five-foot-high effigy of "their" goddess made of gold and ivory—an overwhelming sight for anyone who approached it. Still, the Parthenon was not a temple but a treasury. Here not only the money of the city of Athens was stored but also the funds of the Delian League. The precious statue of the goddess itself was considered a financial reserve to fall back on in times of dire need. It is known that it was eventually taken to Constantinople where it was finally burned around 500 A.D.

Robbed of its most important possession, the Parthenon then became a place of worship—first as a Christian church, later as an Islamic mosque. This could not have been in the spirit of the Parthenon's builders, but things could have been worse. The nearby Erechtheum, commissioned by Pericles in honor of Erechtheus, the mythical founding father of Athens, was used as a harem during the Ottoman empire.

The Parthenon as a gunpowder storehouse; an artist's rendition of the 1687 explosion

A 1929 poster advertising a cruise to Greece

The Parthenon, built to house Athens' treasury and
the funds of the Delian League

"More splendid than anything ever seen before," the Acropolis in
all its former glory; oil painting by Leo von Klenze, 1846

Black cloths signified the night and a machine that resembled a crane helped actors playing the gods to float in the air or "return" to Olympus. However, the stage in ancient Greece was not all that perfect. The elegant solutions demanded by contemporary audiences had not yet been invented. But the apparatus for reproducing thunder and lightening was already well developed and amazingly convincing. These early beginnings do nothing to diminish the achievements of the ancient Greeks, who after all, invented theater.

A Place that Knows No Shame
The Theater of Epidaurus

Greece; *c.* 400 B.C.
Architect: Polycleitus the Younger

"To the hunt—

above all in the circle of the theater,

richer in game

than you could have imagined.

There is the stuff

of love and dallying games

and to touch and

what you will always possess."

Ovid (42 B.C. to 17 A.D.), *The Art of Love*

Mosaic from Antiquity depicting actors performing

Comedy actors in ancient Greece

The birth of the theater reaches back to Thespis, the first known Greek tragedian. He barely emerges from the shadows of legend, but we do know he added a figure to the chorus that sang and danced in Athens in honor of the gods, establishing the first theatrical dialogue and paving the way for drama. This was in 534 B.C., the date from which the history of theater begins. Early Greek theater served a religious purpose. The chorus, through which the gods spoke to the people, guarded the eternal order on earth. "Speaking" parts were subordinated to the singers and used merely to announce the will of the gods expressed by the chorus. Production followed on the heels of speaking parts. The altar stood in the middle of the stage and the chorus slowly surrounded it, as if it embodied Fate which, both infallible and with an eye on eternity, wanders through Time.

Apart from tragedies, comedies were also performed, and theater customs soon became less formal. Centuries later, the Roman poet Ovid described a visit to the theater in Rome:

"Like bees in the native forest and fragrant meadows where they swarm around the wild thyme
decked-out women stream toward the celebration of the play,
My judgment always fails me in masses.
They who come to see, come to be seen.
Yes, a spoiled place that knows no shame."

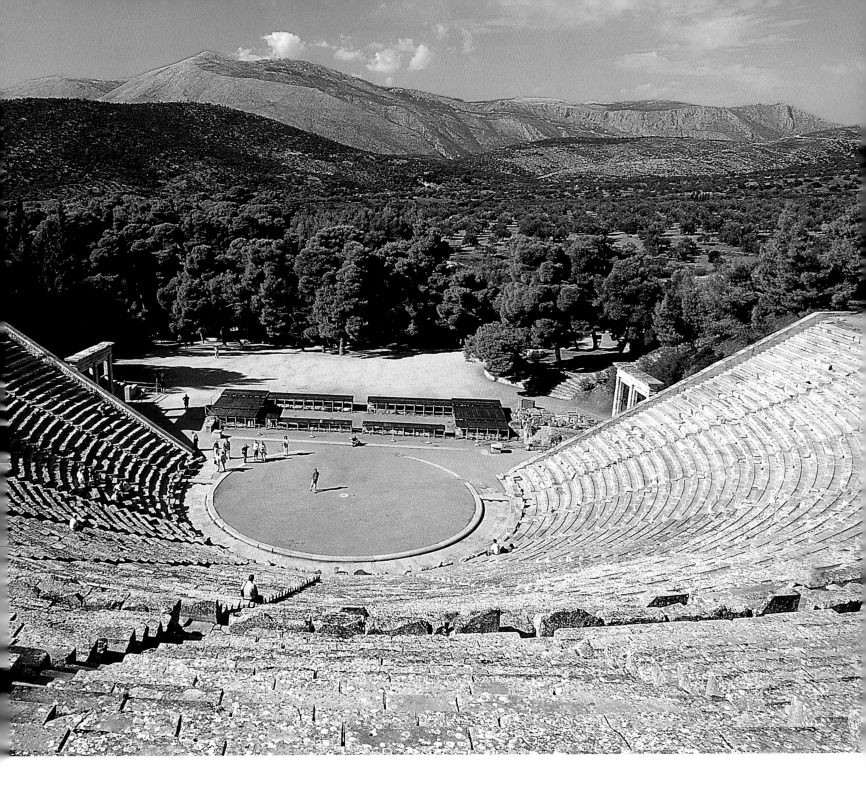

Theater stood at the center of society. It promised education, entertainment, and the occasional amorous adventure. It also had a therapeutic use. Epidaurus was a city, on the northeast coast of the Peloponnese, devoted to the famous cult of Asclepius. A visit to its theater was part of the health program. The priests of Asclepius were also physicians who, although well-versed in surgery, used thermal spas and psychotherapeutic methods to treat patients. These treatments were famous throughout the ancient world and thousands made pilgrimages to Epidaurus to improve their health. They were housed in guest houses. The ruins of one guest house, northwest of the theater, shows that it once had 160 rooms.

One method of treatment involved the "temple sleep." Patients were sent to rest in the temple of Asclepius, a most sacred place. Afterwards the priests asked them questions designed to unlock the secrets of their dreams and lead to healing. The priest-physicians were also convinced that theater could free emotions, thus curing or relieving the symptoms of disease through catharsis.

A stage with a tradition more than 2,000 years old; even today productions are held at Epidaurus

Huge numbers of theatergoers and spa patients must have visited Epidaurus during the feast days of Asclepius. Epidaurus, which is the best-preserved of ancient Greek theaters, was renowned for its acoustics and became a model for theaters for centuries to come. It had fifty-five semicircular rows of seats that could accommodate 14,000 people.

The Birthplace of the Gods
The Mysterious Past of Teotihuacán

Mexico; 1st century B.C.
completed and extended c. 500 A.D.

"When it was still night, when there was as yet no day, and as yet no light, they gathered there. There the gods were summoned to Teotihuacán. They spoke: "Come here, oh gods!" Who would take it upon himself to turn night into day and darkness into light?"

Aztec myth of creation, according to Father Bernardino de Sahagún, *Codices Matritenses*, c. 1590

Long before the arrival of archeologists, travel writers had discovered this mythical place. Back in 1804, following his journey through Central America, the explorer Alexander von Humboldt noted: "The only monuments in the valley of Mexico which are striking for a European due to their size or mass, are the remains of the two pyramids of Teotihuacán."

This imposing ruined city, of which only one-tenth has been excavated, is located about thirty miles northeast of Mexico City in a wide mountain valley some seven thousand feet above sea level. During its golden age, around 500 A.D., the ancient city had a population of some 200,000. It appears to have been not only the earliest and largest pre-industrial metropolis of the entire Western Hemisphere, but evidently the most powerful city in Central America at that time. It was here that the history of Mexico began. For here lay the fertile ground for the political, religious, and economic development of the Mexican highlands. The city's influence reached as far as modern Guatemala, five hundred miles away. Yet we know nothing about its inhabitants, about their way of life, or about the events that took place here.

The people of Teotihuacán left behind not a single written word, so it is not known which language was spoken here, or what the people called themselves and their city. The name Teotihuacán, which is used today, comes from the language of the Aztecs, who settled in the valley several centuries later, and can be translated as "the city of those who became gods." Legends surrounding Teotihuacán had been related long before the Spanish conquest. The Aztecs believed that the world as they knew it had begun in Teotihuacán. They interpreted the abandoned ruins, which they were convinced had been erected by a long-lost civilization of giants, as the cradle of existence, where the

sun and moon had come into being. They thus saw the two pyramids of Teotihuacán, where they regularly made sacrifices, as the archaic shrines of the two cosmic, primordial gods. The Aztecs called the old main thoroughfare "the Road of the Dead" because they believed the ruins along this central axis of the city—which was originally nearly three miles long and forty yards wide—to be the graves of priests and kings. In reality they are the remains of temples.

Contrary to the darkly mythical imaginings of the Aztecs, the vast sea of dwellings that made up Teotihuacán must have been abuzz with activity during its heyday. The city, which lay on the trade route from the highlands to the gulf coast and was blessed with an abundant water supply, had a large market and countless workshops. Art and astronomy experienced an unprecedented surge forward, and time was ordered into a calendar. Bright painting decorated the walls of houses, and Teotihuacán became a magnificent, colorful, and bustling metropolis, which had so much power that it needed no fortifications. The central focus appears to have been the so-called sun pyramid. The gigantic two-and-a-half million-ton edifice made of bricks and earth, stretching almost two hundred feet high, was created without the help of wagons or beasts of burden. Its principal facade is precisely aligned with the point where the sun sets on the day of the summer solstice. The entire city, which is arranged on a grid plan, is oriented towards its four corners. Why this great city began to decline around 600 A.D. is also a mystery. Could the farmers living around it no longer produce enough food? Was it attacked by warlike tribes from the steppe regions to the north? These questions still remain unanswered. We only know that, for the future cultures of Central America, Teotihuacán became the ideal of a glorious past—as classical Athens did for Europe.

Mysterious friezes from an ancient society; a detail from "The Paradise of the Rain God"

Once the largest pre-industrial metropolis in Central America.
The temple ruins along the central axis of the city

Bas-reliefs of mythical figures decorate
the facade of the sun pyramid Quetzalcoatl

The Rock of Death
The Drama of Masada

Israel; originally built *c.* 100 B.C.; further rebuilt as a fortress to escape attack, 36–30 B.C.

"Let our women remain inviolate and our children die without the experience of slavery. Then let us show each other the final proof of our love, which guards the glorious shroud of our freedom. Let us now set fire to the entire fortress with the exception of the storehouses for our food. When we are all dead, they will bear witness to the fact that we did not take our lives because we suffered want, but because we were determined to choose death over slavery."

Speech by Eleasar at the fortress of Masada, in Josephus Flavius, *The Jewish War*, 79 A.D.

Roman soldiers on the Trajan column in Rome

An indescribable massacre must have taken place on May 2nd of the year 73, the day when proud Masada bowed its head to the Romans. On that day 960 men, women, and children chose of their own will to die in the courtyards, chambers, corridors, stairways, and casements of the fortress in order to avoid slavery to the Romans. The tragedy was nothing other than collective suicide.

Since the time when the Roman general Pompey had conquered Jerusalem after a three-month siege in the year 63 B.C., forcing the country to surrender to the dictatorship of Rome, individual Jewish resistance groups had repeatedly rebelled against the detested foreign rulers. But ultimately the cult of the emperor among Roman administrators and extremely high taxes caused an escalation of tensions which finally ignited the entire population: the year 66 A.D. saw the eruption of the great Jewish rebellion. Rome had to come to terms

Shards for drawing lots; the chosen were given the task of murdering their own in order to avoid enslavement by the Romans

with several serious defeats, but then the empire's inexorable war machine was set in motion to bring the Jews to reason with fire and sword.

In 70 A.D. Titus, the son of the Roman emperor Vespasian, marched with his army to the gates of Jerusalem, mercilessly razing the city and destroying the temple. Judea was lost. 960 men, women, and children fled the inferno and retreated to the place which would be the last bastion of the Jews in the war against Rome, the last refuge of Jewish independence: Masada.

Atop the inaccessible rocky plateau which rises like a mighty colossus over the desert of Judea just west of the Dead Sea, Herod the Great had built a fortress which was said to be impregnable. A twenty-foot-high wall of limestone almost a mile long, guarded by thirty-

seven towers crowning the natural, steep chasms surrounding the plateau, which rises more than a thousand feet above the desert, promised protection unmatched by any stronghold of the day. Inside the fortress, and covering an area of 300 by 600 yards, were not only palace and administrative buildings, bathhouses, swimming pools, and a synagogue, but also cisterns, storerooms, stalls, and gardens which together would ensure the supply of food and water even in the event of a drawn-out siege.

But the rebellious Jews of the year 70 A.D. who had retreated to Masada could not be saved by the overflowing storerooms; after they had been under siege by the Tenth Roman Legion for almost three years, they gave up the fight. The situation was hopeless: at the foot of the fortress, the Romans had set up eight army camps, and at the same time they had begun to build an enormous ramp on the west side of the fortress plateau. When the ramp was completed and the Romans sounded the attack, the besieged Jews chose to end their own lives: family fathers killed their own wives and children, and were in turn killed by the ten men who had been chosen by lots to carry out this task. The last took his own life. "Their zeal did not cool when the time came to carry out the plan," writes Josephus Flavius, who based his account on the story told by a woman who, accompanied by an attendant and five children, had survived the massacre by crawling into an underground water pipe. "Fathers forced to murder their wives and children were consoled by the thought of the ill-treatment they would have suffered had they fallen into the hands of the enemy."

Masada, which was only rediscovered in 1838, excavated sometime later, and partially reconstructed, is today an imposing national shrine where Israeli soldiers swear the oath of allegiance to their country.

King Herod the Great's fortress of Masada, a stronghold for the
last bastion of Jewish resistance to the dictatorship of Rome

A fortress with comforts; under-floor heating in King Herod's
bathhouse

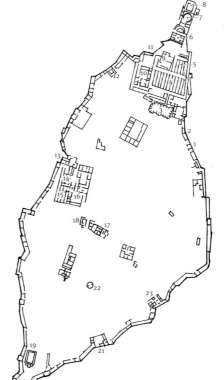

1 East Gate
2 Dolomite Stone Wall with
  Casemates
3 Quarry
4/5 Magazine
6 Upper Terrace of
  the Northern Palace
7 Middle Terrace of the
  Northern Palace
8 Lower Terrace of
  the Northern Palace
9 Baths
10 Administrative Buildings
11 North Gate (Water Gate)
12 Synagogue
13 West Gate
14 Administrative Wing
  of the Western Palace
15 Storage Rooms in
  the Western Palace
16 Royal Living Quarters
  in the Western Palace
17 Small Palace
18 Ritual Bath
19 Cistern
20 Southern Bastion
21 South Gate
22 Columbarium
23 Living Quarters

The Treasury of the Pharaoh
The Cliff City of Petra

Jordan; constructed between 100 B.C. and 200 A.D.

"The Nabatean capital is called Petra and is completely surrounded by steep rock walls, which protect it. Inside, many water sources provide for food and gardens. Outside its walls there is desert almost everywhere, especially in the direction of Judea."

Athenodorus, *Book XIV*, 1st century B.C.

For centuries the city was all but forgotten. Only some nomadic tribes at the change of seasons pitched their black, goatskin tents among the remains of a long-forgotten era. The ruins are the remnants of impressive monuments which once represented the prosperity of a flourishing community: Petra, half-way between the Dead Sea and the Gulf of Aqaba, was once a royal city and the religious center of the Nabateans, a tribe which settled on the Arabian peninsula around 400 B.C. Here, between high, steep, rock walls, which narrow to form dark gorges at the outskirts of the city, the Nabateans, originally camel drivers and caravan guides, found a refuge that was hardly accessible and therefore quite secure against enemy intrusions. Nevertheless, Petra, a settlement made possible thanks to a rich, natural water supply, lay not far off the beaten track.

The city controlled several caravan routes which had to pass through the arid valley of the Wadi Musa on their way from the south to the Mediterranean coast, including the old "King's Way" which Moses and the Israelites are said to have already followed on their flight from Egypt to the Promised Land. The income from toll-collecting and trade in asphalt made the city rich. Petra probably experienced its peak between the second century B.C. and the second century A.D. when it boasted a population of at least thirty thousand. There were paved roads, baths, a bazaar with shops, two theaters, three market places, palaces, gymnasiums, terraced gardens, and a refined drainage system—in fact, some of the original terracotta pipes are still intact today.

The town stretched for some five miles from one end to the other. But its most important remains are the caves and temple and tomb facades carved into its rosy sandstone. The narrowness of the gorges could hardly accommodate large, free-standing buildings. For this reason the inhabitants retreated into the cool bosom of the solid rock—along with their gods and their dead—hence the city's name, Petra, meaning "rock."

Archeologists have counted over eight hundred rock-cut dwellings and tombs. The so-called Treasury of the Pharaoh is considered the most important of these unusual examples of antique architecture. The richly decorated, 130-foot-high, two-story facade, which is artistically chiselled out of the ruddy sandstone (and has repeatedly served as a backdrop for films), focuses attention on the entrance to an unadorned, square room behind which a second, similar chamber is hidden. The complex is named "The Treasury of the Pharaoh" because of nineteenth-century Bedouins who imagined that a Pharaoh's treasure was contained in the ten-foot-high urn which stands on a pedestal over the middle of the facade. This complex was more likely the tomb of a

Like a mirage: the spectacular view of the end of the gorge

Nabatean king, and the urn purely decorative element—which did not preserve it from repeated nocturnal shotgun attacks from would-be thieves hoping to break it and take the imagined treasure.

Conquered by the Romans and declared a provincial capital, Petra lost its importance from the third century A.D. onwards, when caravans found other routes, and trade by sea unexpectedly flourished. Christianity was embraced in Petra after the monk Barsauma had successfully prayed for a "miraculous rainfall," bringing a long period of drought to an end. Yet even the fact that Petra had been elevated to the seat of a bishop could not halt the city's decline. Petra was mentioned one last time, namely in connection with crusaders who set out from there to defend Jerusalem, before the sleeping beauty sank into a seven-hundred-year sleep—to be kissed awake only in 1812 when it was rediscovered by Johann Christian Burckhardt.

"The Treasury of Pharaoh." The richly decorated facade
has been repeatedly used as a backdrop for films
Left: lithograph by David Roberts, 1842–1849

Running Water:
The Divine Source of Life
The Pont du Gard

From Uzès to Nîmes, France; built around the time of the birth of Christ

"The sight of the structure overwhelmed my imagination. I was all the
more astounded that it stands in the
middle of such an arid region. What
power must have been necessary to
transport such enormously large blocks,
seeing that there is no quarry nearby? I
climbed around the three levels of the
great aqueduct, and my respect for it
prevented me from treading too hard.
The echo of my steps beneath the
mighty arches made me believe that I
could hear the voices of those who had
built them."

Jean-Jacques Rousseau, *Les Confessions*, 1770

At some point the time came when Nemausus, the old Celtic god of springs and rivers, could not do the job alone any longer. The settlement which had been founded where his spring bubbles up out of the ground, today known as Nîmes, had developed, since its conquest by the Romans in 121 B.C., into one of the greatest cities in the empire. Along with the remains of the ancient city wall, the Tour Magne, the Maison Carrée, the amphitheater, and other relics of its past, Nîmes possesses more important architectural monuments than any other Roman town west of the Alps.

In antiquity, the people who crowded the forum, the market halls and courtrooms, the baths and temples, the theater and the circus needed enormous amounts of water every day. Since the flow of water from Nemausus's spring at the foot of Mont Cavalier was insufficient to fulfill such a great need, two other sources were tapped: those of the rivers Eure and Airan. There was only one problem: both springs were located almost thirty miles north of Nîmes, near Uzès. Thus, a long conduit had to be built.

Starting in the mountains, the conduit led sometimes underground, sometimes over the ground in order to provide a level path for the water, despite the unevenness of the terrain, and to guarantee the gentle gradient necessary. At places where deep valleys or rivers had to be crossed, the builders created bridges, so-called aqueducts, which held the water pipes at the same angle of inclination. This allowed the engineers to avoid having to channel the water down at a low level and through the river, only to have to pump it back up on the other side — a technically more complex undertaking. They also constructed a "water bridge" of this type, the Pont du Gard, at the point where the pipeline between Uzès and Nîmes crosses over a deep gorge cut by the river Gard, a tributary of the Rhône. Much like a series of triumphal

Roman engineering at its best—the intersection of two aqueducts; oil painting by Zeno Diemer

arches, this monument to the skill of ancient engineers, which even in contemporary accounts was praised as "an architectural wonder," not only served to demonstrate Roman greatness and power but also successfully fulfilled its original purpose for many years.

With its three rows of arches, one on top of the other, the imposing structure stretches to a height of 150 feet. The water channel runs along the top and is covered by stone slabs. Across the lowest row of arches is a footbridge which, during the Middle Ages, was used by pilgrims to cross the river Gard on their way to Santiago de Compostela. The shape of the gorge dictated the length of each row of arches: the

lower six arches are sixty-six feet high and cover a stretch of valley 140 yards wide, while the upper row of thirty-five arches, which are only twenty feet high, measures 270 yards from end to end. The structure's slender proportions make us forget that hundreds of workers had to use winches to lift blocks of stone weighing as much as six tons before the aqueduct could be put into operation and transport vast quantities of water to Nîmes.

The end of the pipeline, the old water distributor at the edge of the ancient city, was not discovered until 1844. The adjoining reservoir was constructed according to the principles devised by Vitruvius, a Roman architect and

"An architectural wonder" that serves as a monument to the skill of ancient engineers

engineer who, in the first century B.C., wrote the only book, which survives from antiquity, on the basic problems of architecture. His recommended system of water pipelines provided both public institutions and the homes of administrators with sufficient amounts of water, during the frequent spells of hot weather, when the reserves of private households had long run dry. Only in the nineteenth century would the western world again be capable of providing a water supply comparable to that achieved in antiquity.

Throw Him to the Lions!
Gladiators at the Colosseum

Rome, Italy; begun 72 A.D. during the reign of Emperor Vespasian; officially opened in 80 A.D. by Emperor Titus

"He was streaming with blood, yet his torn limbs continued to live, and from head to toe there was nothing of his body left to see."

Martial, *Book of Spectacles*, written in 80 A.D. on the occasion of the ceremonial opening of the Colosseum

Even writers of comedies can lose their smile. That is what once happened to the Roman writer Terence in the year 160 B.C. when the performance of one of his plays was suddenly interrupted by a sudden commotion. The reason: someone had spread the word that a gladiator fight was about to take place—a type of competition originally performed with swords (or *gladii* in Latin), later also with spears, nets, or glowing-hot rods of iron, and always ending with the death of the vanquished. The announcement of a spectacle of this kind—organized by rulers hoping to gain the favor of the masses—was reason enough for Romans to drop everything and rush to the Colosseum. After all, great entertainment of the murderous variety was on offer, the excitement and interest frequently heightened by the use of bears, lions, and tigers which, driven wild with hunger and the lash of the whip, pounced on the gladiators and tore them to shreds.

Originally, gladiators were part of the cult of the dead, and the first written mention of them dates from the year 264 B.C. For the funeral ceremony for Decimus Junius Brutus Pera, his sons ordered three pairs of gladiators to fight. In those days it was believed that the sacrifice of a human life reconciled the deceased person with those still living. With time, this religious custom developed into a form of popular entertainment organized by the magistrate. The protagonists were condemned prisoners whose final sentence was to turn their own day of reckoning into an entertaining spectacle. Victims were gathered from the far corners of

the Roman Empire. They were prisoners of war, slaves, criminals, and Christians. Although, men who had ostensibly achieved a certain degree of success in society were not necessarily spared a similar fate. The emperor Vitalis, for example, is said to have punished a disinclined young lover by selling him to the warder of a wandering troop of gladiators. Those who survived several fights in the arena had the chance of not only being pardoned, but also of achieving a dubious kind of fame—possibly one reason why gamblers, adventurers, and outcasts, who had nothing else to lose, volunteered as gladiators.

In Rome, the Colosseum—the largest and most imposing amphitheater in the Empire—was known as the original showplace of fights between gladiators and wild beasts. According to ancient sources, 87,000 spectators could be accommodated in the four-storied oval structure.

Contemporaries marvelled at this "world wonder." With its outer walls towering more than 150-feet high, it became the prototype for all future arenas for spectator sports. The first gallery was reserved for the emperor and his court, the second for noble families, and the third and fourth tiers were given over to "the rabble." Sailors hung an enormous canvas sun shade from the top gallery, which was supported on 240 poles. Inside, an ingenious system of stairways and entrances allowed spectators to access the galleries directly and depart equally swiftly. The arena itself was spacious enough for three hundred simultaneously fighting pairs of gladiators. Underground, there was a labyrinth of rooms and chambers for storing weapons and other supplies; there were cages for wild animals and a subterranean passageway to the emperor's prison for the gladiators.

The Colosseum, which became known by this name only during the Middle Ages, due to the colossal statue of Emperor Nero that stood nearby, was opened with a celebration lasting one hundred days, during which the arena was drenched in the blood of both men and beasts. The highlight of the show was the staging of a sea battle. First the arena was flooded with water, then horses, bulls, and other animals "which had been trained to move in the water as they would on land" were driven into the waves. Finally, gladiators fought hand to hand and from ship to ship until the last man fell—to enraptured cheers from the crowds.

The frenzied atmosphere of long ago has now given way to one of peaceful meditation: the only wild cats to be seen today stretch themselves out in the warm sun while the tourists marvel at the ruins of the Roman Colosseum.

A model of ancient Rome showing the Colosseum (top)

Above: The ruins of the Colosseum in Rome—the floor of the arena
where thousands sacrificed their lives—has not been reconstructed

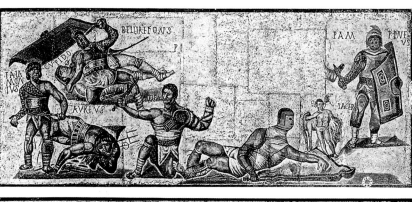

An entrance to the arena, an ingenious
system of stairways and entrances

Gladiators fighting to the death

Shrine of the Planet Gods: The Pantheon

Rome, Italy; 118–128 A.D.

"Of all the temples which are to be found in Rome, none is as excellent as the Pantheon, which is today called the Rotunda. The building is so completely preserved that one still sees it as it was at the time of its creation. They called it the Pantheon because it was dedicated to Jupiter as well as to other gods. And the people called it the Rotunda, perhaps because—as some believe—it represents the world."

Andrea Palladio, "On the Pantheon," 1570

Cleopatra was a beast. The Egyptian queen, who had succeeded in wrapping the most powerful men in the Roman republic around her little finger—first Caesar, then Mark Antony—knew how to strike a pose. At a banquet given in her honor during her stay in Rome, she swallowed half a valuable pearl with a glass of wine in order to flaunt her incredible wealth. Of course her snobbery did not help her one bit. Just like her last lover Mark Antony, Cleopatra's life ended in suicide, at the deadly bite of a viper. But the gesture with the pearl was not quickly forgotten in Rome. The remaining half—which, according to appraisals made during the Middle Ages, was worth 250,000 gold ducats—was given to goldsmiths to work into the ear ornament on a statue of a god, which formed one of the treasures in the Pantheon.

This building, which today is considered to be the best-preserved monument of classical Rome, has a further association with Cleopatra. It originated with the Roman general Marcus Agrippa, the man who had disastrously defeated Mark Antony and Cleopatra in the naval battle near Actium, thus driving the two to commit suicide. Full of pride at the victory, Agrippa financed the Pantheon to create a monument to himself and his family, which also included his father-in-law, Augustus, the godlike first emperor of the Roman Empire.

It is not believed that the Pantheon was really dedicated to all of the gods in the Roman heavens, as its name suggests. It is more probable that Agrippa had the Pantheon built in honor of the seven gods of the planets, including the sun-god Sol, as well as Mercury, Venus, Mars, Jupiter, Saturn, and Neptune. This assumption is corroborated by the fact that the Pantheon, which burned down twice and was built as it now stands only in the 2nd century B.C., has exactly seven wall niches in which each planet god would have had a place. In addition—and this is the most important argument—the double shell structure of the cast cement dome, which is considered a technical masterpiece of Roman architecture, is painted inside with gold stars on a blue background.

Antique visions of the harmony of the cosmos seem to have turned to stone in the architecture of the Pantheon: the height of the spherical interior space is equal to its diameter, and the height of the walls on which the dome rests and the radius of the dome itself measure exactly half of the diameter. With its perfect proportions the Pantheon can be interpreted as a symbol of the cosmos. That could also have been the reason why the building, which has impressed artists and travelers throughout the ages, was already praised in antiquity as "the miracle of Rome." Its spherical interior, which is illuminated only from above—by an opening in the middle of the dome—was the stage for important acts of state in Roman times, during which the throne of the emperor was placed directly under the source of light, symbolizing the divine origin of his legitimacy and power.

Christian emperors forbade the Roman cult of the gods and closed the Pantheon. Yet the temple survived and was transformed into a Christian place of worship. The statues of the gods disappeared, and in their place wagonloads of bones—reportedly of martyrs—were brought in and the building renamed the Church of St Mary and the Martyrs.

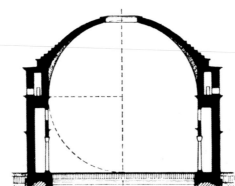

Perfect proportions: the spherical interior space of the Pantheon is equal to its diameter

The final resting place of emperors, martyrs, and the artist Raphael

The Pantheon is one of the best-preserved monuments of classical Rome. It has remained intact for almost 2,000 years

Water, Water, Everywhere!
The Baths of Caracalla

Rome, Italy; 206–216 A.D.

"My lodgings are located directly over a public bathhouse. Now just imagine the noise that I am subjected to, day in, day out: quarreling youths, bawling bathers who try to sing in the bath, the splashing water and crashing waves when someone leaps into the basin, the outcry when a pickpocket is caught in the act, the shrill voice of the hair-plucker. If, then, a sportsman begins to count the number of times he can bounce a ball, then that's more than I can bear. At such times I could curse my own ears."

From Seneca's *Letters on Moral Issues to Lucilius*, 62 A.D.

The baths of the emperor;
reconstruction by Ivanov

The Romans once considered bathing a necessary evil. In fact, even as late as the year 200 A.D., it was still believed that contact with water "did not promote bodily vigor." That is why Scipio the Elder, the otherwise shining victor over Carthage, only washed himself every ninth day. With time—and beginning in Campania, where the first private bathhouses fed by hot springs were opened—bathing developed into an enjoyable entertainment for the general public.

Clever businessmen promoted the breakthrough of this new kind of leisure pursuit by attracting the public to warm-water basins and steam baths with sensationally low entrance fees. And while brothels and taverns sprang up around bathhouses in order to offer bathers further pleasures after they had purified themselves, engineers finally revolutionized bathing culture for good. They invented the hypocaust system—the under-floor heating method by which hot air was piped through cavities in the structure's stonework—making it possible to control the temperature of large basins, floors, and walls in the bathhouses. From then on, baths became more luxurious, more comfortable, and more technically refined from decade to decade. Some bathing establishments in Rome even advertised their modern facilities. Yet only the bathhouses which the emperor himself commissioned, in order to gain the favor of his subjects, were free from the pressure of competing for clients. Their ruins still bear witness to the fact that they represented the unequalled culmination of bath architecture in the history of mankind.

The baths built by the emperor Caracalla in the south of Rome, not far from the Via Appia, are among the most extensive complexes of their kind. The remains of this overwhelming, palatial structure are on a site of some twenty-seven acres. Originally, massive pillars and columns supported the roofs of spacious halls which were decorated from floor to ceiling with frescoes, mosaics, exotic plants, and fine sculptures. Perfumes and spiced wine were mixed with the water in order to make it "finer." Extravagance was the name of the game. The all-pervading aura of luxury was calculated to emphasize the generosity of the man responsible for the baths' creation. Because Caracalla, a cruel despot, wanted to be remembered as a great philanthropist, he made it possible for his subjects to bathe in surroundings as elegant as those otherwise only enjoyed by the richest of the rich. The warm water gushed from gigantic silver spouts, flowing down marble steps and over painted tiles.

The water consumption was enormous. Twice the amount of water stored in the reservoirs of bathhouses built by other emperors could be stored in the vast chambers under the Baths of Caracalla. Under the dome and half-dome ceilings, barrel vaults, and groin vaults, customers not only bathed, sweated, and relaxed. Besides halls for swimming and warm-air halls able to accommodate 1,500 people, there were also rooms for sports and gymnastics, for masseurs and hairdressers, for lectures and meetings—even libraries and shops.

Everyone used the baths. As an institution for the promotion of public health and education, they had become an indispensable part of public life in Rome. Emperors and beggars, lovers and matchmakers, cake-sellers and pickpockets, all flocked to the baths. But even though the toilet seats were made of marble, it seems that, even in those days, it was difficult to discourage bathhouse customers from one utterly profane evil, as we gather from an inscription discovered among the ruins of the baths built by the emperor Titus: "May the wrath of the twelve gods, of Diana and Jupiter, be upon anyone who urinates or defecates in this basin."

The baths in their heyday; reconstruction by Viollet-le-Duc

Focal point in public life, the
Caracalla Baths included rooms
for masseurs, libraries, lectures,
and shops

Mother of the World
Hagia Sophia—
A Shrine to God's Wisdom

Istanbul, Turkey; 532–537 A.D.
Architects: Anthemius of Thralles with Isidorus of Miletus

"Not the sound of swords, nor the victorious battles in the south and west, nor even the trophies of defeated tyrants bathed in blood have inspired me to begin my hymn of praise. No! I wish to sing the praise of the Hagia Sophia, that wondrous temple which outshines all achievements of war, and every representative palace, in a blaze of glory."

Paulus Silentarius, an usher at the court of Justinian,
In Praise of Hagia Sophia, 537

The weight of the central dome is carried
by the surrounding half-domes

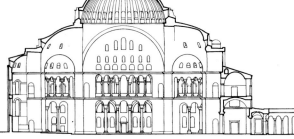

The situation was critical. From one end of the empire to the other, ominous rumblings had risen against the Byzantine Roman Emperor Justinian. The rebuilding of cities leveled by earthquakes, the fortification of the empire's frontiers, and the improvement of the water supply had weakened the treasury. Only through stringent savings and higher taxes could he refill the imperial coffers, but these measures caused new problems. The capital was awash with misery as unemployed civil servants, small landowners, ruined by the new

A report to Emperor Justinian detailing the building progress
of Hagia Sophia, as shown in a medieval manuscript

laws, and retainers of formerly respectable families who could no longer afford servants, came to Constantinople hoping the emperor would restore the justice they felt was their due. Instead, they found bread in shorter supply and of poorer quality. Tensions mounted and finally climaxed in the Nika Revolt of 532.

Nearly half of Constantinople went up in flames before the imperial troops struck back, killing 30,000 rebels in the Hippodrome. But even before the last body could be buried and the final smoldering fire extinguished, Justinian was already planning for the future. The rebels had destroyed the capital's main Christian church, built by Emperor Constantine in 360 A.D. and dedicated to Hagia Sophia—holy Wisdom. Justinian decided to replace it with an imposing new structure in gratitude for his victory over

the insurgents and in commemoration of the victims of the revolt.

Heaven and earth were to be joined in this house of worship, which would surpass all other churches dedicated to the Creator and serve as a reminder of the glory of its builder to all the nations of the world until the end of time. It was a tall order, but one which the master builders successfully fulfilled. Upon completion Hagia Sophia became the world's most magnificent cathedral. Its distinctive feature is the central dome which rises to a height of almost 170 feet. With a diameter of circa one hundred feet and flanked by descending half-domes, the dome became the principle architectural element in religious buildings influenced by Christian Constantinople. No other structure, until our own era, would contain such a large and un-obstructed, light-filled space under a single roof.

At its consecration on December 27, 537, the Emperor proclaimed, "Glory and honor to the Highest who found me worthy to complete such a work." Then he remembered the builder of the first temple in Jerusalem, "Solomon, I have vanquished thee!"

Following its consecration four hundred clerics served in the Hagia Sophia. It was regarded as the heart of the Byzantine Empire and simultaneously as the metropolitan church of the patriarch of Constantinople, who was the highest Christian leader after the Pope. The Emperors of the Byzantine Empire were crowned under its dome, and all important ceremonies of state took place there. Its terrified citizens sought shelter under the dome of Hagia Sophia in 1204 when the crusaders and their army attacked Constantinople. Although the city was successful in repelling the western invaders, it could not hold off the Ottoman Turks. They captured Constantinople in 1453 and converted Hagia Sophia into a mosque, adding four minarets. It continued, however, to serve as an example for architects, and later Islamic religious buildings followed the plans of the former Christian church.

Hagia Sophia, the Emperor Justinian's magnificent church in Istanbul (formerly Constantinople)

The sound of praises being sung has long gone; since 1934 Hagia Sophia has been in use as a museum

The Beginning of Christianity
The Church of the Nativity in Bethlehem

Israel; 6th century, built by Emperor Justinian

"And Joseph also went up from Galilee, out of the city of Nazareth, into Judaea, unto the city of David, which is called Bethlehem, because he was of the house and lineage of David, to be taxed with Mary his espoused wife, being great with child. And so it was, that, while they were there, the days were accomplished that she should be delivered. And she brought forth her firstborn son, and wrapped him in swaddling clothes, and laid him in a manger; because there was no room for them in the inn."

Luke Chapter 2, verses 3–7, 70 A.D.

It must have been a wonderful night. In En-Gedi on the Dead Sea the grapevines were blooming out of season, and the Star of Wisdom lit up the fields surrounding Bethlehem, a small Mid-Eastern city with a colorful bazaar. At the same moment the ox and donkey stood by as everyone who had gathered in the stable, sank to his knees before a manger, and worshiped the Holy Child.

Many legends surround the birth of Christ. According to one, the brothers and sisters of Jesus were present at his birth along with Joseph and the shepherds. Jesus may have had four brothers (Jacob, Josiah, Judas, and Simon) and two sisters (Lysia and Lydia) born of Joseph's first marriage. Another apocryphal story tells of two midwives who attended the birth—Zebel and Salome. Zebel believed that Mary was a virgin but Salome doubted it and wanted proof. That was unwise because "her hand withered and died." But the damage only proved temporary when an "angel appeared unto her and ordered her to touch the babe. From that moment she was cured." This was the first miracle that occurred in the stable of Bethlehem.

The stable is thought to have actually been a cave. In the soft limestone cliffs surrounding Bethlehem such man-made grottoes are not unusual. In the third century A.D. Origines, an early Christian theologian who traveled throughout Palestine and is best remembered for his spectacular self-castration, wrote: "One is shown the cave in Bethlehem where he was born and the manger where he lay in swaddling clothes." In Origines' time it was apparently still possible to enter the cave. Today it is a

crypt-like structure in which a silver star on the floor marks the place of Christ's birth with the inscription: "Here Jesus Christ was born of the Virgin Mary." A five-naved Church of the Nativity rose over this and other caves—the Grotto of the Innocents, the Grotto of the Manger, and the study of St Hieronymus (who translated the Vulgate edition of the bible, the only authorized translation used by the Catholic church).

Despite countless renovations and additions, the Church of the Nativity remains much as it was when it was built nearly 1,400 years ago. The majestic structure, which Christians regard as the "holiest place on earth," had its glory days. During the Crusades the kings of Jerusalem were crowned in the church. Later it fell on hard times, not only because the region was under Ottoman rule and the church suffered neglect (as well as being damaged by frequent earthquakes), but because Orthodox and Catholic Christians could not come to an agreement about sharing the church. In 1810 the disagreement exploded into a bloody conflict between believers of the two faiths. Problems continue but fortunately have not hindered archeological research.

A few years ago more caves were discovered under the church. Researchers have found bones, charred stones from ancient cooking fires, iron-age tools, and pottery shards, which prove that at around the time of Christ, shepherds and their animals had occupied the caves. Nowadays neither the church nor the caves can be accessed by animals. The entrance was lowered to a height of about four feet in the sixteenth century in order to keep camels and donkeys from using the holy place as a shelter.

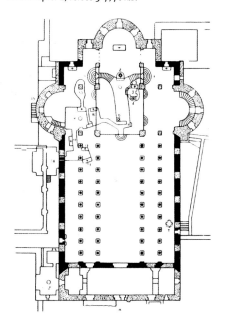

Birthplace of Jesus Christ:
the limestone grotto in Bethlehem

The Church of the Nativity: the entrance was lowered
in the 16th century to keep out camels and donkeys

The grotto in which Jesus Christ is said to have been born

Allah, I Am Here!
The Pilgrimage to Mecca

Saudi Arabia; from the 7th century onward

"I yearn for Mecca and its clear skies.
I yearn for the whispering of time on
every corner and want to walk along
the streets and lose myself among the
holy sites. I can now see myself, my
brothers, how I go through the alleys
of Mecca and recite verses from the
Koran as if they were being proclaimed
for the first time. It is as if I were
listening to a lesson spoken by the
Almighty. What joy! What joy!"

Nagib Mahfouz, *Echo of My Life*, 1997

Mecca is visited by at least 700,000 pilgrims every year

Mecca—the fulfillment of a dream. It is not
only an obligation for every Muslim to make
a pilgrimage to the holy city of Islam at least
once in his life if he possibly can, it is also a
deeply felt need. The instructions that he has
to obey on his journey are precisely defined in
the Koran, ensuring that the pilgrim leaves this
world—and everything that defines him in this
life on earth—behind him, at least for the
duration of his stay in Mecca.

In the holy city, your origins, your education,
and your social class are irrelevant. All pilgrims
are equal. All wear the same white pilgrim's
clothing, and all observe the same religious
rituals in a type of rehearsal for the day at the
end of time when all will stand as equals to be
judged by God.

Nothing promotes solidarity among Muslims
as much as the shared pilgrimage to Mecca.
As many as 700,000 pilgrims are counted
every year. But even for the millions upon
millions of believers who are never able to
visit Mohammed's birthplace during their life-
time, the city in western Saudi Arabia is ever-
present. For each one of their five daily prayers,
they face in the direction of Mecca, regardless
of where they happen to be at that time.

The focus of their prayers is the Great Mosque
with its six minarets and nineteen gates in the
center of the city of Mecca. There it stands,
draped in black silk brocade in the middle of
the mosque's square courtyard and framed by
columned halls surmounted by domes: the
Kaaba, the world's holiest place according to
Islamic belief. The simple, somewhat irregular
structure of stone encloses a single, windowless
room. Its name comes from the Arabic word
meaning "cube."

Imbedded in the wall at chest height next to
the entrance, which is open only on high holy

The floor plan of the Kaaba on ceramic
tile, 18th century

A rich pilgrim on his way to Mecca in
a sedan chair borne by two camels

days, is the greatest treasure known to the Islamic world, the Black Stone. A legend dating back to the beginnings of the Old Testament surrounds this meteorite. Adam, the first of all human beings, desperate after being banished from Paradise, is said to have wandered into the valley where the city of Mecca now lies. Here he found a sign that God had forgiven him: a ruby-encrusted baldachin sheltering a large, shining stone whose splendor filled the entire valley with light. This white, shimmering jewel became black after being touched by hundreds of thousands of worshippers throughout the ages. But in it the sages recognized a symbol of the human soul which shines from beneath the throne of God. Adam walked around this wonderful apparition seven times and erected the Kaaba over it—not only the first structure, but also the first shrine in the world. After it had been destroyed in the Great Flood, it is said that the Kaaba was rebuilt by Abraham and his son Ishmael.

In fact, it is quite possible that the Kaaba was the site of a stone cult, a frequent form of worship in ancient Arabia since time immemorial. Later the new Christian religion is said to have played its part in the story. Images of the Mother of God are supposed to have decorated the Kaaba before Mohammed appeared as a prophet, freed the shrine of all "idolatrous images," and made it the universal center of the Islamic faith. The prophet introduced not only the obligatory pilgrimage, but also the custom of praying towards Mecca. As can be read in the Koran, the holy book of Islam which Allah is said to have personally dictated to the prophet Mohammed between 610 and 622 A.D.: "And wherever you might be, turn your face in the direction of the holy mosque."

The Kaaba is the holiest of holies for millions of people

The Nocturnal Ride to Heaven

Sacred to Three World Religions: The Dome of the Rock

Jerusalem, Israel; 685–691
Architect: unknown

"One night Mohammed rode his winged horse from Mecca to Jerusalem where he was welcomed to the temple rock of the prophets Abraham, Moses, Solomon and Jesus Christ. Together they prayed in the grotto under the holy rock. Then Mohammed re-mounted his horse and rode to heaven at which time the rock freed itself and the Angel Gabriel who accompanied Mohammed had to hold it back with his hand. Mohammed, however, was in the seventh heaven and glimpsed the joy of paradise. The same night he returned to Mecca."

From an Islamic legend, *c.* 632

It is said the Dome of the Rock marks the center of the earth, which may not be far from the truth. The golden yellow rock beneath the imposing dome is believed to be the summit of Mount Moria, which is mentioned in the Old Testament and is, therefore, a significant monument to human history. Almost two-and-a-half thousand years before Mohammed, the founder of Islam, made his legendary ride to heaven, Abraham, the father of Judaism, is believed to have stood at the same spot with a knife quivering in his hand as he prepared to sacrifice his son Isaac. The quick intervention of an angel saved the boy.

About 900 years later King Solomon built the first stone temple of the Jews over the rock. This holiest of shrines sheltered the most important cult object of the Israelites—the Ark of the Covenant—an acacia-wood box containing both tablets of the Ten Commandments. For centuries the temple remained the political and religious heart of the Israeli state. The sacrificial altar may also have stood on the same rock, a theory supported by the evidence of a hole that may have been used to drain off animal blood.

Repeatedly looted, destroyed, and rebuilt (for the last time by King Herod the Great), Jesus of Nazareth entered the temple towards the end of its existence, first as a newborn child when Mary and Joseph, following Jewish custom, presented him to God. He returned as a 12-year old to meet with the temple elders and again as an angry preacher to expel the merchants who had turned the house of God into a "den of thieves." The temple was finally destroyed in 70 A.D. during a Jewish uprising against the Romans. It was never rebuilt. To this day Jews mourn the destruction of the temple at the Weeping Wall—the only part of the original structure still to be seen.

The Romans constructed a temple to Jupiter, their national god, in its place. But this too crumbled away, and the site gradually deteriorated into a rubbish heap in a southeastern corner of Jerusalem's old town. Caliph Omar, who was inspired by the legend of Mohammed's nocturnal ride to conquer Palestine and Jerusalem, had the rock cleared of rubbish, dirt, and crumbling ruins.

Caliph Abd el-Malik gave the order to build the majestic blue and gold Dome of the Rock in 685 in order to show that Mohammed stood higher than the prophet Jesus Christ. He was concerned that his Muslim brethren would be unduly influenced by the grandeur and beauty of the nearby Church of the Holy Sepulcher.

The Dome of the Rock, however, was larger and more colorful. After the Kaaba in Mecca and the Great Mosque in Medina, it was soon regarded as the third holiest shrine and wonder of the Islamic world. The dome, which was once believed to have been covered by ten thousand plates of pure gold, has become synonymous with Jerusalem. For a small fee, guides are happy to show visitors the hoof prints of Mohammed's horse, a reliquary holding two hairs from the prophet's beard, the fingerprint left by the Angel Gabriel, and a footprint of Jesus. And those who lay their ear against the rock can hear the water flowing in the river of paradise.

The holy rock, sacred to Islam, Judaism, and Christianity, lies directly under the cupola

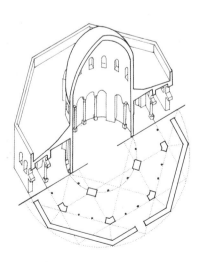

Pure gold — the dome was at one point covered by 10,000 plates of gold

The Cradle of Japan
The Former Imperial City of Nara and the Hall of the Great Buddha

Japan; c. 732–752; Buddha Statue, 749
Sculptor: Kuninaka no Kimimaro

"Yamato is the highest elevation in the land.

Mountains like green walls,

It is laid out step after step

Hugging the hill—

How beautiful is the land of Yamato!"

By the legendary Prince Yamato-Takeru, from *Records of Ancient Events*, 712 B.C.

For generations the people of the Yamato Valley have made their living as woodcarvers or farmers raising goldfish, fruit and rice. Its idyllic landscape of spreading fields and cedar and cypress forests is separated from the city of Kyoto by a chain of low hills. It is far removed from the hectic life of the city. Yamato seems unchanged—as if the passing centuries have left it untouched, imparting the land with a unique charm of its own. It is the cradle of Japan, the heart of the ancient kingdom where, according to the sagas, the Imperial family and other noble clans first touched Japanese soil in the fourth century B.C.

They are said to have arrived from the Island of Kyushu and to have built their first capital, Kashiwara, at the foot of Mount Unebi in the south of the Yamato plateau. The area was dubbed "The Seat of the Sun Clan" in their honor. These rulers traced their origin back to the gods. The leader of the clan was the Emperor, who was also a priest, and who called himself Tenno, the King of Heaven—a direct descendant of the sun goddess. Kashiwara did not remain the capital. According to the religious beliefs of the ruling family, the residence of the Imperial family had to be moved following the death of Emperor Tenno, because the place of his death was thought to be unclean. For this reason, the exquisite landscape of the Yamato plateau gave rise to one new capital after another. Settlements were built only to be abandoned a generation later.

By the eighth century the administration of the Kingdom required a permanent capital and Nara, then named Heijokyo, was founded. Just a few decades after its founding this new capital, which was laid out according to the advice of the royal astrologers, already had more than 200,000 inhabitants. Culture blossomed, but after seventy-five years Nara was also aban-

doned. This time the capital was moved to Heiankyop, which is known today as Kyoto. The residences and palaces of Nara crumbled away. Only the temples, built on the eastern side of the city, survived to bear witness to the importance of the era.

It was while the Emperors resided in Nara that Buddhism came to Japan. Emperor Tenno Shomu, who ruled from 724 to 749 was especially devoted to Buddhism and the only Japanese ruler to place Buddhism above temporal power. Shomu was also responsible for building the most important monument in Japan—the Hall of the Great Buddha. The building is 150 feet high and 225 feet long, making it the world's largest wooden structure. Despite its huge size, the temple appears light and airy.

It took tens of thousands of workers more than twenty years to complete the enormous structure. Tens of thousands more came, including delegations from China, Korea, and India, to celebrate its dedication in 752. Inside the impressive building is the country's most important sculpture, a colossal bronze statue of Buddha, sitting with crossed legs on a pedestal of fifty-six lotus blossoms.

The statue is of enormous proportions: it is nearly fifty feet high, and the face alone is fifteen feet long. It contains 437 tons of bronze, as well as considerable quantities of mercury and gold. According to Japanese historians the completion of the statue exhausted some of the country's copper reserves. The amount of material used also exhausted Nara's subjects who were forced to pay high taxes and volunteer their time. In the meantime troubles of the past have given way to promises of a good future. A considerable number of Japanese still believe that if they crawl through the rectangular hole in the right column behind the Buddha, their admission to paradise will be guaranteed.

An official and lady of the court, Nara dynasty

The largest wooden structure in the
world: the Great Hall of the Buddha

The statue of the Great Buddha was cast using
the design of a master from Korea

A Forest of Columns
The Mezquita of Córdoba

Spain; 785–1009; construction of the Christian cathedral after 1500

"The impression upon entering this Islamic shrine is indescribable. One has the feeling, not of wandering through a building but of being in a forest sheltered under a roof. As far as the eye can see there are rows of columns that intersect and disappear into infinity. One feels surrounded by a lush vegetation made of marble that has shot out of the earth overnight."

Théophile Gautier, *Travels in Andalusia*, 1840

A Moorish vault; the mosque was a forest of columns and arched arcades

When Mohammed, the founder of Islam, died in Medina on June 8, 632, he ruled most of Arabia. The caliphs (which literally means "followers") succeeded in his footsteps. They governed an empire that stretched to the north and west along the south coast of the Mediterranean to the Atlantic. And because the straits between North Africa and Gibraltar seemed the shortest and most easily accessible route to Europe, they soon set their sights on the Iberian peninsula. The plan was successful, and after 711, the half-moon flag was flying over Andalusia and neighboring areas. The new rulers, called Moors because of their Moroccan origin, were warmly welcomed in many areas. And not without reason. They led the country into an economic and cultural golden age, the likes of which its populace had never experienced.

The Islamic invaders introduced oranges, rice, sugar cane, and date palms to the Iberian peninsula. They modernized the irrigation systems and agricultural methods, expanded trade routes, and supported the crafts. Soon there was a worldwide demand for glass, pottery, textiles, carpets, and weapons from Andalusia. Pulsating life infused the cities.

Córdoba was especially fortunate and entered a period of great prosperity. The city in which Seneca was born and where Caesar rose to a high post, became the residence of the emir, the representative of the caliph. As a result, it grew into a metropolis of a million inhabitants in which the fertile mixture of Jews, Christians, and Muslims produced an exciting climate of intellectualism, prosperity, and wealth. The streets were paved, and lanterns provided light. There was a sewage system and running water, 700 public baths, fifty hospitals, and seventeen universities.

As Europe's second most important capital after Constantinople, Córdoba became so prestigious that its emir rose to caliph. The spiritual core of his rule was the great mosque known as the Mezquita. It was built between 785 and 1009 on the site of an earlier temple dedicated to the Roman god Janus, which later became a Christian basilica. With its forest of 856 columns it was long regarded as not only the largest Islamic shrine in the world but also as one of the holiest sites to be visited by Muslim pilgrims. Córdoba was the Mecca of the West.

The mosque contained an original copy of the Koran and a foot bone of Mohammed. Thousands of lamps, some made of upturned bells plundered from Christian churches and filled with aromatic oil, lit up the nineteen naves, bringing a magical sparkle to the columns

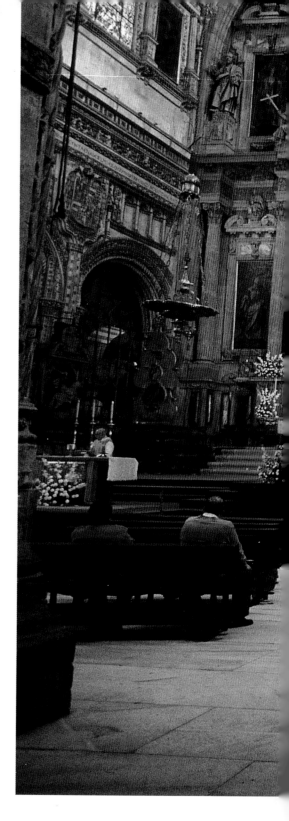

of marble, granite, porphyry, and jasper. Golden stars shone down from the ceiling. Because mosques were always gathering places, philosophy and natural sciences were taught, new laws were announced, and justice was dispensed in its ad hoc courts. All this took place on precious, thick carpets, in the mysterious, glittering atmosphere of the mosque's columns and arched arcades—interrupted only by the muezzin's call to prayer five times a day.

A cathedral inside a mosque: the colorful history of the Mezquita in Córdoba

In 1492 when the Moors were driven out of Spain, it all came to an end. The mosque was converted into a Christian church. A cathedral, rising high above the original roofline, was built in its midst at the expense of twelve naves. Emperor Charles V later regretted having allowed the radical change that destroyed the harmony of the building: "Here something was built that could have been anywhere, but what was destroyed was unique."

"There I Have Seen a Unique Marvel"
The Palatine Chapel, Aachen and the Holy Roman Empire

Germany; c. 800

"As one living stone is peacefully laid on another and their number and size match perfectly, so the work of the Lord who has created this great hall will shine. The completed structure crowns the efforts of a pious people. This testament to human art will stand forever under the protection of God the Almighty and Merciful. Therefore, we pray to God to protect this holy temple which Emperor Charles has built on safe ground."

From the consecration speech in the Octagon of the Palatine Chapel, possibly written by Abbot Alcuin, c. 800

Bas-relief of Charlemagne on the front of the shrine, c. 1215

Since time immemorial the triangle of land, today bordered by Belgium, the Netherlands, and Germany, was famous for the healing power of its warm-water springs. The Romans had already enjoyed bathing in the waters, which at 74° centigrade are the warmest in Central Europe. The spa also gave the city of Aachen its ancient Latin name, Aquisgrana.

The thermal spa, which was believed to heal rheumatism, gout, sciatica, and skin disease attracted Charlemagne who was more than fifty years old at the time. The rich hunting grounds in the area which were Carolingian territory may also have played a role in its appeal. Moreover, the city was valued as a strategic base for the empire that had begun to expand to the east. In any case, Aachen became one of Charlemagne's favorite residences and the capital of his empire.

As early as 769 the first Palatine castle, or "Pfalz," was built in the northern foothills of the High Venn. Such structures were fortified palaces that the ruler used as representative but temporary residences during his travels through his kingdom. Charlemagne was, according to Eginhard, his biographer, a tall man "with lively eyes, possessing authority and dignity." In 794 he ordered the old Palatine castle to be rebuilt and turned into a royal residence that would be grander than anything Franconian rulers, before or after him, would ever know.

Charlemagne made Aachen the center of his empire, a "new Rome" in which architecture and science boomed. His coronation took place in the Palatine Chapel, which is said to have been planned by Charlemagne himself and which took its inspiration from great religious buildings, based on the antique cultures of the Mediterranean region to which he had been exposed on this campaign through Italy.

The Palatine Chapel however would remain unique for its time—for centuries it remained the highest vaulted stone dome north of the Alps.

The master builder of Aachen borrowed forms from Roman, Byzantine, Lombard, and Franconian architecture. In the Palatine Chapel he created a structure that, in the words of one enthusiastic writer, "bridged time and joined nations." The chapel also marked the first time architecture strove to achieve height—a characteristic that would prove significant in subsequent western architecture.

The Palatine Chapel of Aachen would become a model for an entire architectural epoch. Its octagonal shape symbolizes completion and harmony and stands for heaven and the eternal kingdom of God. The circumference of the octagon measures 144 feet, the purported area of the heavenly Jerusalem. The simple marble throne that still stands in its original position in the western part of the upper passage is also full of symbolism. It represents the elevated position of the ruler and his place in the world—at the same time it faces east, the direction of the resurrection of the Savior and the rising sun. For nearly six hundred years, from 936 to 1531, following the tradition set down by Charlemagne, German kings were crowned in the Palatine Chapel.

Aachen became the capital of the Holy Roman Empire, a place of pilgrimage, and a monument to Charlemagne, the founder of the Holy Roman Empire. The city attracted many prominent visitors, including the painter Albrecht Dürer who came to Aachen in 1520 for the coronation of Charles V. He made note of the chapel, which had been enlarged to a cathedral: "There I have seen a unique marvel, the likes of which none who live here have ever seen excelled."

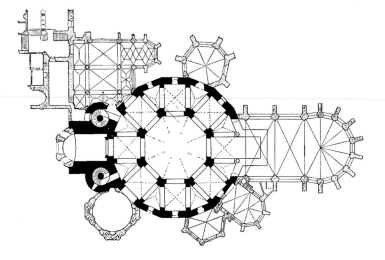

The Palatine Chapel, said to have been designed by Charlemagne, and the simple marble throne on which he was crowned

In the Heart of the Golden City
The Hradčany in Prague

Czech Republic; begun towards the end of the 9th century

"I see a large fortress whose fame will reach the heavens. It stands in the middle of a wood where the waves of the Vltava flow around it. A mountain ridge in the form of a dolphin branches off from a wide rocky mass and slopes down towards the river. There you will come upon a man who is making a lintel out of wood, which we call 'prah' in our language. Since also great lords have to bow at this lintel, name the fortress that you will build there Praha. From this fortress two golden olive trees will grow up to the seventh heaven and will shine omens and miracles down upon the world."

Prophecy of Libussa, 11th century

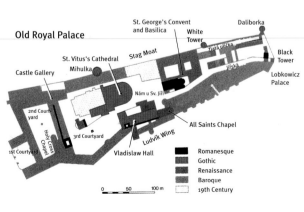

It was a long way to fall. The window of the Bohemian chancellery was about forty-five feet above the moat of the Prague fortress. But, according to eyewitnesses, the Hapsburg governors Jaroslav Borita von Martinitz and Wilhelm Slavata von Chlum got away with only "a terrible fright, their lives, and a few scrapes." Their headfirst departure from the fortress in the company of their secretary on May 23, 1618, was as involuntary as it was unusual, following as it did a bitter argument with Bohemian Protestants. A manure heap broke their fall. That did not change the fact that the incident was interpreted as the revolution of Catholic Hapsburgs against the Protestant nobles. The plunge from the window in Prague triggered the start of the Thirty Years' War.

The Hradčany, the hill fortress in Prague, had been the scene of bloody outbursts of hatred several times during its one-thousand-year history as the seat of saints and icono-clasts, emperors and tyrants. Its origins, however, are unknown. It was most likely founded towards the end of the ninth century to protect a ford in the Vltava and consisted of a three-part, wooden fortification surrounded by a bulwark. As of 973 it was the residence, not only of a duke, but also of the bishop of

the newly founded diocese of Prague. The cathedral still stands inside the fortress walls today—a unique example in central Europe of the coexistence of temporal and spiritual powers.

The Hradčany experienced its first golden age in the fourteenth century. Charles IV, king of Bohemia and emperor of the Holy Roman Empire, had the fortress of Prague enlarged, not only as the imposing focus of his power, but also as a goal for pilgrims. As the cult site for the national patron saint, Wenceslas, the repository for the insignias of the crown, the court church, and princely tomb, the Cathedral of St Vitus became the spiritual center of Bohemia. Along with Rome and Constantinople, Prague was one of the most important metropolises in Europe.

The city would achieve this status only at one other time: during the reign of Emperor Rudolph II. The art-loving and scientifically interested Hapsburg, who established his resi-dence in Prague in 1576, surrounded himself with celebrities from all over Europe at the Hradčany (which would become his prison after his deposition), among them the painter Giuseppe Arcimboldo, the astronomer Johannes Kepler, and the Rabbi Jehuda Löw ben Bezalel, who is said to have demonstrated the wonders of the camera obscura for him. "Whoever yearned for something great," wrote a contem-porary, "came to the Hradčany in Prague, where he could view a remarkable number of exceptional, extraordinary, and priceless and valuable things in the emperor's collection."

The Vladislav Hall, one of the most imposing Gothic rooms of the Hradčany, was often the setting for the high life of the time. Grand enough for coronations, court festivals, and jousting tournaments, proper craftsmen's fairs took place here during the reign of Rudolph II when Persian carpet-makers, Italian jewelers, lace-makers from Brussels, Dutch potters, and armorers from Nuremberg offered their wares for sale.

In the Golden Lane on the north flank of the Hradčany, where Rudolph II's alchemists desperately tried to create gold, Franz Kafka later worked on his prose texts; however, he viewed his native town Prague critically: "This little mother has claws. One must bend to her will, or....we would have to set it alight in two places. One of them is the Hradčany. Then it would be possible for us to escape."

A plunge from this window precipitated the Thirty Years' War

View of the Hradčany with Prague's Charles Bridge on the left

The Vladislav Hall, one of the most imposing rooms of the Hradčany and a venue for tournaments and fairs

Franz Kafka lived and worked in Golden Lane which runs along the northern wall of the Hradčany

53

A Journey to the End of the Earth
The Pilgrimage to Santiago de Compostela

Spain; 1077/1078–1128

"It is with the greatest joy that we see large crowds of pilgrims keeping vigil over the grave of Saint James. By the light of their candles, the whole church is aglow as if illuminated by the sun on a bright day. Some play the lyre or the drum, the flute or the recorder, the trombone, harp, or fiddle, the British or Gallic *rotta*; some sing, others confess their sins, read psalms, or give alms to the blind."

From the sermon *Verenanda Dies*, 12th century

The cathedral's gigantic incense burner was originally used to mask unpleasant human and animal odors

For the Europeans of the Middle Ages, the end of the world lay near Capo de Finisterre on the Atlantic, just beyond Santiago de Compostela, in what today is the province Galicia in northern Spain. But Santiago's impressive cathedral, where according to legend the immortal remains of the apostle James lie buried in the crypt, was always as busy as a beehive—or more appropriately as a barn. "Horses and cows stood in the church, and the people brought their entire households with them. They cooked and slept in the galleries," reported the pilgrim Gabriel Tetzel from Nuremberg, who travelled to Santiago in 1467. It is no wonder then that the gigantic incense burner, which still amazes visitors today, hung in the basilica. While recalling the prayers of the pilgrims "rising to heaven like incense," back then the burner also served to mask human and animal odors with clouds of fragrant incense.

As a place of pilgrimage, Santiago was, after Rome and Jerusalem, the most important long-distance goal for worshippers in the Christian Middle Ages—and it often came to pass that penniless pilgrims would spend the night in churches along the way. The inns could no longer accommodate the ever-increasing flood of pilgrims, which explains why, all along the routes to Santiago from all corners of Europe, typical pilgrim churches can be found—churches with several aisles flanking the central nave and with generously proportioned transepts to shelter as many pilgrims as possible. Travellers could spend the night in the galleries. And the semi-circular path, or ambulatory, separating the main altar from the mandatory group of radiating chapels was used for processions inside the church, during which the faithful were often led past relics.

The pilgrims themselves were members of every social class—from barefoot peasants to well-heeled knights. Needless to say, all manner of riffraff mingled with the pious worshippers: scoundrels and swindlers, bandits and pickpockets were keen on gaining worldly rather than heavenly rewards. A pilgrimage was a dangerous undertaking. Not only were travellers often threatened by robbers who were all too quick to pull a knife. Epidemics and illness also took their toll, as well as accidents involving vehicles, lightning, and floods. Thousands died of exhaustion in roadside ditches and drafty hostels. Those who set out

on pilgrimages could never be sure if they would come back alive. Despite this, the pilgrimage to Santiago became more and more popular.

Its origins can be traced back to the ninth century. At that time a shining star appeared to a hermit, hence the town's name: Santiago de Compostela, or, "Saint James from the field of stars." The vision revealed to the hermit that the apostle James had been buried by angels at the spot where the pilgrim church now stands. A marble sarcophagus was unearthed there, and believers erected the first church at the site. It was the first seed of a town which would soon become world famous. Its importance is demonstrated by a thirteenth-century Arabic chronicle which said that Santiago was "the

A dangerous undertaking: pilgrims to St James often fell prey to robbers and bandits

most important Christian temple in the whole universe" and that it was "for the Christians what the Kaaba in Mekka is for us."

The pilgrims came "from the most distant regions, even from darkest Egypt." Yet there were also those who criticized the pilgrimage. In the fourteenth century, a southern German preacher grumbled that there was nothing to see in Santiago other than "a dead skull, the better part of which is already in heaven." Later, Martin Luther remarked: "One should not run off to Santiago, for no one is certain that Saint James truly lies there—and not a dead dog or a dead horse." In fact, the pilgrimage ritual would later degenerate and almost die out completely, until it experienced a revival in the nineteenth century, which has lasted until today.

The cathedral is described in a 13th-century chronicle as
"the most important Christian temple in the whole universe"

Already the Hour of Death Approaches
The Tower of London

England; begun in 1078. Built on the order of William the Conqueror under Gundolf, the future Bishop of Rochester

Oh Death, oh Death rock me asleep,

Bring me to quiet rest,

Let pass my weary guiltless,

Ghost out of my woeful breast.

Toll on the passing bell

Ring out my doleful knell,

Let the sound my death tell,

For I must die

There is no remedy, for I die,

I die, I die.

Anne Boleyn, second wife of King Henry VIII, before her execution in the Tower of London, 1536

King Henry VIII of England, who had two of his wives executed in the Tower; oil painting by Hans Holbein the Younger, c. 1540

It's no wonder that Great Britain is known as the land of detective novels. When it comes to bloodshed, the English have a unique claim to fame: in hardly any other country is the ancient royal seat bathed in such a demonic light as it is in Great Britain. The Tower on the east side of the old city of London is not a symbol of a glorious past or spectacular festivities. On the contrary, here the shadows of malice and revenge, death and depravity lurk in every corner.

For centuries the defiant fortress was the scene of secret, mostly murderous plots. It was also used as a state prison until 1820, and has gone down in history for the countless executions which took place within its walls. It is not surprising either that monarchs did not want to live here and looked around for more cheerful surroundings. Even today the sparkling splendor of the crown jewels, which are kept in the Tower, cannot bedazzle us enough to let us forget the place's dark past. The fact that the Tower shone in the eyes of the world at least once during its long history, when it housed the royal observatories before they were moved to Greenwich, cannot make up for its troubled past.

From the outset, the Tower was planned as a fortress with dungeons. Near it was the old Roman city wall, which is why Shakespeare believed that Julius Caesar had ordered the Tower to be built. In fact, the mighty stronghold on the north bank of the Thames is around a thousand years younger. The core of the complex, the so-called White Tower, was constructed in 1078 by William the Conqueror—of limestone expressly shipped over the Channel from Normandy. During the following centuries, two ring-walls and numerous towers were built around the royal stronghold with its apartments, halls, and chapel (the oldest existing house of worship in London).

The tragic events which were played out within this fortress fill volumes. In 1473 it is said that King Richard III had his two nephews suffocated with pillows in the Bloody Tower in order to ensure that they would not lay claim to the throne. A similarly hair-raising incident occurred in the Wakefield Tower. King Henry VI, the crowned king of England and France, was murdered there while praying. The official version of his demise was that he had died of melancholy. On February 12, 1554, seventeen-year-old Lady Jane Grey, the legendary nine-day queen, was cut down in her bloom at the Tower, a victim of the executioner's axe. This fate had already befallen the former Lord Chancellor, Sir Thomas More, who had clashed with King Henry VIII on matters of religion. The seafarer Sir Walter Raleigh, the founder of the American colony Virginia, lost his head at the same place after falling from favor with his queen, Elizabeth I. He was just writing his history of the world when the executioner plucked the quill from his hand.

Other prisoners in the Tower came to more subtle ends. It is said that Sir Thomas Overbury's last meal was seasoned with nitric acid and accompanied by wine laced with mercury. Whoever was led as a prisoner through Traitors' Gate into the Tower could well conclude that he had been condemned to death. Not all delinquents were willing to accept this sentence, however. A noble lady from Salisbury is said to have tried to avoid her execution (ultimately without success), much to the confusion of her executioner, by dancing furiously around the blood-stained room. Catherine Howard, King Henry VIII's fifth wife, was condemned to death by her husband, as had been her predecessor-but-two, Anne Boleyn. She proved a more submissive victim to her inevitable fate. The night before her beheading at the Tower, she carefully rehearsed her behavior at the executioner's block in order to make a good impression to the very end.

The execution of the Earl of Stratford, prime minister under Charles I, 1641

Not all Beefeaters and jewels, but an ancient royal seat with a history of murderous plots and bloody executions

ENTRY TO THE TRAITORS' GATE

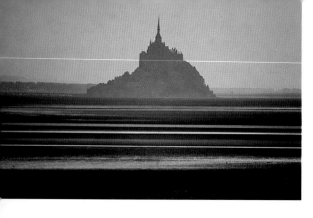

Pyramids of the Sea
Mont-Saint-Michel

Normandy, France; founded in 709; reconstructed
from 1023 onward

**"The Archangel Michael, Prince of the
Church, receives the sainted and leads
them to the Paradise of joy. He had
struck the Egyptians with plagues,
divided the Red Sea, led the people
through the desert into the Chosen
Land. In the holy army of angels he is
the flag-bearer of Christ. At the command of the Lord he will slay the
Antichrist on the Mount of Olives with
all his power. And at his call the dead
will rise on the Day of Last Judgment."**

From *The Golden Legend, Saint Michael, the Archangel,*
by Jacobus de Voragine *c.* 1270

In 709 Bishop Aubert, the religious leader of
the coastal town of Avranches in Normandy,
began to wonder if he could trust his senses.
The Archangel Michael had appeared to him
three times in his dreams. Each time the leader
of heaven's armies had ordered Aubert to build
a church on top of a steep cliff, six miles outside
the city, in order "to celebrate his memory."
Aubert hesitated. Finally a series of miracles
convinced him of the seriousness of the re-
quest and confirmed its validity.

The basis for the legend of Mont-Saint-
Michel is contained in the Legenda Aurea from
the pen of the Dominican Father, Jacobus de
Voragine. It is a collection of holy writings
which became one of the most popular religious books of the Middle Ages. Historical ac-
curacy played but a minor role. Nevertheless,
researchers have confirmed that Mont-Saint-
Michel, which had previously been a sacred
site to a Celtic religious cult, was converted into
a holy place for Christians at the beginning of
the eighth century.

Churches honoring St Michael were tradi-
tionally built on top of hills, places of high
honor in the Middle Ages. In view of the Day of
Last Judgment, which posed a constant threat
to medieval man, it would have been a mistake
to wind up on the wrong side of the revenging
angel charged with enforcing God's justice.
St Michael had already vanquished Lucifer and
driven him out of Paradise. So it is hardly surprising that Bishop Aubert made a pilgrimage
to Monte Gargano in Apulia, the most famous
holy site associated with St Michael to bring
back relics for the new church. He returned
with a portion of an ecclesiastical stole, which
St Michael was said to have laid upon the altar

himself, and a slab of marble bearing the angel's
footprint. The relics ensured that Mont-Saint-
Michel would attract its share of pilgrims for
centuries to come.

The medieval monastery and church are built
on top of a strategically located cliff that marks
the boundary between Normandy and Brittany.
At high tide it is completely cut off from the main-
land and presents a unique example of fortified
medieval monastic architecture. In the first
century after its establishment, hermits' huts
clung to the steep cliffs leading to the holy site.
Later massive buildings replaced them, and
because of the lack of space, the monks were
forced to build vertically rather than horizontally.

The abbey church occupies the highest point
on the cliff and is supported by a massive un-
derpinning that prevents its walls from crashing
into the sea—which has actually happened in
the past. Because of their exposed position
overlooking the English Channel, the holy
brethren often found themselves involved in
wars and were not adverse to trading their
rosaries for swords to fight alongside the brave
knights of old who were defending their coast.

With the passing centuries Mont-Saint-Michel
grew into one of the largest cliff monasteries
in the western world and blossomed into a renowned center of religious learning and culture.
For centuries one of most significant collections of scriptures and one of the most famous
libraries in France were sheltered behind its
walls. It was this cultural significance that
saved the monks from being dispersed and
their monastery from being sacked during the
French Revolution. Until 1863 Mont-Saint-Michel
also served as a prison, primarily for priests
who had opposed the revolution.

Mont-Saint-Michel depicted in the Bayeux Tapestry which
records the Norman Conquest of England, 1066–1082

"The end of the world is nigh." When fire gutted Mont-Saint-Michel in 992 it was believed to signify the end of the world

The Knights' Hall

The Merry Wives of Windsor
The Seat of the English Monarchy

Windsor Castle, England; begun in 1078

"Never a wife in Windsor leads a better life than she does: do what she will, say what she will, take all, pay all, go to bed when she list, rise when she list, all is as she will: and, truly she deserves it; for if there be a kind woman in Windsor, she is one."

Mistress Quickly about Mistress Page in William Shakespeare's *The Merry Wives of Windsor*, 1597

William Shakespeare, one of the many illustrious guests at Windsor Castle; portrait from the 1st edition of his complete works, 1623

Peter de Blois, a knight in the twelfth century, was at odds with his fate. The bread was like lead, he said, there was no fresh fish, and the meat smelled rotten. Worst of all, the wine tasted like pitch. Besides, one had to drink with one's teeth clamped shut in order to filter out all the things that actually shouldn't have been in the wine. From the time of King Henry II onward, when it became a binding tradition for English monarchs to live at least part of the time in Windsor, the history of Great Britain was not one of the most glorious. Not only did the food there leave something to be desired but also the accommodation. Even for the ruling family, life must have been uncomfortable.

Castles were cramped, dark, and drafty. A visit to the "toilet" meant hanging off the outside walls of the castle at a breezy height in a projecting structure—which, in times of war, occasionally became a deadly trap.

Windsor Castle, still one of the residences of the British royal family and the largest inhabited castle in the world, was founded in 1078 by William the Conqueror as part of a defensive system outside the capital. Originally, it only consisted of the "Round Tower." Surrounded by an earthen bulwark and a palisade, the massive structure was enthroned on the commanding limestone hill on the eastern bank of the Thames. An idea of what the "Round Tower" must have looked like on the inside in those days can be gained from a contemporary account: "At ground level were the storerooms and the granary, with crates and barrels and other household equipment. On the next floor were the living quarters and the reception room. A fire was lighted here in the mornings and evenings, and sometimes also during the day when someone was sick. Next to the tower stood the kitchen building, on the lower floor of which pigs, geese, and cocks waited to be slaughtered and eaten."

Yet Windsor Castle, where the long history of England is reflected in its architecture, was subject to continuous modifications. The complex expanded during the course of the centuries. The wooden palisade was replaced by walls of stone, and, in the area around the "Round Tower," stately buildings were erected which soon became the scene of lively festivals. In 1346 the ladies of the court at Windsor celebrated the victory over the French—to the displeasure of a chronicler—by "appearing in stolen dresses and furs, without wasting a thought on the French ladies who had been robbed." Yet worse still, "other beauties, but not the most chaste, dressed themselves in elegant men's suits which also were cut according to French fashion and had tight-fitting hose in two different colors. They wound up their long hair like turbans and moved through the castle in the most provocative manner."

The merrymaking must have been quite racy too on the evening when the Countess of Salisbury once lost her blue garter while dancing with King Edward III in Windsor. The monarch picked it up, calling to the jeering nobles: "Honi soit qui mal y pense," "Shame upon him who thinks ill of it," and promoted the seductive garment to the highest decoration of the country. Still today the gentlemen of the Order of the Garter wear this distinction under their left knee. It's no wonder that, considering the special role of the women in Windsor—who supposedly had a few witches among them—Shakespeare found material for his plays here. The Merry Wives of Windsor was performed for the first time in 1597 in the presence of the queen—in Windsor Castle, of course.

Windsor Castle in the 18th century

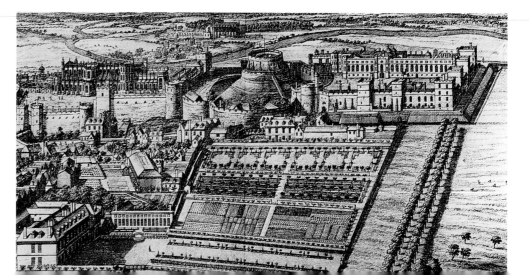

Windsor Castle: seat of the English monarchy and the largest inhabited castle in the world

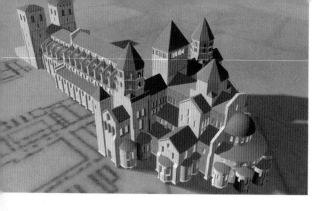

Cluny: The Most Magnificent Abbey Church

Burgundy, France; begun in 1088; consecration of
the main altar in 1095; completed in 1130
Architect: possibly Gunzo of Baume

"The Basilica is of overwhelming
majesty, beauty and grandeur. One
could almost believe that heavenly
beings pass in and out and could describe this house of God as the lobby
of the Angels. Even the simplest monk
is refreshed in this vast breathing
space. Here he may find joy in the
expanse of the spirit of God."

Vita, Hugh, Abbot of Cluny, *c.* 1120

The sight of the abbey of Cluny in the Grosne
valley must have awed early travelers as they
caught sight of it from the Mâconnais hills.
Beneath them stretched a church, larger than
anything they would ever have seen before—
a bold structure of enormous dimensions and
an imposing testament to faith, power, wealth,
and audacity. Six massive towers rose into the
Burgundian sky, and, beyond the lofty vestibule,
a five-nave basilica opened before them, re-
ducing them to the size of tiny church mice.
There was not one transept, but two, along
with countless chapels, altars, paintings,
chandeliers, and sculptures.

The abbey church could accommodate
thousands of worshippers and had an overall
length of about six hundred feet—as long as
two football fields, end-to-end. Critics who
found fault with the dimensions were referred
to a higher authority. According to Abbot
Hugh's Vita, Saints Peter, Paul, and Stephan
personally ordered the church to be built and
laid out its dimensions with the help of a long
thin rope. The saints forgot, however, to provide the necessary funds.

Abbot Hugh saw to the financing, a task
facilitated by the fact that the abbey was at
the peak of its prosperity. It answered only to
the Pope and was, in its early years, independent
of secular rulers, making it a model for the
Western Christian world. A wave of monastic
reform spread from Cluny throughout Europe,
and the abbey was the heart of an order that
included more than 2,000 other monasteries.

Not only did the abbey have jurisdiction over
religious matters, it also become involved in
politics. Abbot Hugh had the task of dealing
with the spiritual leadership of reclaimed
Moorish lands on the Iberian peninsula. Later
he would mediate in the conflict between
Pope Gregory VII and the Holy Roman Emperor
Henry IV who was ultimately forced to travel to
Canossa to seek the Pope's forgiveness. Both
contributed money to the monastery. The King
of Castile sent 10,000 talents of gold, looted
when the Moors were driven from Toledo. King
Henry IV of England and other potentates were
no less generous.

A papal emissary laid the cornerstone on
September 30, 1088, and work began on what
would be the largest structure to be built in
the Middle Ages. Later the monastery was enlarged, and in 1245 the monks of Cluny hosted
a meeting between Pope Innocent IV and
St Louis (King Louis IX of France). The monks
were able to accommodate the Pope, the
Emperor, and their retinues, along with twelve
cardinals, twenty bishops, and the Byzantine
Roman Emperor, without having to give up
their own cells.

Today not much remains of the abbey's
former glory. Cluny became synonymous with
the church's exploitation of the people at a
time when Richelieu and Mazarin were abbots.
During the French Revolution it was decon-
structed and sold eight years later to a demolition company in Mâcon. All that remains
of the church that was once the grandest in
all Christendom, is the south transept and the
so-called tower for baptismal water.

The abbey in the 12th
century; in 1790 it was sold
to a demolition company

The ruins of the monastery of Cluny. The south transept and the baptistery are all that remain of one of the largest structures of the Middle Ages

Dizzying dimensions in "the Lobby of Angels"

Deep in the Jungle
The Temple Complex of Angkor Wat

Cambodia; 1110–1150

"No film, no photograph can prepare you for the overwhelming impression of the temples of Angkor. It is also difficult to speak of them without using effusive language. They are mighty, enormous, wonderful, surprising, awesome. They were built on the idea of godliness. They are the power of the kings of Angkor made stone."

Han Suyin, *About Angkor*, 1972

Angkor Wat after its rediscovery in 1972

The monk Bartolomeo de Argensola, one of the first Christian missionaries to find his way to Cambodia, could hardly believe it. As he stood before the completely overgrown but still majestic ruins of the ancient residence and temple city of Angkor in 1609, he thought that the ideal city described by the Greek philosopher Plato had risen before his eyes—if it were not indeed the supposedly sunken city of Atlantis. Other visitors from the West believed that Angkor was founded by Alexander the Great or by the Roman emperor Trajan, under whose rule the Roman Empire grew far beyond its original borders.

But on their military campaigns, neither Alexander the Great nor Trajan ventured as far as the land that is now Cambodia. The city Angkor, a synonym for a dream turned to stone and at the same time the most extensive temple complex in the world, was created by the Khmer. This people, who used to live not only in Cambodia but also in areas of what is now Thailand, Laos, and the former Cochin China, founded an empire whose culture flourished in the eleventh and twelfth centuries. The heart of their political system, which was economically supported by fishing and rice planting, was at Angkor—at that time a dynamic metropolis with over a million inhabitants.

The majority of the population lived in huts built on stilts (because of the yearly floods brought on by monsoon rains) and roofed with reeds or tiles. Even the king lived in a palace made of wood, as structures of stone were reserved for the dwellings of gods. That is why only the temples have survived the centuries—monumental evidence of a brilliantly developed culture whose last secrets still have not been told.

The largest sacred structure in Angkor is the temple complex Angkor Wat, a city within a city, which had a population of twenty thousand and

was considered the highest expression of the artistic, technical, and religious wisdom of the ancient Khmer. The square-shaped complex, covering more than half-a-square mile, is thought to depict the universe as described in Hindi mythology. The six-hundred-foot wide moat, which surrounds Angkor Wat on all four sides, symbolizes the primeval waters. In the center of the complex is the temple area

proper—with three terraces on various planes surrounded by galleries—that represents the holy mountain Meru. Its five high towers, which resemble lotus buds, represent the seats of the gods and can be seen as symbols of past greatness on Cambodia's national flag.

Hundreds of elephants and thousands of people must have been involved in the construction of the temple complex, which also functioned as a mausoleum. Angkor Wat is believed to be the mortuary of the deified king Suryavarman II, whose reign was of particular significance in the history of Cambodia; never before had the Khmer realm grown as much as it did under this powerful ruler and greatly feared general. But after his death, the country plunged into chaos. Conflicts regarding succession weakened the kingdom, making it an easy target for enemies. In 1432 the Khmer finally surrendered their old capital. "Thus came the downfall of Angkor," in the words of the writer Han Suyin, "which died because of its magnificence, its splendor, its architectural megalomania. A new invader arrived on the scene: the jungle. The trees came and grew over stones and heads and choked Angkor."

The symbol of past greatness—representations of the
Angkor Wat towers form part of Cambodia's national flag

A city within a city—a plan of
Angkor Wat showing the square-
shaped complex with its
surrounding moats and gardens

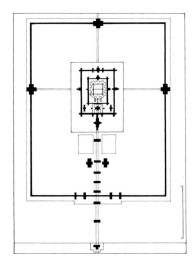

The towers of Angkor Wat display a
striking resemblance to lotus buds

Simplicity as the Ideal in Fontenay Abbey

Burgundy, France; founded in 1118; construction of the church from 1139; consecrated in 1147
Architect: possibly Bernard of Clairvaux

"To what purpose those unclean apes, those fierce lions, those monstrous centaurs, those half-men, those striped tigers, those fighting knights, those hunters winding their horns? Instead of feasting their eyes on stone, the Brethren in the cloister should read the law of God. For God's sake, if men are not ashamed of these follies, why at least do they not shrink from the expense?"

Bernard of Clairvaux, *Apologia ad Guillelmum Sancti Theoderici abbatem, c.* 1127

Bernard of Clairvaux's righteous indignation took the form of terrible tirades, set off by the wasteful grandeur and the excessive size of the abbey church at Cluny. Its height, length, and breadth prompted him to brand it "monstrous," "excessive," and "superfluous." He dismissed its chandelier as "vain trumpery" and damned the glow of its gold as "traitorous to the poor." Nor was he shy about criticizing the art. The paintings lead the monks to immoral digressions. The statues of the saints—the more brightly painted, the holier they were regarded—could only delight a fool. His conclusion: "In a monastery everything that appeals to the eyes, the ears, the sense of smell or taste should be regarded as if it were evil smelling dung." Bernard of Clairvaux, born in 1091, was as acetic as he was quarrelsome and generally feared for his biting wrath.

His self-confidence sprang from the cradle. Born the son of a noble Burgundian family, he decided to renounce the world and enter the recently founded Cistercian order. Thanks to his powerful personality, Bernard soon became the driving force behind the order and was able to bring it to its full flowering.

Named after its parent monastery in Cîteaux, south of Dijon, the Cistercians aspired to return to the old monastic ideals of the their Western founder, Saint Benedict of Nursia. They lived a solitary life in the forest and preached seclusion, simple labor, and poverty. The order forbade every form of luxury—above all architectural. The strict rules of the Cistercians, which Bernard enforced, also applied to all affiliated monasteries. It stipulated that the monks were not to erect any unnecessary buildings and were to refrain from including figurative designs on floors, bell towers, paintings, or sculpture. The only decoration allowed was the crucifix. Those who failed to obey had to pay. In monasteries that retained stained glass windows despite the rules, the abbot, prior, and cellar master were obliged to fast on bread and water every sixth day until the panes had been replaced with clear uncolored ones.

Bernard's campaign for simple architecture went beyond his writings. He is believed to have taken an active part in designing and building the monastery church at Fontenay in Burgundy, which was constructed on land belonging to his uncle. It was a concrete example of his ideals and became the model for all subsequent Cistercian churches in Europe. The former abbey church still bears witness to the simplicity of early Cistercian buildings and rises, as it did 800 years ago and almost unchanged, out of an idyllic, spring-filled forest near Auxerre.

At the beginning of the fourteenth century some three hundred monks inhabited the monastery. Following years of slow decline it was abandoned and then sold. At one point the historic structure was turned into a paper factory belonging to the family of the balloon pioneer Montgolfier. Finally it was purchased by businessman and art collector Edouard Aynard, who restored the buildings to their original design. Aynard's heirs now live in the former monastery, but it is open to the public as a museum and monument to peace and contemplation.

Bernard of Clairvaux—who is believed to have contributed to the design of the monastery church at Fontenay

The pillared hall where the monks would gather

Simplicity as the ideal:
the cloister and church at Fontenay

67

On the Field of Miracles
The Leaning Tower of Pisa

Italy; construction begun in 1173; addition of the belfry in 1350; completed in 1372
Architects: Bonanus, Giovanni di Simone, Tommaso Pisano

"In Pisa we climbed to the top of this strange edifice which all of the world knows—the Leaning Tower of Pisa. It is seven hundred years old, but neither history nor the legends say anything about it, if it was built the way it is standing now on purpose, or if one side of it has sunk. There are also no records which tell us if it ever stood straight. And yet it is the airiest and most beautiful building."

Mark Twain, *Travels Through the Old World*, 1869

Many travelers to Italy have believed it was intentional: that the builder planned a leaning tower, fully aware of what he was doing—out of "willfulness," "cunning," as a "brazen protest against the laws of gravity," or "as a special test" of his art, in order to remain "in the minds of men in time immemorial." Without doubt, the architect succeeded at the latter.

In fact, the campanile of Pisa cathedral was not designed to lean. That was what Johann Caspar von Goethe assumed as he set off on a tour of Europe almost half-a-century before the birth of his famous son Johann Wolfgang. After his visit to Pisa, he noted: "It would have been truly mad to construct the tower as it stands today, especially since its entire inner structure, as well as the different floors into which it is divided and which overhang to the same degree, convince us to the contrary." Even Bonanus, the first builder, who, according to legend, is buried in the foundations of the tower, felt forced to give up on account of the increasing slant: when the third gallery was finished, he stopped work.

Some hundred years later, the architect Giovanni di Simone summoned the courage to continue where others had left off. He built three more galleries and thought he could compensate for the tilt by bending the axis into a vertical position. That did not impress the tower, though. It leaned still further—so much, in fact, that in 1372, when the bell tower was put on top, four steps were necessary on one side and six on the other just so that the belfry could be entered. The diplomat and writer Robert Dvorak says: "Is it not like a symbol of Italy itself, of its art, of crooked, precarious equilibrium, of that which is feared but does not occur; of unforeseen surprises?" Everyone

has been waiting for the tower to topple. It has not yet fallen—but it has not become a world-famous building just because it leans. It is an architecturally fascinating structure that was built for a very specific purpose.

At the time when its foundation stone was laid, Pisa was located directly on the sea and was a powerful, independent port. The Near East, Greece, North Africa, Sicily, Sardinia, and the Balearic Islands were controlled by the republic of Pisa since the Pisans and the Normans together had defeated the Saracens in 1063. To give thanks for the brilliant victory, the Pisans began work on the cathedral; the bell tower was added later. Completed by the additions of the baptistery and the Camposanto, the superb building ensemble in the northwestern corner of the old city was named the "Campo dei Miracoli," or "Field of Miracles." The Pisans wanted to impress the world, yet their plans went awry, as did the tower. The soft alluvial soil is to blame for the tower's predicament, into which not only the campanile continues to sink deeper but also the cathedral itself; its facade has already sunk more than eighteen inches—nothing compared to the seventeen-foot tilt of the Leaning Tower, but nevertheless threatening. Whereas the mathematical genius Galileo Galilei, a native of Pisa, was delighted with the tilt of the tower—which he made use of to try out his famous free-fall experiments—today the world is wondering what can be done to set the tower aright.

But all attempts to save the tower will be in vain, a legend says. This is not a technical problem, but a problem of a much more exalted variety: the Leaning Tower is the revenge of St Reparata, whose church was torn down in the eleventh century to make way for the new cathedral and its campanile.

Soft alluvial soil is to blame for the increasing slant of the Tower

Some lighthearted solutions to the problem of stabilizing the Leaning Tower

From the Mud of the Earth to the Light of Heaven
The Cathedral of Chartres

France; 1194–1220
Architect: unknown

"Cathedrals—palaces of peace and tranquility. What feeling for harmony, what order! The concept of perfection impresses itself upon my mind, the concept of justice. Oh, you eternal stories in stone! The power of this architecture, this density which I so value and which is lacking in my age. And then that great, all-knowing silence. Chartres is wise in a deeply passionate way."

Auguste Rodin, *The Cathedrals of France*, 1914

The world's largest extant labyrinth in an ecclesiastical building is in the Cathedral of Chartres

In the night from the 10th to the 11th of June 1194, an inferno raged through the streets of Chartres. Almost every quarter of the town was ablaze, including the bishop's palace and the cathedral. The morning after, despair over the victims and the largely destroyed town was great, yet greater still was the grief at the loss of a most important relic: since 876, "the robe of Mary," which Charlemagne was said to have received in Jerusalem as a gift on his legendary crusade, had been kept in the cathedral.

In 911, when Vikings besieged the town, it became clear for the first time what power the relic possessed: the bishop of Chartres appeared on the town wall brandishing "the shirt of the Virgin," and the enemy troops fled. Now the people of Chartres believed that the relic, which, since the time of the "Viking miracle" had attracted thousands of pilgrims to their town every year, had been burned. But then, from among the smoking wreckage, the bishop appeared at the head of a solemn procession, bearing the sacred gown. Protected behind the iron door of the crypt, it had escaped the flames. Thus the future of Chartres as a destination for pilgrims had been saved—as well as the commercial life of the town, which was dependent on the crowds. Filled with gratitude, the townspeople rolled up their sleeves and built a new church to honor the Mother of God—a cathedral which, according to the French art historian Marcel Aubert, represents "the triumph of Gothic art."

With the invention of flying buttresses, which support the cathedral from the outside, interior galleries could be eliminated, making it possible for builders to create an uninterrupted vertical space almost 120 feet high. The unknown architect emphasized this verticality and, with carefully calculated proportions that became exemplary for all styles to follow, strove to make the divine notion of beauty in ecclesiastical architecture visible.

Yet the cathedral, which is also cited in connection with esoteric energy paths, is most famous for its 186 large, stained glass windows. Contrary to former building practice, they reach up almost to where the sloping of the vaulted roof begins. They allow light to pour into the church, yet break it into myriad colored rays, creating the impression that the solid walls of stone are dissolving. The interplay of colors produces fascinating effects which transform the celebration of the sacrament into an exalted cult of light.

Around the year 1200, Pierre de Roissy, the chancellor of the school of philosophy and theology at Chartres, extolled the atmosphere in the cathedral as "light that delivers us from evil, and not only shines on us, but also inspires us." The mystical quality of light is based on the concept of God as "the light of the world." Anything that glowed or shined, including the luminous colors of frescoes or paintings on glass, was considered a reflection of the heavens and would transport the viewer skyward.

The light and the vertical emphasis of the walls, it was once believed, would take the heaviness from the stone and transport the worshipper from the mortal realm to the divine. Yet conjuring the supernatural had its price: the Cathedral of Chartres could only be completed thanks to the financial support of generous donors. In 1215, one donor contributed, for example, two silver cups and six silver spoons to help further the building work. Patrons were convinced that their gifts were investments in eternity because, according to one contemporary account, "if the builders believed that the world would someday come to an end, they wouldn't construct such buildings that tower up to the heavens, nor lay foundations that reach down to the profoundest depths of the earth."

"The triumph of Gothic art." The use of flying buttresses resulted in the creation of enormous, uninterrupted vertical spaces

"Light that delivers us from evil, and not only shines on us, but also inspires us." An unprecedented 189 luminous stained-glass windows were designed to transport the viewer heavenward

The Deceptive Image of an Eternal City
Death-Defying: The Cliff Dwellings of Mesa Verde

USA, 200–1300

"We drove through low underbrush, when suddenly the ground opened up. A deep canyon dropped away in front of us. Vertical sandstone walls veined in yellow and brown, with steep slopes further below, dark with vegetation. On the opposite side: a hanging city a pale golden settlement with towers and houses filling out a wide, oval opening in the rocks. It looked so infinitely distant, that it seemed to be a dream, like the deceptive image of an eternal city."

Jacquetta Hawkes, *The World of the Past*, 1963

The paths and steps are frighteningly narrow and steep, suggesting that the people who lived here did not suffer from dizziness or a fear of heights. For their cliff-side dwellings are attached to the walls like swallows' nests over the yawning abyss. One false step must not have been an uncommon cause of death for the Anasazi Indians. Why they suddenly withdrew with everything they owned into the narrow, inaccessible canyons around 1200—a time in Europe when minstrels were still singing the praises of heroic knights—is still an unsolved mystery.

Before 1200 their home was the plateau above the canyon, called "Mesa Verde," or "Green Table," by the Spanish after the discovery of America. Thickly covered with pine trees and juniper bushes, the mesa, covering a massive area of some three hundred square miles, rises approximately 1,500 feet above the surrounding plains. The Mesa Verde is a grandiose landscape of countless canyons cut deep into the sandstone plateau, creating a unique ensemble of steep drops, washed-out rock niches, and caves.

Here, in the southwestern corner of what is now the American state of Colorado (near the borders of Utah, Arizona, and New Mexico), the Anasazi Indians, who were originally hunters and gatherers, found almost ideal living conditions. Water, wood, and wildlife were there for the taking, and for these the Anasazi were willing to endure the thin air at an average altitude of some six thousand feet, as well as the extreme variations in temperature between day and night. Once settled, they ate corn, pumpkins, beans, and turkey. At first the Anasazi lived in brushwood huts; later, they built their first villages

with houses made of logs, branches, and clay. When they retreated into the canyons, their society had reached its zenith. The cliff dwellings were solidly made of sun-dried adobe bricks reinforced with straw and were painted on the inside. As a rule, the houses faced southwest—so that in the cold of night the residents could take advantage of warmth stored in walls that had been bathed in sunshine throughout the day.

Another example of this orientation can be seen at the thirteenth century "Cliff Palace"—the largest cliff dwelling at Mesa Verde and in all of North America. Tucked under the overhanging rocks in a sickle-shaped cavity in the wall of Cliff Canyon, it was once inhabited by 200 to 250 people, in 217 rooms spread over four different levels. The foundations of twenty-three oval-shaped structures have been excavated in front of the main complex. At one time these may have been covered with dome-like roofs and used for cult rituals. The clever exploitation of the scarce space and the technical mastery of the buildings are still widely admired today.

Yet life along the canyon walls, which had already come to a halt around 1300—probably as a result of a long drought—must have been no picnic. The precarious paths may have made it especially difficult for children and the elderly to leave the settlement. Besides the protection the rocks offered, the exposed situation of the cliff dwellings had only one uncontestable advantage: waste disposal. The residents of Mesa Verde simply threw their garbage, as well as their dead, into the abyss—the latter, however, wrapped in large cotton shrouds.

The Anasazi cleverly exploited the protection of overhanging cliffs in constructing their dwellings

The "hanging city" of the Mesa Verde

Carved from the Light of the South
Emperor Frederick II and Castel del Monte

Apulia, Italy; begun before 1240
Architect: possibly Philippe Chinard

"As a landmark which is visible from a great distance, dominating the vast plains, people call it the 'Belvedere' or the 'Balcony of Apulia.' An even better name could be the 'Crown of Apulia,' because this castle stands on a hilltop like a mural crown. It seemed to me to be like the diadem of the Hohenstaufen empire, crowning the splendid countryside when the evening sun made it sparkle purple and gold."

Ferdinand Gregorovius, *A Journeyman's Travels in Italy*, 1877

Emperor Frederick II, the builder of Castel del Monte, is said to have been a "cunning man, wily, dissolute, malicious, and irascible." At least that was how a contemporary saw him, the monk Salimbene of Parma. The church and its servants did not care much for the great ruler, who "had little love for religion," as Pope Pius II observed peevishly in the fifteenth century, not forgetting to mention the emperor's "indecent habits" in which he "secretly indulges." Some circles even saw Frederick II as the antichrist—the son of Satan, who, according to dismal notions about the finitude of human life on earth, was to appear directly before the end of the world. His own curiosity was to blame for this assessment, a curiosity which drove him to look beyond the bounds of his own culture and his own beliefs—an incomparable sacrilege for honest Christians.

Frederick II, simultaneously the "hammer of the world," and, according to the opinions of those who admired him, the "wonder of the world" and "the first modern man on the throne," commanded not only his native Italian, but also French and Provençal, Latin, Greek, Hebrew, and Arabic. His interests did not only include ruling, waging war, and hunting, but also classical philosophy, literature, and medicine, as well as all aspects of Jewish and Islamic culture. Frederick II was a freethinker—and not only a few biographers suggest that Castel del Monte, a building which unifies classical, Islamic, and Judeo-Christian elements, is his legacy in stone.

The design of the monumental castle, which in its austere simplicity is enthroned on the hilltop like an erratic block, appears to be "carved from the hard light of the south." It is thought to be the work of the emperor himself, reflecting his love of geometry and astronomy, and his fanaticism for everything that can be explained theoretically. The east-west axis of the strictly proportioned building, whose walls and corner towers have the prismatic clarity of a crystalline structure, is said to deviate exactly two-and-one-half degrees from the ideal direction—that is, it stands exactly parallel to the tilted axis of the earth. Castel del Monte has often been called "astronomy cast in architecture" for that reason.

Of still greater importance, however, is the mathematical rigor of the ground plan which is based on the number eight. The octagonal, open inner courtyard is enclosed by an eight-cornered ring-like structure in which each of the two floors contains eight trapezoidal rooms. In turn, eight octagonal defensive towers protect the outer walls of the fortress. These elements reflect not only architectonic principles, but represent philosophy in a constructed form. Since the square is a symbol of the world and life on earth, while the circle stands for the otherworldly infinity of God, the octagon represents the intermediary realm between heaven and earth. This corresponds to the Christian notion that the number eight symbolizes the resurrection of man and the bliss of eternal life. This concept, on the other hand, is rooted in the antique idea that the number sixty-four, of which eight is the square root, is a symbol of the heavenly wisdom which orders everything in the world according to a logical plan.

Castel del Monte—an ideal building with transcendental allusions—stands in close relation to the emperor's self-esteem. Throughout his life Frederick II saw himself as a mediator between the different cultures of the known world. And yet in the travel diary of this incessantly active master there is not one reference to a stay at the Castel del Monte. Before the emperor's death on December 13, 1250, the castle, which offered the greatest luxury, every imaginable comfort, and extraordinarily modern sanitary facilities, had only been used twice: once as the setting for a marriage and once as a prison.

A coin depicting Emperor Frederick II

The austere simplicity of Castel del Monte, the "Crown of Apulia"

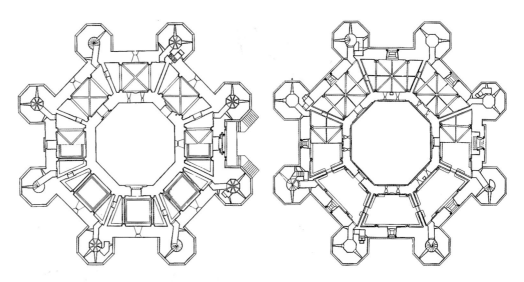

Reflecting Frederick II's love of geometry and astronomy, the ground plan was based on
the number eight which in turn reflects the Christian notion of resurrection and eternal life

Rise! Rise, You Bravest of Knights!
Fortress and Monastery in One: The Malbork

Poland; begun in 1272

"For centuries, the calmly-flowing waters of the Nogat river have mirrored the Malbork—an imperious monument of a turbulent past, animated by myths and legends, visited by kings and emperors, destroyed and rebuilt several times. The key to the beauty of its architecture, which is so similar to that of a Gothic cathedral, is one of the Malbork's greatest secrets."

Mariusz Mierzwinski, Director of the Malbork castle museum, 1992

The history of the Teutonic Order and the Malbork begins in the Holy Land—in the port of Acre near the modern metropolis Haifa. It was there in 1190 that merchants from Lübeck and Bremen founded a hospice to care for German knights fighting in the third crusade. Eight years later, this brotherhood of Hospitalers evolved into a spiritual order of knighthood, the "Teutonic Order," which was soon to become involved in politics, eager, by whatever means, to gain worldly power.

Hermann von Salza, a crafty and capable thinker and Grand Master of the Teutonic Order from 1209 to 1239, transformed his knights into a military organization with a view to founding the Order's own state. It was impossible to achieve this goal in Palestine, however, as the age of Western rule there was almost at an end. His plan also miscarried in Hungary, where the Teutonic Order responded to a call to help defeat a heathen tribe: King Andrew II recognized the threat they posed and drove out the valiant warriors. Instead, in 1226, an invitation came from Duke Conrad of Masovia, a region along the lower Vistula river. He wanted to subjugate the heathen ancestors of the Prussians and hoped to enlist the help of the Teutonic Order, for whom the fight against heathens in Europe was as important as the crusades against infidels in the Holy Land. As payment, he offered the knights a dominion of their own within his territory.

Hermann von Salza seized the opportunity and more: after the Teutonic Order had defeated the heathens, he demanded—and won—complete control over the Baltic Sea, much to the dismay of the Duke of Masovia. But in order to expand their sphere of influence, the knights of the Teutonic Order needed a strong base for their operations. They chose a site on a mountain ridge between Gdańsk and Elbing, near where the famous Amber Road crosses other trade routes. Here, between the Nogat river and swamplands further inland, they created the Malbork, a fortified monastery dedicated to the guardian of the Teutonic Order, the Virgin Mary.

Originally simple, the Malbork would eventually be developed into one of the most powerful fortresses in Europe. For in the year 1309, the Grand Master of the Teutonic Order, who had previously lived in Acre, then in Venice, established his seat here. Having become the center of the realm, which included not only Pomerania, Livonia, Estonia, and Gotland, but also the Hanseatic towns Gdańsk, Torun, Elblag, and Kaliningrad, the Malbork was the scene of vibrant courtly life. There are accounts of sumptuous banquets in the Great Refectory, that gravity defying, most audaciously built hall of all crusaders' castles, where the ceiling vaults rise up into space like delicate palm fronds. But there were also reports of treachery and murder—specifically that of Werner von Orseln, the Grand Master, who was slain at the entrance to the castle's chapel.

But Malbork's days of glory as the residence of the Grand Master were not to last long: in 1454 the Order came to mortgage the fortress to its mercenaries, who in turn relinquished it to the Polish king. From then on, almost all Polish monarchs stayed at the Malbork while in Pomerania—until the fortress came under Prussian control in the aftermath of the first division of Poland in 1772. It was then used as barracks and a granary, and finally fell into disrepair. Rebuilt in the nineteenth century by the Prussians (among them the planning officer and writer Joseph von Eichendorff), and by the Poles after its destruction during World War II, the great stronghold is now viewed ambivalently: on the one hand as "a monument to Polish nationalism," on the other as "a symbol of German expansionism to the east."

A detail on the crypt bars in the monastery chapel

The stronghold at Malbork was rebuilt by the Prussians in
the 19th century and again by Poles after its destruction
during World War II

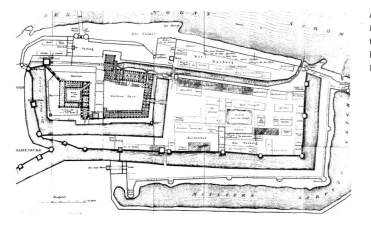

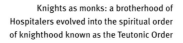

As the center of the realm,
Malbork was initially the base for
the powerful Teutonic Order and
later became the seat of the
Polish monarchy

Knights as monks: a brotherhood of
Hospitalers evolved into the spiritual order
of knighthood known as the Teutonic Order

Silk, Saffron, and Sandalwood
Venice, Its Wealth, and the Doge's Palace

Italy; begun in 814; expanded from the 13th century onward

"Like a unique diamond in the center of a jewel, the Doge's Palace thrusts itself into the foreground. Such architecture has never been seen anywhere else. Everything about it is new. One feels freed from the bounds of tradition. One understands that there is a whole world beyond that of classical and medieval forms, that human creativity is limitless, that, like Nature, it is capable of violating all rules and, precisely for that reason, is capable of bringing forth a perfect work."

Hippolyte Taine, 1864

The end of Venice coincided with the carnival. As Napoleon dissolved the Republic, the counselors were putting on their masks

In 1204 the moment of truth had come for Venice. For in that year the army of crusaders under the leadership of Venice invaded the Byzantine capital of Constantinople. The victory, bought with streams of blood and merciless brutality, made the maritime republic a world power. Venice controlled three-eighths of the Eastern Roman Empire, behind the scenes powerful Venetian figures pulled the strings of the "Latin empire" established in Constantinople, and Venetian merchants dominated commerce throughout the eastern Mediterranean.

After 1380, when Venice had succeeded in pushing aside her rival Genoa, the lagoon city was acknowledged as the center of world trade. The goods which were bought and sold there are evidence of exotic abundance: alum from Asia Minor, cotton from Cyprus, emeralds from Egypt, rubies from Ceylon, ivory from Ethiopia, cloves from Java, indigo from Baghdad, pepper from Malabar—almost everything could be had. Even the slave trade played an important role. It is hardly surprising that, in a city like this, luxury came to be a matter of course.

Prosperity was visible not only in the splendor of people's clothes, jewels, and gondolas, but also in the city's architecture. Facades, ceilings, stairwells—every available surface was decorated and covered with gold. This was also true of the Doge's Palace, the seat of the head of state where all decisions for the well-being of the republic were made. Originally erected as a wooden citadel in 814 and surrounded by water, the former fortress, which once guarded the entrance to the Canal Grande and the Rialto, was transformed into a generously expanded building of stone grand enough to reflect the power and wealth of Venice.

The facade, with its rows of arcades, windows, and delicate diamond patterns in pale yellow-white and rosy marble, has an oriental character, and at the same time is the allegory of Venice: in the same way that the entire city rests on a foundation of oak piles anchored to the floor of the lagoon, the Doge's Palace, supported on slender columns, seems to hover over the earth. The countless paintings and frescoes which decorate its interior celebrate the triumph of Venice over and over again. These include *The Conquered Cities Pay Homage to Venice, Venice as Ruler of the World, Venice Receives the Crown as a Sign of Her Power,* and *The Apotheosis of Venice.*

Needless to say there are also portraits of all of one-hundred-and-twenty doges, the chief magistrates of Venice between 697 and 1797, who gave the palace its name. But according to the constitution which declared that the republic is everything, that the individual must serve her unconditionally, and that no cults of particular individuals could be tolerated, the doge was not considered a ruler, but a "slave of the republic." It was not he who ruled, but an aristocratic oligarchy, the Council of Ten, and the senate.

A slave to the Republic: the doge Leonard Loredan, by Giovanni Bellini, *c.* 1507

The doge was merely a figurehead who had to submit to numerous restrictions. He was not allowed to become involved in matters of trade and could not leave the city. His correspondence was censored, private contact with foreign dignitaries was forbidden, and, with the exception of flowers and aromatic herbs, he was not permitted to accept gifts. The doge was a prisoner in a golden cage, a thought which moved the writer Joseph Victor von Scheffel to write the following lines in 1855: "The Doge's Palace is a curious marvel which already on its exterior clearly expresses that a Venetian doge is not a prince who can live according to his whims and pleasures, but the principal administrator of a sinister, severe republic which only puts these rooms at his disposal more or less in the same way that another city gives its mayor the third floor of the town hall as an official residence."

The Doge's Palace as the embodiment of the
splendor and power of the Venetian state

The inner courtyard with its imposing flight of stairs

Sanctuary of Dreams
The Alhambra and Poor Boabdil

Granada, Spain; construction begun in 1300 under
Ibn al-Ahmar; rebuilt from 1333 to 1354 under Jusuf I

"Who can do justice to a moonlight night in such a climate and such a place? The temperature of a summer midnight in Andalusia is perfectly ethereal.... But when moonlight is added to all this, the effect is like enchantment. Under its plastic sway the Alhambra seems to regain its pristine glories. Every rent and chasm of time; every moldering tint and weather-stain is gone; the marble resumes its original whiteness; the long colonnades brighten in the moonbeams; the halls are illuminated with a softened radiance—we tread the enchanted palace of an Arabian tale."

Washington Irving, *The Alhambra*, 1832

It has been described as a "palace of pearls," as "a portrait of paradise," and called the "heavenly Jerusalem." But in reality it is "Qal' at al Hamra"—"the Red Fort"—a name that refers to the glow of the setting sun reflecting from its walls. It is a fortress, one of the mightiest that was ever built on the Iberian peninsula. The awe-inspiring structure crowns a ridge shaped like the prow of a ship, one of the foothills of the towering, snow-topped Sierra Nevada which thrusts deep into the valley.

Massive walls and monumental towers dominate the hill above Granada and betray no hint of the lovely gardens and apartments protected in their shadow. Inside the formidable defense structure, which formerly contained a town with houses, administrative buildings, army barracks, stables, mosques, schools, baths, cemeteries, and gardens lies the heart of the Alhambra. The Moorish royal palace, a "crystal Elysium," in which the legendary richness of Eastern architecture and decoration comes into full flower, rises majestically next to the old fortress and representative building erected under Emperor Charles V.

The Alhambra protected its precious treasures behind battlements and crenelated towers—a necessary precaution in the time of the *Reconquista*, the name given to the renewed Christian conquest of the territories which had been under Islamic rule since the eighth century. In the thirteenth century Granada became a refuge for Muslims fleeing the carnage of what the Christians called the "Crusade against the Infidel," and the Muslims named the "Holy War." The city became the residence of an Islamic King and the last bastion of Mohammedanism in Europe. The royal palace, the Alhambra, is the epitome of Islamic art. It is an enchanted monument to Moorish culture on Western soil—as if the Islamic world wanted to concentrate all of its power in one place.

The Islamic palace has neither a representative facade, nor a main axis upon which various parts of the building are arranged, providing a complete contrast to its neighbor, the princely residence of European Christendom. It even lacks wings of interconnecting rooms. Instead, various inner courtyards surrounded by apartments seem to be arranged at random. Fountains splash softly, and there are picturesque views onto hidden gardens in which cypress and lemon trees provide shade and flowers lend a dramatic show of color. The architecture is human in scale. Its lofty pavilions, rooms, and baths appear intimate, manageable and inviting. Is this the secret of the Alhambra?

The early residents of the palace were already caught in its spell, as the sad legend of Boabdil, the last Moorish ruler of Granada, illustrates. Worn down by the long siege of the city by the Catholic monarchs, King Ferdinand II of Aragón and Queen Isabel of Castile, Boabdil capitulated and handed them the keys to the city on January 2, 1492. Having thus transformed his city into the graveyard of Islamic culture in Europe, he saddled his horse and rode away, never to return. He turned back only once to gaze upon the Alhambra from a point known as the "Hill of Tears" (La Cuesta de las Lagrimas) where he broke down and wept over the loss of his paradise. His mother, who appeared to be made of sterner stuff, chided him not to "weep like a woman over what he was unable to defend as a man."

Boabdil, the last Moorish ruler of Granada, hands the keys to the city to the new rulers, the Catholic King Ferdinand II of Aragón and Queen Isabel of Castile

"An enchanted monument to Moorish culture," the Lion Court in the Alhambra

A detail of one of the Alhambra's richly decorated, lofty vaults

A Wall Built of Blood
The Great Wall of China: The Longest Structure in the World

China; begun *c.* 800 B.C. and completed during
the Ming dynasty (1368–1644)

"A wall that stretches across half
the earth! A wall from Philadelphia to
Kansas City, a wall from Constantinople
to Marseille! Whether you see it by the
light of the stars or the moon, through
a cloud of dust, through the veil of
a rain shower or through falling flakes
of a snowstorm—it remains forever a
huge, gray, unbelievable, immovable
ghostly reminder of the past."

William Edgar Geil, *The Great Wall of China*, 1909

It is said that it is even visible from the moon.
Astronauts have still to confirm this fact, but
one thing is certain, the Great Wall of China,
with its dozens of branches leading off to the
left and right, is the longest structure that man
has ever succeeded in constructing. To this day
it has never been completely or accurately
measured. It is estimated to have been twice
as long in its original form—up to one-eighth of
the earth's circumference—than the approximately 1,500 miles that now remain.

The wall stretches from the Kansu province
in the west to the Gulf of Chihli in the east,
wending its way through deserts and mountains in between. The basis for conjecture
about the original length of the giant fortification comes from Chinese writings. The Chinese
call it "The Wall of 10,000 Li," and a *li* is equal
to 547 yards. But 10,000 *li* is also a figure of
speech signifying that something stretches

The dragon as a symbol of the Great Wall, which wends
its way across the countryside

on forever, beyond the imagination of mere
human beings.

Its beginnings go back to Chinese pre-history
and are not found in any written record. The
history is based on oral tradition with its reliance on legends and sagas. It appears that
the first stretches of the Great Wall were constructed between 800 and 500 B.C. They were
protective earthworks made of clay, built to
prevent tribes from the barren North from
invading the fertile South, which was still
splintered into countless rival fiefdoms.

Following the unification of China in 221 B.C.,
Emperor Shi Huangdi had the individual protective walls joined to form one long wall that
separated two totally different cultures. On one
side were the nomadic tribes of Central Asia
who were largely shepherds. On the other was
the highly civilized agricultural society of the
newly formed Chinese Empire. In the centuries
that followed the wall was partially destroyed,
rebuilt, restored, and enhanced by the tradition
of watch towers. By the time of the Ming dynasty

(1368–1644) the wall served not only as a fortification against the Mongols but also as a trade
route.

The top of the crenelated wall, in places fifty
feet high, provided a well-protected road on
which "five horses could pass abreast," according to the account of Father Matteo Ripa,
a missionary from Naples who lived in China
at the beginning of the nineteenth century.

The Great Wall was thus an important traffic
artery in whose shadow market towns grew and
blossomed. But the construction of this world
wonder also cost hundreds of thousands of
lives. According to a Chinese saying about the

The Great Wall of China—a fortification and trade route in one

wall, "tears of the people" have dampened it from top to bottom. Each stone is said to represent one death—a bloodletting that wiped out generations of Chinese.

Gruesome tales are still told of how the Great Wall was built. Overseers whipped farmers and soldiers forced to work on the wall until their skin hung in shreds. Anyone who laid two stones together so that a nail could pass through the space between them was beheaded. The mortar used to build this all-encompassing monster was mixed with human blood, a theme echoed by Guo Moruo, China's most famous Maoist poet. Following the Japanese invasion in 1937 he wrote, "We are neither cowards nor presumptuous. But we believe we must conquer our enemies. We must build a new wall out of nothing less than our own flesh and our own blood."

The top of the crenelated wall hid a well-protected road

The Flower of Italy
Florence and Its Cathedral Dome

Italy; 1296–1436; dome by Filippo Brunelleschi; 1418–1436
Architects: Arnolfo di Cambio, Giotto, Andrea Pisano,
Francesco Talenti, and Giovanni Ghini

"The city is delightful, so that it is
appropriate that it should be called
'Beautiful Florence, the Flower of Italy.'
Magnificent buildings, some dedicated
to God, others for the use of man rise
in view. First one sees the wonderful
Cathedral of Santa Maria del Fiore,
covered in marble and topped by
an extraordinary dome created by
the excellent Florentine architect
Brunelleschi."

Leon Battista Alberti, *On the Art of Building*, 1452

In the fourteenth century, Florence was not only one of the largest but also one of the richest cities in the world. The mighty Florentine Peruzzi Bank, for example, had sixteen European branches, including one in London and another on the island of Cypress. The Florentine *gulden* was considered the most important and stable currency in the Western World. Commerce and trade flourished in the metropolis on the Arno despite the rivalry among its leading families that often escalated into blood feuds. Not even the plague, that wiped out two-thirds of the

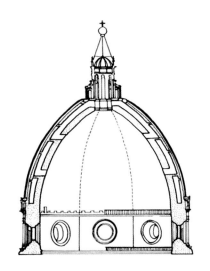

Transection of the first independently supported dome in the history of architecture

population within a few months in 1347 and 1348, could stop the city's growth.

When Florence unscrupulously brought half-a-dozen neighboring cities, including Arezzo, Pisa, and Livorno, under its hegemony, it became the leading power in central Italy. Nowhere else could artisans and merchants accumulate so much political influence—a situation that

prompted Swiss historian Jacob Burckhardt to call Florence of that time "the first modern state in the world." Art blossomed alongside the prosperity.

Since 1296 the citizens of Florence had been tinkering with their cathedral, adding onto and altering the structure. Now they wanted to clothe it in glory. The new cathedral had to be imposing, a symbol of the city's power and zest for life. Thus Florence, whose buildings were almost exclusively built of the local *pietra-forte*, saw a new monument to its self-confidence rise in the middle of the city. The cathedral became a veritable mountain of white, red, and green marble, and it appeared to have been conceived by a painter rather than a builder. It was dedicated to the Virgin Mary and evoked the flower of the lily, *del Fiore*, on the city coat of arms in its name.

The soaring interior can accommodate 25,000 worshippers, making it Christendom's fourth-largest church after St Peter's in Rome, St Paul's in London, and the cathedral of Milan. Its enormous dome, which rises toward heaven like "the bud of a flower," dominates the skyline of Florence. It was an epoch-breaking achievement, an engineering marvel that inspired Michelangelo in his design of the dome for St Peter's in Rome. It is made of brick laid in a herringbone pattern and held together by fast-drying mortar. The dome, which rises almost 350 feet into the air, with a diameter of 125 feet, revolutionized architecture. It is the first independently supported dome in the history of architecture.

In earlier domes, such as those on the Pantheon in Rome and the Hagia Sophia in Constantinople, the weight was distributed to and supported by load bearing structures. In Florence's cathedral the weight is borne by only eight, white marble ribs that span the dome from its base to the lantern in its center. Architects are still amazed that, given the technical knowledge available at that time, Filippo Brunelleschi, a goldsmith, builder of fortifications, and a defense engineer, could have constructed such a masterpiece. The achievement also amazed Brunelleschi himself who, doubting his mastery, entrusted his creation to the protection of Mary, the Mother of God. He would position himself behind the dome and stare at it imploringly, as if by staring he could safeguard his masterwork from collapsing.

Early drawing of the view over Florence
with the Cathedral dome, *c.* 1480

"A marble mountain" — Brunelleschi's masterpiece

The Lost City
Machu Picchu

Peru; c. 1450

"This city, which is built over an abyss, is a cosmic vision of nature. Its important role as a shrine is reflected in its ritual-like elegance, in the expression of the eternal uttered by its very stones. As the realization of a bold architectural dream fitted into the fantastic mountain world of the Andean peaks like a valuable jewel, Machu Picchu should be considered one of the greatest monuments of the Incas."

Hector Velarde, *The Architecture of the Incas*, 1960

The "Rock of the Hanged," the "Chapel of the Mummies," the "Window of the Snakes"—at every step of a walk through the ruins of Machu Picchu the stony witnesses of the past are encountered with names rich in intriguing allusions. Yet all of the names are from the twentieth century. The terraced city, which is perched on an almost inaccessible cliff-top, high above the wild canyon of the Rio Urabamba in the middle of the Peruvian Andes (7,500 feet above sea level) was only discovered in 1911.

For many explorers, "the skyscraper of ancient Peru," as it is sometimes called, is still the most unimaginable and mysterious of all forgotten cities. For as in the case of Teotihuacán, the imposing ruined site near Mexico City, there is no written record of Machu Picchu. What was the original name of this city with its thousands of steps? Who built it? And when? Was it suddenly abandoned? And, if so, why? What rituals took place here? Wild speculation abounds—including the fantastic belief that Machu Picchu is the creation and dwelling place of winged humans.

What we now know for sure is that Machu Picchu had no more than a thousand inhabitants and was a city of the Incas. This people, which in the fifteenth century became ever more influential through military expansion and skillful diplomacy, controlled a tightly structured empire when the Spanish conquistadors finally defeated it in 1572. It stretched along the Pacific coast from modern Columbia to Chile. Machu Picchu, the city of colored granite, which was

decorated with fountains, palaces, places of sacrifice, and temples, but which also had shops, workshops, a solar observatory, and prisons, was not the capital city but a fortified administrative center.

Most probably it was founded by Pachacutec, the ninth Incan ruler, who was worshiped as a descendent of the sun-god and ruled between 1438 and 1471. At that time, the city might have been considered a type of pioneering agricultural enterprise; Machu Picchu is the first Incan settlement which spreads out towards the forest. It is famous, above all, for its "hanging gardens" which cling to the high cliffs and descend, cascade-like, into the dizzying abyss, and which supplied the city not only with potatoes and corn, but also with the "green gold of the Andes," the intoxicating leaves of the coca plant. But what significance did Machu Picchu have apart from its unusual location? Did the Incas consider the city, which opens downwards like an amphitheater, to be the mythical birthplace of its ruling dynasty? Did its walls protect the "casa del sol," the empire's most important shrine to the sun? Perhaps the Incan rulers attempted to make contact with the gods here. Was Machu Picchu the "forbidden hiding-place" of great magicians, sorcerers, and sooth-sayers, the "university of the idolators" so vehemently and persistently cursed by Christian missionaries (who incidentally never found them)? Maybe the last Incan ruler barricaded himself in this unconquerable eagle's nest, surrounded by his countless courtesans, the "sun maidens," in the face of attack by European conquistadors, and forbade his people, whom he had left behind in the area around Machu Picchu, to show the conquerors the secret paths to the cliff-top city.

Whatever the case, the Spaniards never set foot in Machu Picchu. And so today the lost city stills guards its secrets like a giant sarcophagus.

Hiram Bingham, the American explorer who discovered Machu Picchu

High in the Peruvian Andes lies Machu Picchu,
terraced city of the Incas

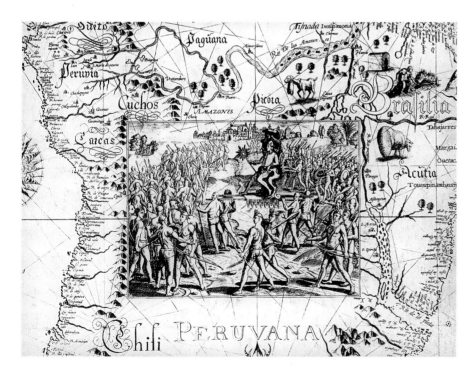

The Inca ruler Atahualpa and his empire, which is believed
to have stretched from modern Columbia to Chile

Healing Herbs and Valuable Vines
The Medieval Hospital Hôtel-Dieu in Beaune

France; opened on January 1, 1452
Architect: Jacques Wiscrère

"Oh you, the poor and sick, bear patiently the pains of the flesh and the scarcity of food, and give thanks to God. For it is less dreadful to suffer hunger and be burned and cut by physicians in this world, than later to burn in the fires of hell with the rich and powerful."

Thomas von Kempen, *The Valley of the Lilies*, c. 1450

Saint Hildegard of Bingen recommended the use of wormwood as a remedy for gout, pains in the chest, coughing, general feebleness, and other illnesses unknown to us today. One recipe instructed one to press the leaves of the plant and cook the juice with honey and wine. This elixir was believed to be an almost magical cure-all. It cleared the eyes, invigorated the heart, warmed the stomach, and cleansed the bowels—according to that pious lady, the first famous woman homeopath in history.

When the hospital Hôtel-Dieu, in the Burgundian town of Beaune, France, admitted its first patients on January 1, 1452, other types of essences were also being brewed in the establishment's pharmacy—opium, mandrake root, and henbane. A sponge would be soaked in an anaesthetic substance to numb a person "who was to be sawed open or cut into"—at that time an unfortunately frequent and rather dubious pleasure for surgeons.

Towards the end of the Hundred Years' War between France and England, which raged from 1337 to 1453, the population suffered grievously at the hands of destitute bands of soldiers on marauding rampages. Thousands lost everything they owned, and death crept stealthily across the country in the form of famine and epidemics. Ghastly war wounds, which had become more numerous and far more dreadful since the invention of gun powder in the fourteenth century, gaped and festered. The indescribable misery was surely the reason why Nicolas Rolin, the powerful chancellor of the duchy of Burgundy, founded the hospital in Beaune, his mother's birthplace, at precisely that time.

In keeping with the medieval concept of God as the ultimate healer, the institution was

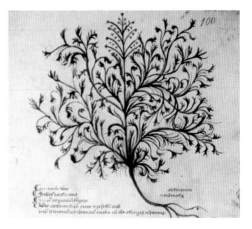

Wormwood, a medieval cure-all; taken from a 13th-century manuscript

called Hôtel-Dieu, the "House of God." This name also recalls the devotion of those who cared for the sick there: heavenly paradise, rather than financial gain, was to be their main reward. Nicolas Rolin, too, strove to prove himself in the eyes of God. He was known for his charismatic personality and was as esteemed as he was feared. It was rumored that he endowed the hospital in an urgent bid to save his soul—his way of making amends to a people which he had at times ruthlessly exploited. It seems that he intended to mend his ways. He spared no cost in equipping the hospital: the medical instruments he purchased were the most modern that money could buy. And with its four wings, its surprisingly noble inner court, the leaden embellishments of its gables, and the colorfully glazed tiles of its steeply sloping roof, the Hôtel-Dieu was more reminiscent of an aristocratic residence than a hospital for the poor.

Rolin also spent generously when it came to furnishing the interior; he commissioned Rogier van der Weyden, official painter to the city of Brussels, and one of the most highly regarded artists of his day, to decorate the panels of the altarpiece. At the heart of the hospital, which also included smaller chambers for noble patients, is the "hall of the poor:" a church-like room over 150 feet long and forty feet wide where sickbeds line the side walls under a colorfully painted, arched ceiling. In order to save space and share body warmth, one bed was always shared by two patients. Anyone lacking the means to pay for care was taken in free of charge. In order to finance this rather costly form of charity, Nicolas Rolin had acquired some of the finest vineyards on the Côte-d'Or. Even today, the proceeds from their harvests are still the most important source of funding for the present municipal hospital of Beaune.

The Virgin and Child depicted with the founder of Hôtel-Dieu, Nicolas Rolin; oil painting by Jan van Eyck, c. 1433/34

An early poster advertising a tour through Burgundy

The embellishments and colorfully glazed tiles of the inner court

God as the ultimate healer; the hospital was called the "House of God"

Science, I'd Like to Lovingly Embrace Thee
Oxford University: One of the Intellectual Centers of England

England; begun in 1474
Master of work: William Orchard

"For nearly one term I went to bed drunk every night and began drinking again immediately when I woke.... I only had to be sober once a week when I read an essay with my tutor."

Graham Greene, *A Sort of Life*, 1971

A long time ago, farmers drove their oxen across the river at the point where the Cherwell flows into the Thames some fifty-six miles northwest of London. The idyll lives on: gentle hills and lush meadows still lend the picturesque river landscape its incomparable charm. Above the undulating green countryside rises the unmistakable silhouette of Oxford with its countless spires. The Romantic poet John Keats called Oxford "the most beautiful town in the world." It is not surprising that this so richly blessed corner of England is an ideal place for study.

Oxford is the oldest university in Great Britain, dating from the twelfth century. Many also claim that the purest English is spoken here. After the market town had developed into an important center of trade under the Normans, the country was governed from here for almost 100 years. Scholars flocked to Oxford, as well as some religious orders who founded several monastery schools. Anyone who wished to complete a regular course of study had to go to Paris, the only university in western Europe at the time. That would change when King Henry II ordered all students of his country to return home from the metropolis on the Seine and inaugurated his own university in 1167, the first in England. He merged Oxford's various monastery schools, which had meanwhile earned a considerable reputation, and modeled this newly-created university on the university in Paris. The four classical disciplines were taught here: theology, medicine, law, and grammar. "Great scholars," according to the wishes of Henry II, should be nurtured at Oxford University "so that we should not want for persons who are suitably qualified to serve God, the church, and the kingdom."

As of the middle of the thirteenth century, the first colleges were called into being. Dons and students studied and carried out research in the colleges, but they also lived together under one roof. Nowhere has the organization of learning in the form of colleges been reflected more magnificently in architecture than in Oxford and in Cambridge. Based on the model of medieval monasteries and their cloisters, the chapel, dining hall, students' rooms, and teaching facilities are grouped around a quadrangle. A perfect example of this type of building ensemble can been seen today at Magdalen College.

The forty colleges which make up the university are housed in some six hundred buildings, almost all of which are listed as national monuments, spread out over a total area of some two square miles. At the end of the fifteenth century, the great humanist Erasmus of Rotterdam strolled over the campus; at his side the young student Thomas More, who would later become Lord Chancellor under Henry VIII and invent a new literary genre with his novel *Utopia*. The list of prominent personalities who studied at Oxford is long. Jonathan Swift, the writer of *Gulliver's Travels* studied there, as did John Locke, the forerunner of the Enlightenment, and Aldous Huxley, the author of *Brave New World*. Oxford's matriculation lists have included the names of twenty-three British prime ministers, ten Indian viceroys, and several hundred bishops.

Erasmus—one of the many prominent personalities to study at Oxford

Although the academic qualifications of Oxford graduates are beyond question, the same cannot be said about their athletic prowess. At the traditional boat race on the Thames, where Oxford University has vied the eight from Cambridge University every year since 1829, Cambridge has won more points overall.

Oxford University, England's first university, was created
when King Henry II merged the town's monastery schools

A vaulted ceiling in the Divinity School

The Soul of Russia
Moscow and the Kremlin

Moscow, Russia; erected in several building phases, beginning in 1474

"What can be compared to the Kremlin which, protected by crenelated walls, adorned with the golden domes of its cathedral, stands on the steep mountain like the crown on the head of the menacing czars? The Kremlin is Russia's altar. One cannot describe it, not its dark passageways, not its magnificent palaces. One has to see and feel all of it."

Mikhail Yurievich Lermontov, *A Hero of Our Time*, 1840

1 Cathedral Square
2 Cathedral of the Dormition
3 Cathedral of the Annunciation
4 Church of the Deposition of the Robe
5 Palace of the Facets
6 Cathedral of the Archangel Michael
7 "Ivan the Great" Bell Tower
8 Teremnoy Palace
9 Church of St Lazarus
10 Upper Cathedral of the Saviour
11 Cathedral of the Twelve Apostles and
   Patriarch's Place
12 Amusement Place
13 Arsenal
14 Senate Building
15 Great Kremlin Palace
16 Armory Chamber
17 Terem Palace
18 Statue of Lenin
19 Palace of Congresses
20 Tomb of the Unknown Soldier
21 Obelisk
22 Alexander's Gardens
23 Great Stone Bridge
24 St Basil's Cathedral
25 Lenin's Mausoleum
26 Red Square
27 State Historical Museum
28 Revolution Square

Perhaps the irony was not intentional when the Russian author, draftsman, and actor Vladimir Vladimirovich Mayakovski said at the beginning of the twentieth century: "It is well known that the earth begins with the Kremlin—it is its center." For the soul of the Russian people lives in Moscow, in the Kremlin. Alexander Pushkin must have felt this one hundred years before when he wrote: "At last our goal is in sight: Moscow lies before us, mighty and majestic, shining so near in the luster of its white walls, in the glimmer of its golden domes and crosses! Oh, how I trembled with joy as the city with its towers, its shining liveliness, and all of its colors stood so impressively before me once again! How often in my deepest sorrow, in my nights of wandering have I thought of you! Moscow. How this name seizes the Russian heart with vehemence! What doesn't speak or ring out from its sound?"

Moscow is the Kremlin, and it has stood from time immemorial as the symbol of an entire country. Here is the heart of a giant empire which stretches from the Black Sea to the Bering Sea, from the Karelian highlands to Vladivostok. The Kremlin, the point at which the streets of the city converge from all points on the compass, was the residence of the czars as well as that of the archbishop of the Russian-Orthodox Christians. It has always been the heart of Moscow—the seat of power.

The Kremlin is a citadel built on an irregular ground plan covering some seventy acres. Behind the defensive walls, which stretch for nearly one-and-a-half miles and are punctuated by twenty towers up to sixty feet high, there are several historic palaces and cathedrals—and a series of twentieth-century administrative buildings. The first fortification of the Kremlin was referred to in 1156: at that time the buildings were made of wood, protected by oak palisades, and covered only a tenth of the area they occupy today. Continually burned down and then extended, the Kremlin took on its present form around 1500, in the first major building phase during the reign of Ivan the Great. The czar not only summoned architects to Moscow from the artistic centers of Russia but also—more significantly—from northern Italy. They transformed the former fortress complex, which until then had had a primarily defensive function, into the stately seat of the most important ruling dynasties in eastern Europe and the golden "third Rome" of Orthodox Christendom.

It was ravaged and plundered by the Tartars in 1571, and rebuilt and expanded with several sumptuous new buildings between 1624 and 1736. Napoleon reported to his wife, Marie-Louise, on Monday, September 6, 1812: "I was unable to form a picture of this town in any way. It once possessed fifty palaces in the French style, furnished with unbelievable luxury, several imperial palaces....but everything has now disappeared. Since yesterday a fire has been devouring the city." When he and the rest of his Grand Armée turned their backs on the smoking ruins, he ordered that the Kremlin be blown up—a command which, for the most part, was sabotaged by the people of Moscow.

Although Moscow had had to cede its role as the capital city to St Petersburg in 1712, the Kremlin was not only restored, but even extended by adding the Great Kremlin Palace, which dominates the southern flank towards the Moskva River, between 1838 and 1849. After the revolution of 1917 the seat of government was moved back to Moscow, and the Kremlin became "the fortress of the revolutionary dictatorship"—which, even in the eyes of Leo Trotsky, was "an utter paradox." According to Trotsky they were at least able to agree on one "decisive" adjustment: the carillon on the Saviour's Tower was changed. Instead of the bells playing "God Save the Czar," the "International" can now be heard every fifteen minutes.

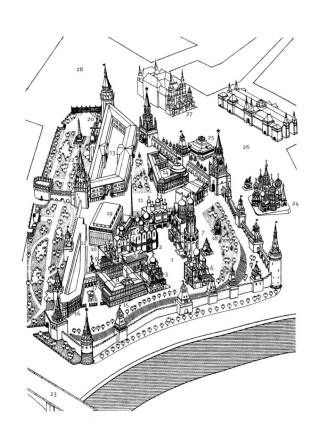

The Kremlin, a citadel whose walls protect
numerous palaces and cathedrals

"Urbi et Orbi"
Rome and St Peter's Cathedral

Italy; begun in 1506
Architect: Bramante; facade: Maderna; dome designed by
Michelangelo; baroque styling by Bernini

"The head and crown of all churches
is undoubtedly St Peter's, and if the
ancients thought it was a misfortune
not to have seen the Olympian temple
of Jupiter, the same could more readily
be said of St Peter's. For this building
is larger than the temples of the Greeks
and Romans, and surpasses them in its
architecture and splendor. I never go
there without praising God that he made
me so fortunate as to see and know this
miraculous work."

Johann Joachim Winckelmann, *A History of the Art in
Antiquity*, 1764

The writer Charles Dickens almost didn't dare
say it. From a distance, Rome, a city which he
had set out for "full of feverish anticipation,"
reminded him of his native London. A sacrilege—
possibly caused by a low-lying bank of clouds
which shrouded the silhouette of St Peter's on
the day that Dickens arrived on the Tiber.

Over a period of 174 years, thirty popes had
pushed ahead with the construction of the
largest church in Christendom. Michelangelo
planned the mighty dome, stretching some four
hundred feet into the sky, thus making St Peter's
the commanding symbol of Rome. The dome
shelters what is believed to be the grave of
Peter, the leader of the apostles, who, according to legend, suffered a dreadful martyrdom in
the year 64 or 67 A.D. in the imperial gardens
near the Vatican Hill, when it is said that he
was crucified upside down.

In 326 A.D., the first church was raised on
this spot—a basilica with the central nave
flanked on either side by a pair of lower aisles.
Having been restored many times, the thousand-
year-old building almost collapsed towards
the middle of the fifteenth century. At that time
the papacy was as powerful as never before.
In 1452, Pope Nicholas V wanted to rebuild
the Vatican as the permanent residence of the
popes, who had previously resided in
the Lateran Palace. It was then decided to build
a new church as well: it was to be as grand as
a "monument made by God himself," which
would make the world "embrace the faith with
the greatest devotion." A mausoleum modeled
on the Pantheon was envisioned.

Pope Julius II had these plans carried out
in 1506, and at the same time constructed
palaces for numerous cardinals who, according
to a contemporary account were "no longer
willing to live in *locis obscuris* and small

'huts.'" The new house of God was constructed
on the foundation of Old St Peter's church.
The cathedral can accommodate sixty thousand
worshippers and gave new meaning to the old
greatness of Rome. The eternal city had now
been resurrected as the glorious center of the
world, this time as the seat of God's representative on earth. With its imposing architecture,
St Peter's not only stands for divine majesty. It
is also the earthly counterpart to the "heavenly
Jerusalem" and a focal point for the story of
the passion and the salvation of Christ.

Today each newly elected Pope still presents
himself to the public for the first time on the
central balcony of St Peter's; it is from here that
the sovereign pontiff gives his benediction
"Urbi et Orbi" ("To the City and the World") and
proclaims beatifications and canonizations. And
at the entrance hall to St Peter's, the ceremonial
opening of the Holy Door still marks the beginning of the church year, an event which is celebrated all over the world.

Planned by the most important architects of
two centuries and decorated with magnificent
altars, precious mosaics, and world-famous
sculptures, the construction of St Peter's cost
immense sums of money. In order to finance it,
the pope sold indulgences: sinners could pay
to free themselves from punishment for their
sins. It was this practice, among others, which
prompted Martin Luther's fundamental criticism
of the church. It angered him that the people
were led to believe that God would accept money
as a form of atonement—a further reason for the
reformer to regard popes as "impudent" and to
refuse allegiance to them. The construction of
St Peter's Cathedral, which was actually meant
to be a manifestation of an all-embracing
Christendom, thus actually contributed to
dividing the church.

Designed by Michelangelo, the dome of St Peter's Cathedral
reaches four hundred feet into the sky

Old St Peter's being
demolished

"Urbi et orbi"—the central balcony from which
the Pope delivers his annual benediction

A procession to the altar; the dome shelters what
is believed to be the grave of the martyred St Peter

Bizarre Roofscapes and Intertwining Stairs
The Château of Chambord in the Loire Valley

France; 1519–1559 (unfinished)
Architect: Domenico da Cortona (?)

"In my life I have seen a great deal of splendid architecture, but never anything more beautiful and rich than this. The park in which the castle stands is replete with forests, lakes, streams, pastures, and hunting grounds. And at its center is this beautiful building with its gilt spires, its wings with their roofs of lead, its pavilions, its terraces, and its galleries. We leave the place filled with wonder, with astonishment, indeed with bewilderment."

Geronimo Lippomano, Venetian envoy to the French court, on his visit to Chambord, 1577

Ground plans of the château, dated 1576

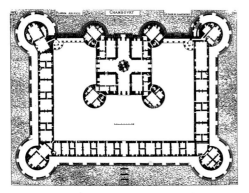

The sculptor Auguste Rodin once described the Loire as the "artery of France,....the flow of light and happiness." As France's largest river, it meanders from its source in the Cévennes mountains over more than six hundred miles of countryside until, wide and powerful, it finally empties into the Atlantic Ocean to the west of Nantes. The region along the section between Gien and Angers is famous as one of the most delightful in all of Europe—and as the Garden of France. The Loire Valley is "as fragrant as Italy" and "as filled with blossoms as the valley of the Guadalquivir

King François I ordered the construction of the luxurious Château of Chambord, depicted in this 16th-century miniature

in Andalusia," enthused the writer Léon Gozlan.

Historically important towns, powerful monasteries, and mighty churches line the riverbanks. But over three hundred castles and châteaux can also be discovered hidden among the vineyards, roses, and poplar trees. The fertile countryside, blessed each year with rich harvests, originally attracted the Romans. Towards the end of the fifteenth century, it became the region favored by the French monarchs—a land of kings in the heart of France. Important administrators and their families followed the court to the Loire Valley, and their châteaux sprang up all around. Whereas residences for the nobility had once been built primarily for purposes of defense, now their

main *raison d'être* was to provide suitably magnificent settings for a luxurious lifestyle.

It is not really surprising that the châteaux of the Loire Valley outshine all buildings created before them in opulence and splendor. King François I, a Renaissance sovereign—who had refined French court etiquette and had a passion not only for beautiful women and the hunt, but also for art—built his dream castle among the forests near Blois, where game abounded. On a site where a medieval castle had once stood, he ordered the construction of a palace magnificent enough to represent all the regal glory of France: Chambord, a dazzling stage for a court reveling in the pleasures of life, a monument to *la joie de vivre*.

The bizarre roofscape with its gables, chimneys, and turrets is a veritable labyrinth extending over the four-hundred-and-forty individually conceived, interlocking passageways, galleries, chambers, and halls. The king's critics grumbled that Chambord was not a castle where one could live long-term, and saw the extravagant palace as a reflection of the self-absorbed lasciviousness of its master. The emperor Charles V saw it with different eyes. In 1539, on his visit to the then half-finished (and today still unfinished) castle, where he was received with pomp and glory by François I, he declared Chambord "the quintessence of all that can possibly be created by the art of mankind."

The staircase at the center of the three-storied main structure is considered the greatest wonder of Chambord. It consists of two separate yet intertwined sets of stairs, making it possible for those ascending and those descending to pass without getting in each others' way. Its design is probably the work of Leonardo da Vinci who, upon the invitation of François I, spent the last years of his life near Chambord, at Amboise, as "the principal painter, architect, and engineer in service to the king."

Ironically enough, François I himself is said to have spent only forty days at Chambord. The French marshal Moritz of Saxony, however, lived for many years in those hallowed halls. The dissolute lifestyle of his court at Chambord became legendary, as did a particular group of exotic residents there: the marshal's brigade of lanky Africans disguised as Tartars, mounted on steeds of dapple-gray.

An aerial view of Chambord's bizarre
wilderness of gables, chimneys and turrets

Leonardo da Vinci's staircase: two
separate yet intertwined sets of stairs

The Dark Heart of the Spanish Soul
King Philip II of Spain and El Escorial

Spain; 1563–1586
Architects: Juan Bautista de Toledo, Juan de Herrera

"In the countryside at the foot of the Sierra Guadarrama, the massive, granite Escorial is merely the largest stone. Only the smoothness of its edges makes it stand out from the surrounding cliffs. Yet on spring days, there is a time when the sunlight is broken up by the craggy peaks of the sierra and white, blue, violet, and crimson light pours down the slopes and into the valley. Then El Escorial, heeding the call of a higher power, once again merges with the quarries from whose very womb it was born."

José Ortega y Gasset, *The Rise and Fall of Spain*, 1921

There was once a time when the light, the smoke, the animals, and the people all shared the same entrance to houses in the small village of Escorial. Iron used to be smelted on the slopes of the Guadarrama mountains, some twenty-five miles northwest of Madrid. "Escorial" actually means "slag-heap," and yet the world associates the name not with poverty and distress, but with wealth and majesty.

For two years the advisors to Philip II had searched for a suitable site to construct a complex which would reflect the king's notion of the office of a Christian ruler: it was to be not only a palace, but also a monastery, a church, a learning institution, a library, an art gallery, and a mausoleum. They found what they were looking for near Escorial. In the following years, a gigantic, rectangular complex measuring some six hundred by five hundred feet would rise out of the plateau. It comprises three hundred rooms, sixteen inner courtyards, fifteen cloisters, eighty-six staircases, eighty-nine fountains, and thirteen chapels.

According to popular tradition, the ground-plan resembles an oversized grate—the torture instrument on which Saint Lawrence met an involuntary and untimely end. Philip II felt that he owed something to the heavenly intercessor because, in the year 1557, he had won a decisive battle against France on the feast day of that saint. At the center of the imaginary grate stands a basilica which, with its commanding dome, was inspired by Michelangelo's design for St Peter's in Rome. Evidently the king spared no cost: he invested 5,260,560 gold ducats in the construction of El Escorial. Despite this sum he was exceptionally cautious. During the construction, he personally inspected every invoice, making notes in the margins such as "that's fine," if he considered the amount to be paid fair, and "he's lying" if he disagreed with the workman. Yet when the masons and plasterers were finished, their work earned no praise. On the contrary: even today the weighty coldness of El Escorial is overpowering. "No one will seriously think that this is a beautiful palace," noted the French writer Alexandre Dumas. His compatriot Théophile Gautier put it even more bluntly: after the pyramids, El Escorial is "the largest heap of stones on the globe," "the most boring and gloomy structure imaginable," "the ideal model for barracks."

The interior of El Escorial sheltered not only the throne of the most powerful nation on the globe at that time, but also a veritable treasure trove of important artifacts, objects, and books from the world of learning. Philip II collected writings of the ancient Greeks, Romans, and Arabs as well as land and sea maps, and the works of great thinkers who studied antiquity, archeology, alchemy, and astronomy. In an age when reformers were loudly denouncing the church, and English admirals were ringing in the defeat of the Spanish Armada, Philip II had created for himself a bastion of stone in which he cemented the old visions of worldly greatness and religious faith. His modest private chambers were grouped around the choir of the basilica so that he could see the altar from his bed. When Philip II died in that very bed on September 13, 1598 following a severe illness, he left behind 7,422 relics of saints. "There would have been enough to convert China to Catholicism having finished in South America," jested those who mocked their king's piety. But when Philip II died, Spain's glorious age of discovery and conquest also died with him.

The ground plan is said to be laid out in the form of a grate, the torture instrument on which St Lawrence died

El Escorial was not just a palace, but also a monastery,
a church, a learning institution, a library and a mausoleum

Royal caskets in the El Escorial mausoleum

The Queen of Villas
The Country Residence "La Rotonda," near Vicenza

Italy; 1566(?)–1580
Architect: Andrea di Pietro della Gondola, known
as Palladio (1508–1580); completed by V. Scamozzi

"The location is one of the most charming and appealing that can be found. The house stands on a hilltop which is easily reached and which is bordered by the Bacchiglione, a navigable river, on one side. On the other a range of gentle hills surround this site, lending the whole a theatrical setting and all the slopes are cultivated, and bear much fruit and excellent grapevines."

Andrea Palladio, *The Second Book on Architecture*, 1570

A farmer and his wife in the 16th-century style in Italy

Johann Wolfgang von Goethe was enthusiastic: "Today I visited a splendid house, the Rotonda, which is situated at a pleasant altitude, a half-hour outside Vicenza," he wrote in his travel diary on the evening of September 21, 1786, adding: "Perhaps architecture has never raised luxury to higher heights." The lordly villa, which crowns the hilltop like the Acropolis, is the acknowledged masterpiece of the architect Andrea Palladio.

Most likely a native of Padua, Palladio threw himself into the study of the architecture of antiquity with passion and good cheer: fundamentally influenced by Vitruvius, a Roman architectural theorist who wrote his famous ten volume *De Architectura* in the first century B.C., Palladio soon became known as the re-discoverer of antiquity. His playfully varied treatment of traditional architectural forms and his treatise, *The Four Books on Architecture*, paved the way for architectural styles of the future. He was commissioned to build the Villa Rotonda around 1566 by Paolo Almerico. Almerico was an ambitious nobleman, a retired monsignor in the service of two popes who had now returned from Rome to his native Vicenza. He already owned a lavish town palace there but aspired to a villa in the country. While other aristocratic families were fleeing the towns in the face of the plague and the difficulties encountered procuring basic supplies, it seems that his main motivation was a wish for rest and calm. In all probability, he also hoped to create a monument to himself and thus gain the admiration of his fellow citizens, something that was not unusual in the sixteenth century.

While planning the villa, Palladio took the surrounds and the hilltop site into consideration, knowing that his client would want to both see and be seen: "Since wonderful views can be enjoyed from every side, whereby some include the immediate vicinity, others, on the other hand, reach further, and still others end only at the horizon, porches have been added on all four sides," wrote Palladio. These porches, which have survived unchanged since Palladio's time, and which, with their rows of columns, are reminiscent of Greco-Roman temples, face the four points of the compass.

The main showpiece of the villa is the large hall, or rotunda, at the center of the cross-shaped ground plan, which is sumptuously decorated with stucco work and paintings. Light only enters this "holy of holies" through the long corridors and through some small openings in the dome. It crowns the villa and, despite the fact that domed vernacular structures were not uncommon in antiquity, it lends the

structure a sacral character—surely a conscious allusion to the owner's career. However Paolo Almerico's dream of securing his fame through the Villa Rotonda lasted only a short time. His son sold the architectural masterpiece to the Capra family, which gave the villa a new identity—although without changing the structure of the building in any way. The Capras purchased the surrounding fields, so that the demonstratively noble, isolated residence was transformed into a manor house, a traditional "villa di campagna." This change is reflected in

Coat of arms of the Almerico family

the inscription chiseled on the villa. It tells not only about the social status of the family but also about their agricultural property: "Mario Capra, who relinquished this house and all the goods within it, the fields, valleys, and hills on this side of the road, strictly according to the rule of primogeniture, sets this down to eternal memory, while he suffers and endures." The maudlin tone of the closing words received little sympathy from Goethe: a man "who commanded so much wealth and determination" could surely also have learned to suffer and endure "with less extravagance."

"La Rotonda" near Vincenza takes its inspiration
from the architecture of antiquity

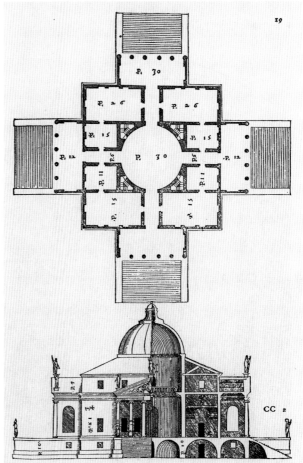

Taken from the *Four Books on Architecture*
by Andrea Palladio

The Evil Spirit on the Throne of Fire
Il Gesù, the Jesuit Church in Rome

Italy; 1568–1584
Architects: Giacomo da Vignola (ground plan) and Giacomo della Porta (facade), members of the Jesuit order

"As I was preparing the altar, I had to think of Jesus, and I felt the urge to follow him. It seemed to me that because he is the head of society, is the reason to live in poverty, more so than all other human reasons. This thought gave me so much strength, I felt I could resist all temptation and hostility."

St Ignatius of Loyola, *Spiritual Diary*, February 23, 1544

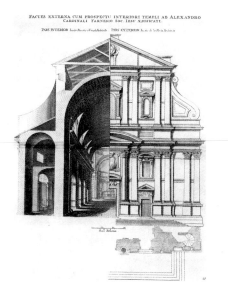

In his youth Don Iñigo de Oñez y Loyola (Ignatius of Loyola's original name) was devoted, according to his own account, to "the superficiality of the world." He fought several duels "with the vain desire to gain honor in this way." He barely escaped prison because of diverse fights and dubious affairs with women. His transformation from hooligan to holy man only took place after he turned thirty. As an officer in the service of the Spanish viceroy he had taken part in the defense of Pamplona against the French and was wounded in the leg. As he lay in his bed in the family castle

The founder of the Jesuit Order

he had occasion to review his life. He also had two books at his bedside, the *Legenda Aurea*, a collection of stories about the lives of the saints, richly illustrated and embellished with fantastic tales, and the *Life of Jesus*, which enthusiastically recommended making a pilgrimage to Jerusalem.

Ignatius of Loyola, the wounded knight, was electrified. He decided to make his own pilgrimage to Jerusalem and to emulate the deeds of the saints. In the words of one of his biographers: "The spirit of holy aspiration possessed him because he realized God, the good spirit brings joy, and Lucifer the spirit of evil brings sadness." As soon as he had recovered, Ignatius traded his sword for a cross and set off for Jerusalem. He studied theology upon his return and gathered others with similar beliefs around him.

He joined the priesthood and later traveled to Rome to offer the services of his followers to the Pope. He was successful, and in 1540 the society he had founded was recognized as a religious order, called the Society of Jesus. The order devoted itself to spreading the Christian faith as disciples of Jesus Christ. For this reason they stressed the power of words. Preaching was a tool of the utmost importance in the society which warned others not to be blinded by "Lucifer, the spirit of evil on the throne of fire" but to follow "Christ the Lord and practice virtue."

Their conviction guaranteed their success, not only in Europe but increasingly in other parts of the world. They followed seafarers and conquistadors and traveled as missionaries to India, Japan, China, Africa, South America, and Canada. But their spiritual center remained the church of Il Gesù in Rome, which became a model for many Catholic churches, especially in Latin America.

The ceiling fresco in the nave shows the triumph of Jesus over heretics and the devil. Because the sermon was so central to their teaching, they gave great importance to the acoustics of the church. The faithful were to hear each word loudly and clearly. For this reason they constructed their church with a single closed nave in which the worshippers were drawn into the mass. A dome was placed at the intersection of the nave and transept.

In their missionary zeal the Jesuits expanded the use of the church to include presentation of extravagant religious plays accompanied by music. The theme of these pageants always stressed the conquest of the church. Il Gesù remains the heart of the worldwide order of Jesuits and a symbol of the triumph of Catholicism over the Reformation and heresy. The founder of the order is buried there. On March 12, 1622 Ignatius of Loyola was canonized.

The founder's shrine above his grave

The splendor of Il Gesù became a model for many Catholic churches around the world

Detail of the magnificent *trompe l'œil* ceiling painting

103

The Brilliance and the Misery of the Mogul Empire

A Dream in Marble: The Taj Mahal

Agra, India; 1630–1653
Architects: Mohammed Isa Afandi, Ustad Ahmed Lahori

"The Great Mogul called the architects to him and set his wish before them to build a magnificent and gigantic tomb for his dead wife. It is further reported that the ruler gave his architects thirty million rupees for the task and made it known that more would be available if needed."

From a report by the Portuguese missionary Friar Sebastiano Manrique, 1642

India is an enormous treasure trove. For this reason Islamic conquerors from Persia and Afghanistan had long cast their eyes on the land south of the Himalayas. Wild hordes descended to pillage the towns and loaded with booty, returned to the distant lands from which they had come. Mohammed of Ghuri was the first who would not be satisfied merely with gold, gems, and slaves.

In 1192 he swept into India, captured the city of Delhi, destroyed its Hindu temples, pillaged its shrines, and settled down in the city to establish the Sultanate of Delhi. His descendants, however, were unable to maintain their grip on power.

The establishment of an Islamic empire on Indian soil would have to wait until the arrival of the Moguls, a tribe most recently at home in Kazakhstan, who traced their ancestry back to Genghis Kahn. In 1526 Babur, leader of the Moguls, declared himself ruler of Hindustan and founded the Mogul dynasty.

At the height of its power the Mogul Empire stretched from Kabul in the east, to the Gulf of Bengal in the west, and from Kashmir in the north, to Bombay in the south. The Moguls were famous for their cruelty. Akbar, Babur's grandson, had 30,000 unarmed farmers hacked to death because they had supported an uprising against him. A few years later he resorted to even greater cruelty to punish a province that had revolted against him. Once he had reestablished his power over it, he had a pyramid built out of 2,000 insurgents'

skulls—a graphic warning to other would-be dissenters.

The blood of their victims did not, however, prevent the Moguls from enjoying the beautiful things of life. Babur was more than just a brutal general. He had a literary bent and devoted himself to his beloved gardens. Akbar, in turn, was interested in philosophical discourse and dialogue between Islam and Christianity. Shah Jahan, his grandson was fascinated with architecture. He commissioned the construction of the Taj Mahal in Agra, the Mogul capital, located two hundred miles south of Delhi.

The Taj Mahal is the most perfect example of Indian-Islamic architecture. It is a work that employed the genius of many different artists from many different cultures. A total of 20,000 workers are said to have labored on the construction of the Taj Mahal. It is finished in white marble from Jaipur and set off with panels inlaid with semi-precious stones in red, green, and blue. On a clear day the magnificent monument sparkles in the sun like a magical palace from *A Thousand and One Nights* and its image is reflected in the blue water of the pool in its geometric garden.

The Taj Mahal is neither a palace nor a mosque, which its four minarets might lead one to believe. It is a mausoleum. The astounding building with its dome, high portal, and window niches was commissioned by the Great Mogul Shah Jahan for his beloved wife Arjmand-Banu-Begam who died at the age of thirty-eight giving birth to her fourteenth child. The Taj Mahal is a monument to eternal love and a reminder to the ladies of the Harem of Shah Jahan's love for Mumtaz i Mahal, the "Chosen One of the Palace," whose name the building bears.

The crypt in the Taj Mahal contains the remains, not only of the beloved wife, but of Shah Jahan as well. Originally Shah Jahan had planned to be buried on the opposite side of the river Yamuna in a mirror image of the famous Taj Mahal—but built of black marble. His grand plan was never realized. Shah Jahan's love of building had pushed the Mogul Empire to the edge of ruin.

The facade of the Taj Mahal: white marble inlaid with semi-precious stones

The Taj Mahal was built as a monument to eternal love

Buildings flanking the Taj Mahal

The brutal general with a passion for beauty

On the Roof of the World
The Winter Palace of the Dalai Lama

Lhasa, Tibet; 1645–1694

"The heavens over this place resemble an eight-spoked wheel of the law, a good omen; the ground resembles an eight-petalled lotus, a symbol of happiness; the mountains resemble the eight symbols of fortune, a sign of prosperity!"

Princess Wencheng, wife of Songtsen Gampo, the first king of Tibet, writing about Lhasa, 7th century

The highest mountain ranges in the world reach into the skies and are covered with glistening snow which never melts. They are very nearly invincible. Below the peaks, there are mighty crags, steep, rocky slopes, and icy turquoise lakes. Tibet, where the Brahmaputra, the mother of the Indus and Ganges rivers, rises from within the mountains, has often been described as a "land of snow." And yet it also has another side: infinite steppe pastures, the almost untouched habitat of nomads, their sheep, yaks, and mules. Vast spaces and a sense of being deeply rooted in age-old traditions and ways of life are the two familiar faces of Tibet. The first known report about the country, which dates from the ninth century, describes Tibet in euphoric tones: "High mountains, pure earth, an overwhelming land. A place where wise men

The 14th Dalai Lama

become heroes, where decency rules, where horses grow light-footed."

The documented history of Tibet begins in the seventh century A.D. Songtsen Gampo, who founded his kingdom in the year 629, developed Tibet into a great power which was to keep its neighbors, especially China, on their guard for the following two hundred years. His formidably efficient army is said to have numbered 100,000 warriors who were armed to the teeth and who unceremoniously invaded one principality after the other. The Tibetan realm

ultimately extended as far as the Himalayas, to Turkestan, and to the borders of the Chinese province of Sichuan.

While the kingdom struggled to come to terms with its rapidly expanding territory, Songtsen Gampo moved the seat of the Tibetan rulers from the Yarlung Valley in the fertile south, to a side valley of the Brahmaputra, to Lhasa. He built his residence on the Marpori, the "red mountain," high over the town. This is where the imposing landmark of Tibet, the Potala Palace, can be seen today. The audacious, labyrinthine structure with its typically Tibetan sloping walls and flat roofs comprises thirteen floors which tower 360 feet into the sky and enclose, or so it is said, 999 rooms. Writers have struggled time and again to find words to describe it: "It is near and yet somehow unreachably distant and surreal, like a manifestation of an unearthly reality;" "majestic, peculiar, incredible, like a never-ending optical illusion, a monument from another world;" to cite just two descriptions.

It was the winter palace of the Dalai Lama, the religious and political head of the country. Actually consisting of two complexes, the Red and the White Palaces, the Potala Palace was not only a residence, but also a school, a library, a workshop, an arsenal, a prison, a treasury, a monastery, and a goal for pilgrims. Its up to fifteen-foot-thick walls enclosed over thirty temple rooms which were richly decorated with wall paintings, wooden columns, and carvings.

In 1959 the tradition of the Potala Palace as the heart of Tibet came to a bloody end; a revolt exploded against the foreign rule of the People's Republic of China, which has occupied Tibet since 1950. The rebellion was mercilessly crushed. Chinese artillery demolished parts of the Potala Palace, Chinese troops slaughtered tens of thousands in the streets of Lhasa. The Dalai Lama and 70,000 Tibetans fled to neighboring countries. But the suffering of those who remained has still not come to an end: "The word 'hell' is too weak to describe what happened during those years," remarked a British witness. Chinese soldiers plundered hundreds of monasteries, the Tibetan religion and culture were suppressed, entire regions of the country, to put it cynically, were "ethnically cleansed."

With these developments, which still cry out for political resolution, a Tibetan prophecy of the eighteenth century became reality: "When the iron bird flies and horses run on wheels, our people will be dispersed like ants all over the world."

Dominating the wintery landscape,
the Potala Palace in Lhasa, Tibet

The throne of the Dalai Lama was abandoned
after he was forced into exile in 1959

The Sun on Earth
The Royal Palace of Versailles

France; 1661–1710

Architects: Louis Le Vau, Jules Hardouin-Mansart (as of 1678), Robert de Cotte, Charles Le Brun (interior design), André Le Nôtre (landscape architecture)

"As an image, I chose the sun. It is without doubt the most vital and beautiful symbol of a great sovereign because of the brightness which surrounds it, the light which it sheds upon other stars which are its court, the joy which it inspires in all places, its perpetual movement, in spite of which it still seems to hover in constant calm because of its unchanging path, from which it never strays."

Louis XIV, *Memoirs*, 1715

The dramatist Molière presented his play *Le Malade imaginaire*, in the garden at Versailles

The French finance minister Nicolas Fouquet had no idea that anything was wrong. In 1661, he threw a wild party at his newly built château, Vaux-le-Vicomte, for Louis XIV and six thousand other guests. Yet only a few days later, he was put into prison on the order of the Sun King. He spent the following nineteen years, which would also be his last, in far less comfortable confinement. His crime could not have been a lack of hospitality: the food and drink at the ball at Vaux-le-Vicomte was said to have been sumptuous, as was the entertainment. In the garden, the comic dramatist Molière had presented his play *Les Fâcheuses*, which he had written especially for the occasion. As a grand finale, a fire-breathing whale had risen out of the canal, its wondrous appearance the prelude to a spectacular display of fireworks.

Louis XIV of France, the Sun King

Still, the host might have felt slightly taken aback when the king took leave of him at daybreak with the following rather sinister-sounding remark: "I cannot invite you to come and visit me. It would be uncomfortable for you in my house." The words hinted at what Louis XIV had seen in Fouquet's castle: *lèse-majesté*. The Sun King shone less benevolently, and not only at the sight of the magnificent gardens with their glowing mother-of-pearl fountains. The richly decorated interior of the splendid castle, whose architecture presented an innovative transition between the court and the park

beyond, also aroused his envy. It was unbearable to him that one of his subjects could be the proud owner of such an inspired interplay of landscape and architecture.

The first thing Louis XIV did following Fouquet's arrest was to engage in his own service the three artists who had transformed the mansion Vaux-le-Vicomte into such a glittering box of treasures. He instructed them to create a residence which, in its entirety, would be the perfect work of art representing the power of absolutism in every detail from the palace itself to the furthest corner of the park. Thus the most sprawling and grandiose palace in the western world came to be created on a sandy plain some ten miles southwest of Paris: the palace and gardens of Versailles, the Olympus of French monarchs for one hundred years.

In the space of a few years, 22,000 workers and 6,000 horses produced a vast complex of buildings and courtyards set in a thoroughly planned, artificial landscape. Nature was made to conform to severe geometric patterns as an allegory of absolutism which tolerates no deviations and sees in every manifestation of "disorder," even in the irregular forms characteristic of naturally growing plants, a symbol of treason and revolution. That is not to say that no *joie de vivre* could be felt inside the palace: Louis XIV, although feared as a statesman, was affable in his private life and liked to have a good time. He had plays performed three times a week at Versailles, often playing the part of Zeus, the father of all gods, himself (or the roles of other protagonists corresponding to his royal status). And in his *Grand Appartement* there was a billiard table where he enjoyed testing his skill against the best players of the court.

Beyond his private rooms, however, a rigid code of etiquette prevailed which was soon to be imitated at all European courts. No one was particular when it came to hygiene, though. During the reign of the Sun King, there was only one single bathtub at Versailles—and that was in the apartment belonging to the king's German sister-in-law, Liselotte von der Pfalz. Moreover, in the absence of toilets, the corners of many different rooms were used for urgent bodily needs—making it necessary for the entire palace to be cleared out and freshly wall-papered at regular intervals.

Versailles, the Olympus for French monarchs

The Great Hall of Mirrors

In the gardens nature was made to conform
to severe geometric patterns

As Big as a Mountain
Final Resting Place of Heroes: St Paul's Cathedral in London

England; 1675–1697
Architect: Christopher Wren

"We were just saying how little time we had to reflect upon life and death when we rounded the corner to face the massive walls of St Paul's. There it was once again—as big as a mountain towering over us, gloomier, colder and more silent than ever. And barely had we stepped inside than we felt utterly freed from the hustle and bustle outside—more so than in any other building in the world."

Taken from Virginia Woolf's *Abbeys and Cathedrals*, 1932

The site has a long history. The Romans had built a temple here, dedicated to Diana, the goddess of hunting. In 604 London's Christians built a church over the ruins, where Melittus, the first Bishop of London, was anointed into his holy office. The church was destroyed several times by fire and each time rebuilt. Soon it became the heart of the English capital. For centuries St Paul's was the scene of the public meetings that took place every three years, which all citizens were required to attend. But they streamed to the church at all times of the year.

People gathered to hear important announcements from the pulpit, which had been built on the exterior wall of the old cathedral. It was a kind of mediaeval *Times* where representatives of the people held passionate speeches and demanded that citizens be allowed greater

involvement in government. Heralds announced important decrees, royal marriages, births, and deaths. Priests read papal bulls, proclaimed church edicts, and the bishops invited sinners to atone for their sins. Here, Jane Shore, the mistress of King Edward IV, had to publicly confess her sins—the very same spot where Martin Luther's writings would later be burned.

The interior of the church resembled a market place more than a house of worship. Peddlers selling leather goods, wool, pottery, and wooden forks and spoons set up stands in the nave. Londoners haggled over prices around the altar and tried to avoid the imploring stares of beggars and cripples, while pick-pockets plied their

dubious trade in the aisles. But the state of affairs was to deteriorate even more. Following the outbreak of the civil war in which Cromwell's Parliamentary troops clashed with armies of the king, Oliver Cromwell further debased St Paul's by turning the church into a stable for his cavalry.

St Paul's, filthy and partially in ruins, was destroyed in the great fire that devastated London in 1666. For architect Christopher Wren it was a dream come true. As early as 1663 he had proposed rebuilding St Paul's, but to no avail. Following the fire, nothing stood in the way of his plans except the smoldering ruins which were soon cleared away.

The building that replaced the destroyed church was destined to become the spiritual center of the British Empire. Its 330-foot-high dome, based on St Peter's in Rome, dominated the skyline of London up until the late twentieth century. With its awe-inspiring height, impressive size and clarity of its interior, St Paul's, along with Westminster Abbey, remains the venue of choice to this day, for the nation's most important ceremonies, such as state funerals and royal weddings. George Frederick Handel and Felix Mendelssohn-Bartholdy once played its mighty organ. Many famous people, including Admiral Nelson and painters John Constable and William Turner are buried in the crypt. "Like majestic turned-down beds, the tombs lie between the columns," wrote Virginia Woolf. "Here is a dignified final resting place," she continued, "to which great statesmen and national figures can withdraw, dressed in their robes of office to receive the acclaim of the public. They are still wearing their medals and ribbons, signs of civil ceremony and military pride. Their tombs are respectable and well cared for. No rust or drop of paint to spoil them. Even Nelson looks smart."

Pushing for attention: St Paul's Cathedral in London,
the spiritual center of the British Empire

The Crimson City
The Imperial Palace in Peking

People's Republic of China; begun around 1300 and substantially altered in the 17th century

"When the ruler holds court his table is placed before the throne and he sits at the northern end, facing south. The Empress sits to his left. His sons, grandsons and other blood relations sit on somewhat lower chairs to his right. The noblemen lounge on carpets, and in front of the hall, there is a great gathering of people from various countries bearing all sorts of rare things."

Marco Polo, writing about the court in Peking, from *The Wonders of the World*, 1299

When Marco Polo returned to Europe in 1295 after an absence of more than 20 years, no one believed the tales he told. The Venetian merchant claimed to have been in Persia, India, and China and to have studied the customs, habits, and characteristics of the various people he had encountered along the way.

The tales he brought home seemed simply too fantastic. Not only did he describe fabulous riches, but told of men with dog's heads, of evil spirits that caused mirages in the desert, and of milk that could be dried to a mysterious powder and, miraculously, could be re-mixed with water to produce milk again. He even told of a land that he visited where alchemists produced gold from paper extracted from the bark of the mulberry tree. All this sounded so fantastic and exotic that his stories about fabulous palaces and the life within them were also doubted.

Marco Polo, however, reported truthfully when he described Peking. "The city is built along a grid pattern and its perimeter is twenty-four miles long, so that each side is exactly six miles long. The layout is so regular, and the streets are so straight, that the entire city resembles a chess board. Everything that is precious and rare in the world, finds its way here. This is particularly true of goods from India, such as precious stones, pearls and spices. The most costly goods are brought to the city from other provinces so that golden fabrics and silk textiles of all types can be produced in incredible quantities."

Even then the Imperial Palace—known as the "Forbidden City"—formed the heart of Peking.

It was called this because no one except palace officials or those belonging to the court were allowed to enter it. Since the expulsion of the Mongols, who had first raised Peking to a capital, the Forbidden City had been the residence of the Emperor of China. Moats and a high wall separated the palace from the teaming life outside.

In the course of half-a-century the palace had grown to become the most significant structure in the Far East. It contained more than 9,000 pavilions and palaces, most of which were built of wood or brick. The crimson color of the buildings symbolizes the light of the Polar Star. The 100-foot-high Throne Room, that had repeatedly been the showplace for imperial coronations, marriages, birthday and New Year festivities, is also full of symbolism. The twenty-four columns that support the roof represent the hours of the day. The eighteen incense burners on the terrace symbolize the provinces of China. The bronze turtles and cranes stand for longevity and good fortune. For many of the rulers this wish did indeed become reality. The average Chinese Emperor reigned for twenty years. Hundreds of concubines saw to their every desire; countless comedians, jugglers, and magicians assured they never suffered from boredom.

China's last Emperor, Pu Yi, was the only one whose luck ran out. He ascended to the throne as a child in 1908 and was forced to abdicate at the outbreak of the revolution in 1911. Following a communist "re-education" the "Son of Heaven" spent his last years as a gardener working for the city of Peking.

Shunzhi, the first of the Manchu Dynasty emperor's to live in Peking

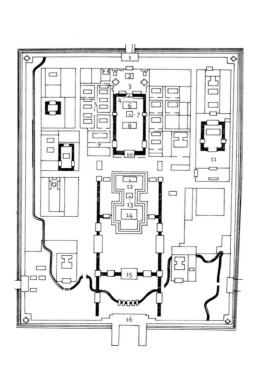

1 Gate of Divine Pride
2 Pavilion of Imperial Peace
3 Imperial Garden
4 Gate of Earthly Tranquility
5 Six Western Palaces
6 Palace of Earthly Tranquility
7 Hall of Union
8 Palace of Heavenly Purity
9 Palace of the Culture of the Mind
10 Gate of Heavenly Purity
11 Palace of Peace and Longevity
12 Hall of the Preservation of Harmony
13 Hall of Perfect Harmony
14 Hall of Supreme Harmony
15 Gate of Supreme Harmony
16 Meridian Gate

Life in a golden cage: the Imperial Palace which
only court officials were allowed to enter

Urban Planning at Its Best
The Spanish Steps in Rome

Italy; 1723–1726
Architect: Francesco de Sanctis

"Behind the fountains rise the Spanish Steps. They are as broad as a whole street and as high as the surrounding houses. At one time they were very much disparaged because of the muggings which happened here in the evening and at night. Now lanterns have been installed and a soldier hired to stand guard. Since then no one has heard of such complaints for a long time, although the lanterns burn only dimly and the soldier always sits in the sentry-box in the evenings."

Hans Christian Andersen, *In the Foreigner's Quarter*, 1842

Louis XIV and the pope didn't see eye to eye. Ever since 1577 there had been an ongoing discussion about the idea of building a monumental flight of steps to connect the Piazza di Spagna and the Church of the Holy Trinity, which towers above the square. But the plan's realization was hindered by several diplomatic skirmishes. The place of worship which formed part of the French embassy next to the papal court was considered a French national church, and, according to the French, stood on French territory. The hill is a Roman zone, countered the pope and wouldn't agree to allow the Sun King—should the Steps ever be built—to erect an equestrian statue of himself on the site. The battle fronts had become so hardened that at first everything just stayed as it was.

Whoever wanted to walk from the church down to the square was obliged to use a treacherously steep footpath along which Roman housewives usually hung up their washing. Only after Louis XIV had departed this life could the muddle of territorial feuds and national pride be done away with. Now the steps could be built—based on a design by a Roman architect and with the money of a French diplomat who had the steps decorated with the fleur-de-lis of the French royal coat of arms. Rome had gained a new architectural ensemble and has continued to benefit from such enlightened urban planning ever since.

The Spanish Steps, which were named after the nearby Spanish embassy, flow like a cascade from the church down to the square. The architect couldn't get enough of the elegant interplay of steps and landings, of sweeping movements to the outside and inside, of terraces which invite one to "tarry a while." From a distance the en-

semble of the Spanish Steps, with the double-towered facade of the Church of the Holy Trinity and the obelisks, seems like an enormous stage set. And, occasionally, the scenes which are played out here strike us as being somewhat theatrical too. On the balustrades young lovers swear their eternal devotion, on the terraces musicians give samples of their skills, and exotic beings flaunt themselves—like the young man whom the writer Ernst Jünger met on the Spanish Steps: "Today he was wearing a suit of white silk with crimson stripes, a red floppy hat, a red tie, a blue shirt, sky-blue socks, white shoes. He was accompanied by a young girl in a garish red jacket and a youth who was also so extravagantly dressed. He stopped with them on one of the steps and used colored pencils to touch up their make-up. By the way, I don't believe that these people achieve much when it comes to eroticism; their main energies are wasted on the show."

Artists and writers have always felt at home around the Spanish Steps. Baudelaire, Gogol, Liszt, and Thorwaldsen drank their espresso at Café Greco, Goethe had lodgings in the Via Corso and, in 1821, John Keats died in a room overlooking the Spanish Steps. He must have often looked down at the goings-on below and also at the misery which has always been at home here: "By day they swarm with beggars with withered limbs," wrote Hans Christian Andersen of the Spanish Steps in 1842. "Some support themselves on their hands and hop along like frogs, others sprawl on the stones and show their physical defects." But on a few days of the year, joy and sorrow are equally hidden from view. In the spring the flower sellers bring cartloads of azaleas into the city and transform the Spanish Steps into a sea of flowers.

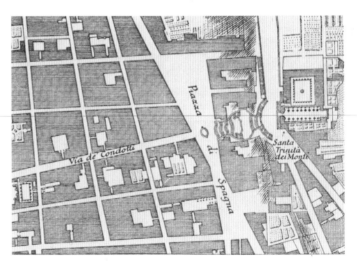

Historical plan of the Piazza di Spagna with the Spanish Steps

"By day they swarm with beggars with withered limbs"
(Hans Christian Andersen describing the Spanish Steps)

Tent of the Field Marshal
Prince Eugene and the Upper Belvedere in Vienna

Austria; 1700–1724
Architect: Lukas von Hildebrandt

"Like an enchanted castle it lies deserted in the stillness of its garden. It is a true 'Sleeping Beauty' castle full of splendid salons with white and gold stucco ceilings and flowered or striped wall-paper. Indeed, as if enchanted — as if it has nothing to do with the loud and busy life outside — a place of dreams and tranquillity."

Arthur Rössler, *As If Enchanted*, 1909

The Relief of Vienna in 1683, Martino Altomonte

He was described as small, puny, and ugly. Prince Eugene was born in Paris and grew up at the French court. Liselotte von der Pfalz, the King of France's sister-in-law at Versailles, described him as a dirty and troublesome child, "who showed no promise, whatsoever." The church beckoned—at least he was still Catholic. The last hope waned when the twenty-year-old prince decided, against his family's wishes, to turn down the religious career they had prepared for him and to seek his fortune abroad.

Prince Eugene set off for Vienna where he joined the imperial army (that needed every man available), in the summer of 1683 to defend the city against the Ottoman army which stood at its gates. Within a short period of time, Eugene proved his courage in battle and was on his way to an exemplary military career. On December 14, 1683 Emperor Leopold I gave him a dragoon regiment and promoted him to colonel. Ten years later the prince from Savoy was a field marshal and the supreme commander of the Hapsburg troops.

His clever, well-planned military campaigns always ended successfully, winning the formerly penniless foreigner fame as the "Ottoman vanquisher" and turning him into a popular hero. He was celebrated in song and verse as the "noble knight." He was also said to possess a large library of beautifully bound books. His contemporaries said he corresponded regularly with respected intellectuals such as Voltaire and Montesquieu. At the same time Prince Eugene was described as a modest man who placed little value on the honors, wealth, and fame he had acquired.

Nonetheless, he wanted to live according to his station. In 1700 he began the construction of an imposing summer palace, south of the city, near the race track where the wall marking Vienna's defenses had stood. The Belvedere, based on the palace of Versailles, would have suited a reigning prince. It was a spacious complex made up of two palaces: the dominant "Upper Belvedere," built on the hill and used on formal occasions and the more intimate "Lower Belvedere" at the foot of the hill which served as his residence. Gardens connected the two palaces. A contemporary visitor, who claimed to have experienced "nothing more beautiful" than a nocturnal gathering in the lighted gardens of the Prince, described the park as having, "a large cascade and four pools with jets d'eau and four fields containing box trees trimmed into fanciful figures."

The view from the palace was grandiose, taking in the towers of the Danube capital and the hillsides of the Vienna woods beyond them.

"Here the field marshal enjoyed a short respite between wars," wrote Hugo von Hofmannsthal. "The city of his emperor, whom he served with glory and obedience, was to spread out before the windows of this resting place and its ancient, honorable cathedral rises in greeting. The magnificent staircase and the light-filled salons were to be filled with paintings glorifying his deeds and with statues that spoke allegorically of his fame and his greatness, his wisdom and his modesty." The symbolism was carried even

The noble officer, Prince Eugen

further on the ceilings of the Upper Belvedere which were painted to resemble splendid Turkish tents, and in the figure of Hercules that appears repeatedly commemorating Prince Eugene himself—the hero that Liselotte von der Pfalz had so underestimated.

The landscaped gardens
between the Upper and
the Lower Belvederes

Sleeping Beauty in the Pine Forest
Dominikus Zimmermann and the Wies Church

Germany; planned: 1743/44; built: 1745–1765
Architect: Dominikus Zimmermann

"A simple portal opens and the visitor finds himself in a festive 'banquet' hall filled with glowing colors. It effuses so much light that it barely seems to be made of solid matter. It appears to be composed of the same substance as the flowers outside, and as the clouds that gather over the surrounding mountains."

Taken from the guidebook: *Schatzkammer Deutschlands* "Treasure Trove of Germany," 1973

Gratitude for the successful completion: the Master Builder Dominikus Zimmermann's votive picture, 1757

It seems to be in the middle of nowhere. The road south, which leads to the mountains, disappears into an area of marshes and small lakes and the forest threatens to swallow all signs of life. The landscape belongs to the Ice Age, but in its midst is a light and friendly island. Those who follow gleams of light midst shadowy forests, emerge from the spruce-lined path into pastureland awash with dandelion, sorrel, lady's mantle and goldenrod. Yet it is not the bounty of nature but a church that dominates the scene—the Wies Church known as the "Flower of the Meadow."

This is the heart of the Bavarian region known as Pfaffenwinkl or "Parson's Corner" because it has more monasteries than any other region in Germany. The abbot of the nearby Steingaden Monastery, who commissioned the building, was convinced that the meadow was also a place where good fortune resided. Delighted with the completed building, he scratched a message in the glass of an abbey window with his signet ring, "Hoc loco habitat fortuna." He added a second line, "Hic quiecit cor," "here the heart finds peace."

The beauty and harmony of the church, whose lively design imparts a sense of joy that is best described by a summer day, has captured the hearts of visitors for more than two hundred years. Yet tears marked the beginning.

On June 14, 1783 a pious farmer's wife named Maria Lory, whose farm was next to the meadow, noticed that the Christ figure in her parlor had "drops on his face," which she believed to be tears. Terrified by the apparition she spread the news of her weeping wonder throughout the neighborhood. It wasn't long before the lachrymose Christ began performing miracles: crippled limbs grew straight, the blind could see and the dumb could speak. The parish priests were skeptical and believed the stream of pilgrims would soon subside to a trickle. But the opposite occurred. Pilgrims from all over Germany, Bohemia, Hungary and neighboring provinces in France and Italy made their way to the miraculous meadow. Officials finally decided to build a church there and commissioned Dominikus Zimmermann for the task.

The renowned architect and master of stucco work was already sixty years old when he received the commission—the Wies Church, however, would prove to be his masterpiece. Starting with the altar where the suffering figure, believed once to have wept in the parlor of the Lory farm, was housed, Zimmermann produced a joyous symphony of light and color, celebrating Christ's triumph over suffering and death. He chose a harmonious arrangement between a basilica and central plan where everything appearing heavy or angular was banned. Instead, round and oval shapes predominate and a passion for light and life characterizes the building.

At the beginning of the twentieth century, the essayist Josef Hofmiller wrote: "The ceiling is like an open sky, white parapets aspire upwards and green trees, clouds and angels shimmer against the heavenly blue. Everything is in motion, white statues, colored figures, fluttering drapery and arms that point, signify and gesticulate. Everything seems limitless and yet contained: the space, light, colors, forms, lines. One's eyes can never get their fill at the Wies Church. It has been described as "a celebratory hymn," "a church of joy" and "a place of redemption."

For its creator the Wies Church became his first stop on the way to eternity. Dominikus Zimmermann was never able to part from his creation. During its construction he built himself a simple house near the church where he lived until his death in November 1766. His son, Franz Dominikus, had married Maria Lory some years earlier, who by that time was widowed and also remained on the spot—not as an architect but as an innkeeper.

The goal for all pilgrims: the high altar with the *Ecce Homo*

Entry into heaven: Rococo fresco with the empty
throne at the Last Judgement by Johann Baptist
Zimmermann, the master builder's brother

Thomas Jefferson and His Country Home
The Wise Man of Monticello

Charlottesville, USA; begun in 1768
Architect: Thomas Jefferson

"Spring has come late this year. The oats still haven't been sown, only a little tobacco planted, and nothing has been done in the garden. The wheat has suffered badly. Nothing can be seen in the countryside apart from the maple, the weeping willow and the lilac. Flour costs eight dollars in Richmond, or so I have been told. And the price for our produce is falling."

Based on Thomas Jefferson's first letter from Monticello to his successor as president of the United States of America, March 1809

He loved the woods and the wilderness of Virginia: "I have so many happy memories of this area that no other place could ever compete with it in my heart." And he never wanted to leave this corner of the world, although he led an eventful life which took him to many fascinating places. The son of wealthy landowners, he had been elected to the Virginia Assembly at the age of twenty-six, acting out his first major role on the political stage in 1776: Thomas Jefferson, a budding lawyer of thirty-three, drafted nothing less than the American Declaration of Independence. It won him the respect of the nation and launched his brilliant career. He went on to become governor of Virginia, ambassador to France, secretary of state under George Washington, vice president under John Adams, and finally Head of State. From 1801 to 1809 Thomas Jefferson held the highest office in the nation as the third president of the United States of America.

Yet during all that time, with the exception of his stay in France as a diplomat at the court of Louis XVI, he kept his main residence near the small, peaceful town of Charlottesville, some eighty miles southwest of Washington.

The brick building, with an octagonal dome and a portico modeled on classical temples, stands slightly elevated among the idyllic green hills of Virginia. This stately country home is "Monticello," Jefferson's refuge for over fifty years. Here he not only indulged in leisure pursuits; with his overwhelming need to create, he was constantly inventing and fixing any manner of things. One of his favorite pastimes was to remodel buildings. Jefferson himself had designed Monticello as a young man—inspired by the Villa Rotonda near Vicenza, which he had visited on a trip to Italy. Inside, Jefferson's love for technical detail can be seen. There are automatic swinging and sliding doors, hidden closets, and narrow staircases which make use of every available space. The greatest showpiece is in the entrance hall: a mechanical clock which tells both the time and the day of the week. Jefferson worked on his house over a period of decades, constantly created new designs, and had walls removed and rebuilt. "Monticello was, without a doubt, a great passion in his life," says one of his biographers, who also tells how Jefferson often put up as many as fifty guests at a time in his country home.

After his presidency, Jefferson withdrew completely to Monticello. He spent his time landscaping the garden, helping his grandchildren with their schoolwork, and sketching designs for the buildings of the University of Virginia, which he founded in Charlottesville in 1819.

"I have said good-bye to politics forever," he wrote in a letter. "Instead of the newspapers, I now read Tacitus and Thukydides, Newton and Euclid, and feel better than I ever have before." For Jefferson the house on the verdant hill must have been a paradise on earth. "Nowhere am I as happy as here, with no other society. All of my wishes end here, and here I will hopefully end all of my days." His wish was to be granted. On July 4, 1826, exactly fifty years to the day after the signing of the Declaration of Independence, Thomas Jefferson died at his house in Monticello. Today his grave in the garden (for which he not only wrote the inscription but also designed the gravestone), is a place of pilgrimage, a shrine for the American nation.

Thomas Jefferson's draft of the American Declaration of Independence

A president's refuge: Monticello, Jefferson's
residence in Charlottesville, Virginia

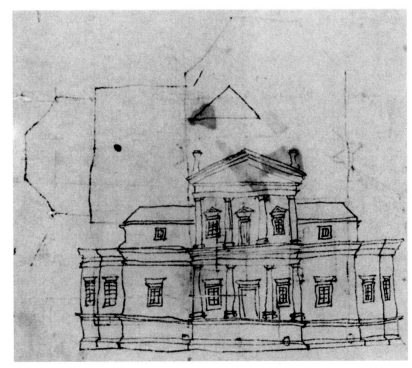

Jefferson's drawing of the first
version of Monticello's facade,
the president was inspired
by the Villa Rotonda in Italy

The Seat of Power
The Capitol in Washington, D.C.

USA; 1793–1867
Design: William Thornton
Other architects who worked on the structure: Benjamin
Henry Latrobe, Charles Bulfinch, and Thomas Ustick Walter

"Where does the journey lead? To
the Capitol, naturally, through broad
avenues that reach to the stars and
wide tree-lined streets that lead to the
next meeting place. I notice a fondness
for monuments. But I soon recognized
that all these symbols, so suspect to
Europeans, are not stale history drawn
from schoolbooks but recently experienced reality and the expression of joy
at becoming one nation made up of all
the world."

Translated from Wolfgang Koeppen's *Journey to America*, 1959

Its name originates in the West and is borrowed
from the highest of Rome's seven hills, the
Capitoline, which was the political and social
center of the metropolis on the Tiber. In ancient
times a temple to the empire's gods crowned
the hill. Later, in the Middle Ages, poets were
honored there, and today the mayor of Rome
resides on the Capitoline Hill.

Washington, D.C., America's capital on the
Potomac since 1790, has little in common with
Rome. But the nation's founding fathers were
able to draw many symbolic parallels: "Ancient
Rome was imperial in its dimensions. Its dignity
and importance should be an example to the
capital of our nation, because Washington is the
Rome of the present." Nowhere is this parallel
more evident than in the Capitol, the seat of
the United States government.

The impressive complex crowns the hill at
the end of an imposing avenue and, thanks to
its enormous dome, dominates the skyline of
the city. The dome is 222 feet high, made of
cast iron, and weighs more than 4,000 tons.
The resemblance to the dome of St Peter's in
Rome is no mere coincidence.

This is where the political heart of the
nation beats. The Congress of the United
States of America meets under the dome. It is
the country's legislative body, divided into two
houses, the Senate (comprising 100 members)
and the House of Representatives (with more
than 430 members).

The circumstances surrounding the building
of the Capitol are a perfect example of the
"unlimited opportunities" for which the USA
is famous. William Thornton, upon whose plans
the Capitol is based, was not trained as an architect, but as a physician. He submitted his
plans only six days before the deadline for
the competition entries. Nonetheless, George
Washington, the nation's first president, chose
Thornton's plan because of its "size, its simplicity and utilization potential."

Although the majestic dome and two spacious wings were built later, the building was
widely praised and honored as "the foundation
for American democracy," "a self-confident
expression of an equally self-confident constitution," and as "a recognition of independence
and freedom writ in stone." It was viewed as a
symbol of a system of government that "granted
equal rights and equal opportunities to all."
Those who were somewhat less impressed
labeled the architecture "pathetic" and noted
that politics in the Capitol often deviated from
the high ideals they purported to follow. "Virtue
in America was fragile, as it was elsewhere,"
wrote the American historian Edmund S. Morgan.

"Americans could preach modesty and promote
speculators; promise freedom and keep slaves."

In light of such condemnation the criticism
voiced by Charles Dickens, who visited the
Capitol in 1842, seems mild by comparison.
He merely complained that the representatives
chewed tobacco and spat on the floor.

George Washington, the first president of
the United States of America

"Washington is the Rome of the present;"
the Capitol dominates Washington, D.C.'s skyline

The first session of the new Senate in the Capitol, woodcut, 1859

Dreams of Glory and Grandeur
Napoleon and the Arc de Triomphe de l'Etoile

Paris, France; 1806–1836
Architect: Jean-Francois Chalgrin

"I salute the regiment that approaches the Arc de Triomphe, then I leave the vaulted arch. In front of me is the Champs Elysées! Ah, an ocean! An enormous crowd stands on both sides of the magnificent avenue. Probably two million, reaching as far as my eyes can see—an excited mass of people under the Tricolor."

Charles de Gaulle, *Memoirs*, 1942–1946

The famous star-shaped intersection at the heart of the French capital could have turned out quite differently. In 1758 there was a plan to build an architecturally daring "établissement" in the shape of a giant elephant on this open space! Its voluminous body would have contained a ballroom, theater, and restaurants. But even the pleasure-loving Parisians found this idea a bit too bizarre. Instead, Napoleon commissioned a more realistic monument.

At his order the massive triumphal arch dedicated to the *Grand Armée* was begun in 1806 in the center of the *Place de l'Etoile*, today known as the *Place Charles de Gaulle*. Later the Tomb of the Unknown Soldier was added at its base—the first monument of this type which would be copied by other countries around the world.

The decision to build the huge arch came on the heels of the Battle of Austerlitz, also known as the Battle of Three Emperors, in which Napoleon won a victory over Russia and Austria. For Austria the defeat was devastating: Hapsburg Emperor Franz II lost his territory in Germany and Italy. Napoleon then founded the Confederation of the Rhine in Germany, uniting sixteen kings and ruling princes under a French protectorate. In Naples, Italy he deposed the Bourbon rulers and put his brother, Joseph, in their place. His Corsican family occupied most of Europe's thrones and Napoleon held the West in his power. The occasion called for more than just a celebration. Napoleon wanted to record his victory permanently for generations to come.

It was no accident that Napoleon looked to ancient Rome for inspiration for his triumphal arch. According to Klaus Lankheit, an art historian: "The emperor saw himself as the heir of the Roman Caesars. His government administration copied Rome with a senate and prefects; he borrowed from Roman law and had François

Gérard paint him in the pose of a triumphant hero crowned with laurel leaves. For his capital he demanded imperial forums, grand avenues, baths, temples, monumental statues and triumphal arches."

The Arc de Triomphe, which placed Paris on a par with Rome, is one of the mightiest triumphal arches ever built. With its height of around 150 feet and its width of 135 feet, it is the perfect culmination for the Champs Elysées and symbolizes the self-confidence of its builder, who was then at the zenith of his power. Foreign observers joined in its praise. The German poet Heinrich Heine wrote: "Napoleon is not of the wood from which kings are carved. He is made of marble, the stuff of gods."

The entire nation was in a jubilant mood, but the construction dragged on. When cannon salutes and the pealing of bells from all the city's churches welcomed Marie Louise of Austria, Napoleon's second bride in 1810, the monument to the glory of France had barely risen above its foundation. The construction site was hidden by plaster casts of statues and draped with giant canvases, painted to show what the monument would eventually look like.

Napoleon never lived to see the completion, and construction actually came to a halt following his defeat at Waterloo in 1815. It was the "Citizen King" Louis-Philippe of the House of Orleans who finally completed the monument. He inaugurated the Arc de Triomphe in 1836 as a symbol of French military fame.

Perhaps it would have been one small consolation for Napoleon after his death to know that, when his ashes were brought over from St Helena, the funeral procession passed through the Arc de Triomphe on its way to the Hôtel des Invalids. Only one other Frenchman ever received this honor—the writer and poet Victor Hugo.

Drawing by Charles Steuben depicting Napoleon's death on the island of St Helena

Napoleon dedicated the Arc de Triomphe to the *Grand Armée* and France's victory over Russia and Austria

The Home of England's Democratic Traditions
The Houses of Parliament

London, England; 1834–1860
Architects: Charles Barry and Augustus Pugin

"Yesterday, at around noon, we took a carriage to drive to the Houses of Parliament which, as far as I can judge, must surely be the most extensive building ever to have been constructed. It is indeed vast, and the tower, which has not yet been completed, continues to rise into the sky. To be quite frank I must admit that I was more impressed by the wonderful interior than with the external design."

Nathaniel Hawthorne, *English Notebooks*, 1857

House of Commons, lithograph, 1862

The mood was tense. The members of the House of Lords had agreed to reduce the number of "unnecessary spectators" attending their debates by excluding the fair sex from all future sessions. In response, a number of blue-blooded ladies under the strict leadership of the Duchesses of Queensberry and Ancaster turned up for action. To prove that neither men nor laws could keep them away, they marched to the main entrance of the House of Lords at

Big Ben, the world famous clock tower

the stroke of nine in the morning, but were promptly turned away. In protest, the ladies proceeded to lay siege to the House. Their blows and kicks resounded at the door while inside, the gentlemen struggled to hear what the speakers were saying. But the Lords still held firm, so the ladies resorted to a trick. For half an hour they kept completely silent. When the Lord Chancellor had the door opened, convinced that they had gone away, all of their bottled-up rage exploded into the chamber. Wildly brandishing umbrellas, they occupied the gallery and barked commentaries throughout the debates. The Lords were thoroughly intimidated and took back their decision to exclude women—and democracy scored another victory.

The Lords should have known that they were walking on difficult terrain. The scene of the event, Westminster Palace, was still considered one of the residences of the English monarchy even after other seats had been established following a fire in the palace in 1512.

Yet after the departure of the monarchs, another spirit stirred within the ancient walls. The palace became exclusively the seat of Parliament, and even the sovereign, according to the remarkably democratic constitution, has to play by its rules. When King Charles I stormed a session in the House of Commons in 1642 in order to arrest five of his delegates, the Speaker ordered him to leave, brusquely reminding him of the independence of Parliament. Since then it has been forbidden for any reigning British monarch to set foot in the House of Commons.

The present Houses of Parliament, where the House of Lords and the House of Commons still sit today, represent the democratic tradition of Great Britain. The imposing buildings on the shore of the Thames—including Big Ben, the world-famous clock tower—are quite a bit younger than one might suppose. They were only erected in the nineteenth century after the ancient Westminster Palace building was irreparably destroyed by another disastrous fire in 1834—an event captured in a famous painting by the artist William Turner.

Opinions on the Gothic Revival architecture of the new Parliament building were divided. During his days as a correspondent in London, Theodor Fontane reported: "Critical voices bluntly express that the thing is totally spoiled, both spiritually and physically. There is a lack of proportion between the heights of the buildings. And then the endless ornaments! One looks to find a purpose for these curlicues and can find no other than that they are there in order to swallow dust and smoke and to accommodate many thousand of swallows' nests." The American writer William Dean Howells countered: "Who could ever say that the Houses of Parliament are anything but beautiful? I find them dignified and majestic. They could only have been built in this style, rising high up into the gray skies, against which they stand out clearly."

The English writer Virginia Woolf was looking for majesty and dignity less in the building than in the demeanor of the delegates during their sessions—and was bitterly disappointed: "Listening to all that chatter, laughter, and general good cheer, the demonstrations of impatience and the lack of respect, one could think that they had gathered at a cattle market."

The Houses of Parliament, a symbol of the democratic
tradition of Great Britain

The House of Lords

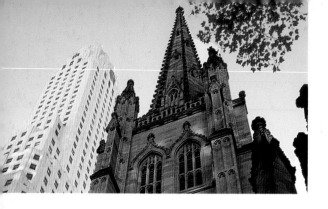

In the Shadow of Skyscrapers
The Old Symbol of a New City: Trinity Church

New York City, USA; 1841–1846
Architect: Richard Upjohn

"I've never seen Wall Street before at five o'clock in the afternoon. The tall shady canyons are nearly deserted; the little church sleeps at the foot of the cliffs, surrounded by its cemetery. Suddenly, the doors of the buildings release dark waves, a rising tide of humanity submerges the streets, and we're carried off in a whirl.... At this hour it is impossible to force pedestrians to respect the traffic lights, so to intimidate the women, who are most agitated, they've chosen handsome policemen with coaxing smiles."

Simone de Beauvoir, *America Day by Day*, 1947

Today it seems as if it has been swallowed by the surrounding skyscrapers. The office buildings of Manhattan's Wall Street dominate the sky above Trinity Church, and it is hard to believe it was once the highest building far and wide. The soaring tower of Trinity Church dominated the skyline of Manhattan until the nineteenth century, and for more than fifty years remained the true symbol of New York City. A church had already occupied the site at the end of the seventeenth century. At that time the rest of the wall that was eventually to give the street its name was still visible. It had been built to protect the Dutch from the encroachment of British settlers. This early church was destroyed in the fire that devastated nearly half of New York in 1776.

A new church was built on the same spot a short time later but collapsed after its completion, making way for the third and, until now, final church building on the site. Trinity Church, which presently stands in the shadow of Wall Street's skyscrapers, is a three-nave basilica made of chiseled, natural stone blocks. Fake battlements top the walls.

The stained glass windows are believed to have been the first manufactured in the United States, and its bronze doors (based on a design by Richard Morris Hunt) bear more than an accidental resemblance to the doors of the Baptistery in Florence. Richard Upjohn, the church's architect, was born in Shaftesbury, England and apprenticed to a cabinetmaker. When his business failed, forcing him deeply into debt, he sailed to America. There his fortunes improved. He worked as a technical draftsman and eventually settled in Boston as an architect. His buildings, inspired by medieval European models, soon became famous as America's foremost exponents of neo-gothic architecture. Trinity Church is his masterpiece. In a survey conducted in 1885, Trinity was ranked fourth among the most important buildings in America.

The cemetery surrounding Trinity Church contains the oldest graves in the city and is the final resting place of many famous Americans, including Robert Fulton, who invented the paddle-wheel steamer and launched his first model on the Hudson river in 1807. Alexander Hamilton is also buried in the cemetery at Trinity Church, which at a current real estate price of $15,000 per square yard, would make the church the richest in the world—at least on paper. Hamilton is famous as the author of the *Federalist Papers*. As America's first Secretary of the Treasury, he was responsible for rescuing the fledgling republic from the ravages of inflation.

Trinity Church now plays only a minor role in the largely secular business world that now surrounds it. The cathedrals of modern America are the office towers of the financial district. The author Tama Janowitz ironically wrote in *Slaves of New York*: "My bank is one of these money institutes on Wall Street, an unusually threatening structure built in neo-Fascist-religious style. In the back there must be one of these giant organs or, at least, a baptismal font. Had they any sense at all at my bank, they would immediately commission me to change the interior into a chapel."

In the shadow of such palatial banks Trinity has become somewhat of a curiosity. But New Yorkers believe the church follows the futile doings of the stressed-out bankers who rush past it, looking on at the time when the famous stock market crashed in 1929. After all, no amount of praying could turn the clock back.

19th-century Manhattan's highest building: Trinity Church viewed from Wall Street, lithograph, 1857

Overshadowed by Manhattan's skyscrapers:
Trinity Church today

The stained glass windows of Trinity
are believed to have been the first
manufactured in the United States

The Stuff of Fairy Tales
Neuschwanstein Castle and Its Tragic King

Bavaria, Germany; 1869–1892 (incomplete)
First design by theater painter Christian Jank
Architects: Eduard von Riedel (until 1874),
Georg Dollmann (until 1884), Julius Hofmann

"I plan to reconstruct the old castle ruin at the Pöllat Gorge in the style of an old German stronghold, and I have to admit that I am very much looking forward to living there one day. Raised on a pinnacle and surrounded by mountain air one enjoys a magnificent view of the Tyrol mountains and far into the plain. This place is one of the most beautiful one can find, holy and unapproachable."

King Ludwig II of Bavaria in a letter to Richard Wagner, March 15, 1868

Young, handsome and King of Bavaria: Ludwig II in his royal garb

The king was young and beautiful. Whenever he presented himself to the public with his majestic appearance, his dark hair and shining eyes, women fainted by the dozen. Contemporary accounts idolize the 22-year-old monarch as "the ideal young, royal adonis, whose moving beauty made thousands of women glow with a magic power." In the hallways of the Munich royal palace mothers from respected families paraded their grown-up daughters, hoping to accidentally meet the adored king. Even women of dubious morals made their advances to him. One opera singer was particularly bold and had already managed to get Ludwig to invite her to go boating with him on the artificial lake of his winter palace. On that occasion she purposely fell into the water, hoping to be saved by the king himself. But instead of proof of his love she only got a severe cold. Ludwig had a servant rescue the wet diva and walked away in silence. There was no subsequent invitation. He did not like such affairs and had other things on his mind. As a child he had immersed himself completely in the mythical world of Germanic sagas, and as a 15-year-old had discovered the operas of Richard Wagner. Like many of his contemporaries he had a strong romantic inclination for the Middle Ages. Inspired by the sagas, the Wartburg with its Hall of Singers and a visit to the construction site at Pierrefonds near Compiègne, which the French architect Viollet-le-Duc was just rebuilding in 14th-century style, he now wanted to create his own fairy-tale retreat—just for himself: a sumptuous dream place, where figures from sagas would come to life: Lohengrin, Parsifal, Siegfried, Tristan, Tannhäuser....The place he selected could not have been better: Tannhäuser is supposed to have spent the night at the castle of the lords of Schwangau on his return from Rome. During the time of Ludwig, only a few sad remains were left of this castle. He had it blown up, so that the construction site lay eight meters below the level of the ruin. In the two years that followed, the hissing of a steam crane and the noise of locomotives transporting building material turned the mountain forest near Füssen into a witches cauldron. The bizarre architecture of the castle, designed by the stage painter Christian Jank, was built around a revolutionary, new steel construction with cast-iron columns. Behind the scenes, one of the most modern hot water systems of the time and a heating system that could be regulated were installed. The interior design does not hint at the technology hidden behind the walls—here the Middle Ages reigned: the furniture is dark and heavy, the walls are decorated with frescoes depicting scenes from the heroic deeds of the German sagas. Neuschwanstein—the setting for a Wagnerian opera? Not quite. It was first and foremost a place of retreat for Ludwig, whose egocentric pleasure in decoration and dream was later picked up by Walt Disney and used for his fairytale empire. Neuschwanstein was where the king could forget about the real world, in which he could no longer reign with the absolute power of monarchs of old. In the event of his death he had ordered Neuschwanstein to be destroyed. But his order was not followed: only a few weeks after Ludwig's mysterious death in Lake Starnberg on June 13, 1886, the first tourists were walking through his dreamworld and standing in his bedroom.

The Hall of Singers at Neuschwanstein Castle, inspired by a similar room at the legendary Wartburg Castle

The salon of the fairy-tale Prince

Neuschwanstein Castle, a vision from
times of yore, girded in a shroud of mist

The City of Glass
The Royal Greenhouses of Laeken

Brussels, Belgium; 1879–1892
Architect: Alphonse Balat

"How much we cherish thy roofs,
thy skin of glass,
That shelter the wealth of the Earth,
its riches,
Protect the evergreen plants from
the cold,
Daring the jasmine to bloom in
our clime
And coaxing with your warmth
The scented pineapple for our sweet
enjoyment."

Abbé Delille, *Gardens, or the Art of Beautifying
the Landscape*, 1782

Much has been written about the curse of the Gardens of Laeken. And it is easy to believe in a mysterious influence. Marie Christine of Austria and her husband Albert of Sachsen-Teschen, the last Hapsburg governor, built the Laeken Palace in 1782 in the beautiful wooded landscape north of Brussels. They wanted a French-style residence—and their wish was realized in stone, in the form of a cool, rational and elegant residence, a seat of power and a symbol of absolute rule. The park, however, was not laid out in the baroque fashion of the day but in the form of an English garden which simulated wild and untamed nature. Many voices warned that the garden posed a threat, symbolized unpredictability and rebellion, and predicted a coup.

A short time later, the garden did indeed strike its first blow. The Austrian governors lost their power, paving the way for Napoleon. When he occupied the country he made Laeken his residence and thoroughly restored the palace. But he too fell victim to the curse of the garden: just a short distance away is Waterloo. Following Napoleon's defeat, the territory of what we now call Belgium became Dutch and the garden found a new owner and a fresh victim.

King William I, a grouchy member of the House of Orange moved into Laeken and assured his place in posterity by building an orangery. It was barely finished when the patriots revolted and sent William back to the Netherlands. After an interim period of relative peace King Leopold II rose to the throne in 1865. He was a nature lover and the first resident of Laeken who apparently came to terms with the revengeful garden.

Leopold set out to enlarge the garden, buying parcel after parcel of land until he had increased the area to some eighty acres. Massive greenhouses rose in the garden against the lush green background of the wooded park. The greenhouses formed the largest connected

The five domed towers of the Congo House

King Leopold II of Belgium

The Winter Garden with its glass cupola in 1876

The Winter Garden: the greenhouses
formed the largest complex of glass
covered buildings in Europe

glass structure in Europe. They were kept at a constant temperature throughout the year and contained everything from orange trees to rubber plants, rhododendrons to exotic plants. The gardens of Laeken grew into a city of glass, a tropical Brabant.

Leopold spared no cost. The exterior construction of the representative Winter Garden with its eighty-foot-high glass cupola—which not only housed palm trees but provided room for royal receptions—cost the king half-a-million gold francs. The sum apparently caused him

little concern because he continued to plan for further expansion. Next to the Winter Garden Leopold built the Congo House, a glass pleasure palace with five domed towers that presented the excitement of Central Africa, and at the same time resembled a Byzantine church.

Later Leopold commissioned a real church, the Église de Fer, in light, airy glass. It was based on the king's own design and provided an artificial home for tropical plants in the sacristy. A long glass corridor connected the church to the palace.

Leopold II died in his own magic green world, in a private apartment in the Palm House on December 17, 1909, never having completely succeeded in escaping the lure of the garden. His private life had been shadowed by tragedy: his only son, the heir to the throne, had died at the age of nine of pneumonia, following a fall into the pond in the garden of Laeken.

Figurehead of the American Dream
The Statue of Liberty

New York City, USA; 1871–1884
Sculptor: Frédéric-Auguste Bartholdi

"Here at our sea-washed, sunset gates shall stand

A mighty woman with a torch, whose flame

Is the imprisoned lightning, and her name

Mother of Exiles.

From her beacon-hand

Glows world-wide welcome;

Her mild eyes command

The air-bridged harbor that twin cities frame.

'Keep ancient lands, your storied pomp!' cries she

With silent lips. 'Give me your tired, your poor,

Your huddled masses yearning to breathe free,

The wretched refuse to your teeming shore.

Send these, the homeless, tempest-tossed to me,

I lift my lamp, beside the golden door.'"

Poem by the Jewish immigrant, Emma Lazarus, engraved on the pedestal of the Statue of Liberty, 1886

The mother of the nation weighs 254 tons; including her pedestal, she is nearly three hundred feet tall and braced by a corset made for her by the engineer Gustave Eiffel, who was later to build the tower in Paris that bears his name.

Since 1886, the "personification of freedom" has welcomed all those who arrive by ship at New York harbor. In the first half of the twentieth century, this greeting was extended above all to European emigrants who, during the great waves of immigration, first trod upon American soil in New York. That is why "Miss Liberty" is not just the symbol of New York. The "statue of the goddess of liberty who bears the beacon of the enlightened spirit into the world," according to her official description, is a symbol for all of America. The copper lady was not born in America, but in Europe. The individual parts of the massive sculpture were cast in a Paris backyard under the watchful eye of her creator, the sculptor Frédéric-Auguste Bartholdi, who came from Alsace on the French-German border.

Bartholdi belonged to the illustrious social circle of the history professor Edouard de Laboulayes, president of the French organization against slavery. At a dinner party in Glatigny in 1865, to which Laboulayes had invited liberal-minded politicians and scholars of his country, it was decided that a gift should be presented to the United States in 1876 to mark the one hundredth anniversary of independence from the English crown. This gift was to be the Statue of Liberty. Their motives were not entirely without interest. After the revolutions of 1789 and 1830, France once again became a monarchy under Emperor Napoleon III, and Laboulayes and his friends wanted to roll the propaganda drum for their own political goal: the founding of the third French republic. Bartholdi, who had discovered his partiality for colossal sculpture during a journey to the pyramids at Giza, won the commission and designed the figure with a diadem and a glowing torch—both symbols of the Freemasons, of which Bartholdi was a member. He also found the ideal site to erect the monument on a visit to New York: an artificial island beyond the southern tip of Manhattan, created from piled-up ballast which had been jettisoned from ships before entering New York harbor.

Since the project's organizers ran out of money, the figure was not finished in time for the anniversary of the Declaration of Independence. The ambitious monument was only completed in 1884 after the newspaper publisher Joseph Pulitzer, founder of the eponymous journalism prize, had successfully campaigned for money in France and in the United States.

Packed in France into two hundred crates, the Statue of Liberty embarked on the same voyage that millions of immigrants would make later in history. On arrival in New York, she was unloaded on Bedloe's Island, the former name

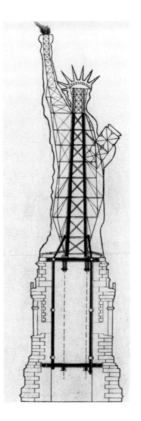

The corset which braces the statue was made by Gustave Eiffel who later built the Eiffel Tower in Paris

of Liberty Island, then assembled, and finally inaugurated on October 28, 1886, in the presence
of Grover Cleveland, the American president.

At first "Miss Liberty" was not warmly
welcomed. Among other things, she was scorn-
fully likened to a "sleepwalking neurotic with
a candle," and to a "has-been matron in last
season's ballgown." New York suffragettes did
not react jubilantly to the unveiling of the goddess of liberty either. They protested that, after
one hundred years of independence, women in
the land of unlimited possibilities still were not
allowed to vote. In the meantime the Statue of
Liberty has conquered many hearts; she has
become a figure with which the entire American
nation identifies. Incidentally, a small-scale version of the statue has also stood in Paris since
1889—a gift made by Americans living in France.

One Must Have Spectacles
The Burgtheater in Vienna

Austria; 1874–1888
Architect: Gottfried Semper

"At the Burgtheater I caught my first glimpse of stage lights. I was nurtured there (for fifty old Austrian crowns a night) and fed a rich diet of arts from this institution of Emperor and King. And there the most famous actors of their time lulled me to sleep with their classical speeches."

Max Reinhardt, from his *Memoirs* in which he claimed to have been born in the third balcony of the Burgtheater, 1943

The theater auditorium

Vienna is best known as the city of the waltz, but the capital on the Danube also has the theater in its blood. This was the case long before 1888 when the new Burgtheater, the most famous stage in the German-speaking world, celebrated its opening.

Spectacular productions were common in the baroque period when breathtaking water and fireworks displays, complicated stage machinery, and fabulous costumes characterized court festivities. At the same time *Hanswurst* (John Sausage), a popular Viennese character, parodied society (while madly swinging his fly swatter) and entertained his audience with ribald tales of problems afflicting the common man. The Viennese, who love a good joke, especially at someone else's expense, were delighted. The church provided *Hanswurst* an unexpected source of competition in Abraham a Santa Clara, a Capuchin Monk whose passionate sermons lambasted Viennese society and turned his pulpit into a sort of popular stage.

Theater was everywhere in the imperial city. It even penetrated the walls of the palace where Empress Maria Theresa herself took to the stage and is believed to have stated, "One must have such spectacles." So it is not surprising that her son, Emperor Joseph II, founded the Burgtheater in 1776.

The theater was first housed in the former building used for imperial balls at the Hofburg on Michaelerplatz. It was to be a National Theater, which would not distinguish between social standing and was open to all the people, not just the aristocracy.

Mozart wrote *Abduction from the Seraglio* for the Burgtheater. It soon became known as a theater stage, and the quality of its productions made it famous in the German-speaking world. The Burgtheater developed the Viennese talent for *double entendre* into a new art form. The city's coachmen were soon as familiar with the theater's productions as they had previously been with prices of wine in the Vienna Woods.

The reputation of the Burgtheater grew despite the fact that the Hapsburg rulers determined its program and demanded that all plays end with the "Vienna conclusion," a form of happy ending that compensated for the public and personal tragedies the imperial family was forced to endure. Thus all tragedies, including *Romeo and Juliet,* were given a happy ending.

At the end of the nineteenth century the theater's former home on Michaelerplatz had to give way to an extension to the imperial palace. The Burgtheater moved to its present quarters on the Ringstrasse, which replaced the wall that had formerly enclosed the city.

Kaiser Franz Joseph I, who was dedicated to beautifying the city and imperial palace, commissioned an imposing theater structure with room for more than 1,000 spectators. The Emperor also sought consolation from Katharina Schratt, one of the theater's actresses, during the increasingly frequent absences of Empress Elisabeth, his globe-trotting wife.

The theater rose on the site of the Löwel Bastei, a fortress that had survived the city's most furious battle against the Ottoman invaders in 1683. The building was not an immediate success. The acoustics left much to be desired, and critical Viennese audiences made fun of the overly lavish decor. But the tradition established

Max Reinhardt, Austrian theatrical director

in the old Burgtheater soon vanquished the problems of the new theater. It is still the dream of every dramatist writing in German to have his play produced on its stage, and actors covet the title "Burgtheater Player" more than any royal decoration.

Gottfried Semper, the architect, proved prophetic when he answered his critics with the statement that, "every theater should be rebuilt after sixty years when it doesn't first burn down." After only fifty-seven years, the Burgtheater was destroyed in a bombing raid in 1945. It was rebuilt following the war. The acoustics are now perfect, and even Vienna's harshest critics have accepted the lavish decor.

The most prestigious stage in the German-speaking world: the Burgtheater in Vienna designed by Gottfried Semper

The original Burgtheater at Michaelerplatz for which Mozart composed "The Abduction from the Seraglio"

Showy and Tasteless?
Gaudí and the Sagrada Familia

Barcelona, Spain; begun in 1882
Architect: Antoni Gaudí (1852–1926)

"In the east blossoms a temple—a mystical specimen—like an enormous flower, and it is astounding to see that it was created here among such coarse, evil people who mock it and its god, and who brawl and jeer at human and divine things. But still the (so precious!) temple grows and thrives among misery, madness, and murkiness, and waits for the believers to come."

Joan Maragall, *Ode to Barcelona*, 1909

Gaudí 's vision: a model of the Sagrada Familia. The church remains incomplete

The Number 30 streetcar could not stop quickly enough. On a June morning in 1926, the old man who crossed the tracks in the city center of Barcelona, completely lost in thought, had not reacted to the shrill ringing of the bell or to the cries of warning. A short time later, after the police dispersed the crowd of onlookers which had gathered around the mortally injured man, no clue as to his identity could be found in the pockets of his shabby black suit. A vagrant? A penniless pensioner? Only the next day, when friends discovered him in the hospital after a long search, did they know who the old man was: Antoni Gaudí, the most famous architect in Spain. They wanted to transfer him to a more exclusive private clinic, but he refused: "My place is with the poor," is what he is supposed to have said before he died.

Whether he really said that or not is immaterial. It belongs to the many legends that surround Gaudí, which would later culminate in attempts to have him canonized. He was pious, that much is certain. As a practicing Catholic, Gaudí believed in the necessity of divine retribution and mercy, in the infallibility of the pope, and in the authority of the bishops. It was these convictions which had ultimately qualified him in the eyes of those who entrusted him with the building of the Sagrada Familia, the Church of the Holy Family.

Gaudí had just turned thirty-one when the men knocked on his door in 1883. They were members of the "Spiritual Community of the Devotees of St Joseph," an extreme right-wing Catholic society which rejected democratic aspirations and promoted nationalist thought. It is said that their president, Jose Maria Bocabella y Verdaguer, was so convinced of their aspirations that he even refused to eat French food, as it came from the land of Voltaire and Napoleon. The goal of the society was, "with the intercession of St Joseph, to pray to God for the triumph of the church in these difficult and perilous times." In order to give weight to their plea, they intended to erect a church, a symbol of anti-modernism, a "temple of atonement" which would lead the people back to the path of virtue.

The orthodox Gaudí, who liked to think he was more Catholic than the pope, seemed the right man for this task. The society gave him carte blanche, and Gaudí drew up plans, letting his imagination run loose and his boldness show clearly. This building was going to be different from anything that had been built before. Disregarding every convention, he blended Eastern and Western decorative elements, and distorted and molded the

facades—ultimately creating a fantastic, bizarre structure infinitely rich in pictorial ornamentation: butterflies and dragonflies, castles and monsters, snails and turtles.

The walls and towers of the Sagrada Familia are a mirror of the world, an expression of mystical visions. Gaudí was not able to see the construction through to completion, but nevertheless, his incomplete work received lavish praise: "This man could do anything he wanted with stone," said the French architect Le Corbusier. Others call the structure (on which work still continues today) "ecstatic architecture" and "the last Gothic cathedral." In Barcelona, people could not quite warm to

Antoni Gaudí

the "grotesquely overloaded heap of stones." Salvador Dalí even spread the rumor that, during the civil war in 1936, the rabble had snatched Gaudí's corpse from its coffin buried in the crypt, tied a rope around his neck, and dragged him down the street—because as the architect of the Sagrada Familia he had become the henchman of anti-democratic reactionaries.

"In the east blossoms a temple—a mystical specimen—like an enormous flower"

A structure infinitely rich in pictorial ornamentation; the main portal

A Page from History
The Berlin Reichstag

Germany; 1884–1894
Architect: Paul Wallot (1841–1912);
rebuilt 1995–1999 by Norman Foster

"Beauty in the city on a rainy day,
Partly on the Havel and partly on the
Spree,
Gleaming domes of synagogues, church
towers and dance *palais,*
And gilding the embankment (who
knows if you've been told)
Stands proud the Reichstag building—
all that glitters is not gold."

Adapted from Kurt Tucholsky, *Home, Sweet Home,* 1914

The Reichstag, as it was, photographed from the air before
World War I

The Reichstag stands on a formerly sandy stretch of land in the curve of the River Spree. Frederick the Great, the "Soldier King," let his troops use the land for military exercises. It was also the starting point chosen by hot-air balloon pioneer Montgolfier for his first flight on September 27, 1799. By the time the Kroll establishment opened the doors of its pleasure palace to the west of the site in the middle of the nineteenth century, the place had lost all claim to being taken seriously. But then the land was claimed for the Reichstag.

Since the founding of the German Reich in 1871, which gave Berlin the status of an imperial city, the parliament had been temporarily housed in a wing of the royal porcelain factory (KPM or *Königliche Porzellan Manufaktur*). The threat of throwing all its china into the street had induced the company to cede space to the legislators. The building on Leipziger Straße was only to serve until permanent quarters could be found.

What Berlin really wanted was a representative home for its parliament. After a competition for the new building failed to produce a suitable plan, a second was launched. The winner was the Frankfurt-based architect Paul Willot. A sum of thirty million gold marks, financed by French war indemnification payments, was set aside for the construction of a building based on an Italian Renaissance palace. It was no easy task for Willot, who had to contend with the envy of his colleagues and the constant meddling of the Emperor. He modified his plans several times but still failed to win unanimous approval when the building was finally completed.

Those who praised it called it "a mirror image of the powerful popular movement which gave birth to the German Reich." But detractors weren't lacking. Emperor Wilhelm II condemned the building, calling it the "Reich Monkey House." Another critic, referring to the heroic sculpture that decorated the facade, called it a "first-class hearse."

The ambivalence of its critics foreshadowed its history, just as the fate of the Reichstag mirrored that of the German nation. On November 9, 1918, Philipp Scheidemann, a Social Democrat, stood at a window of the Reichstag reading room and declared Germany a republic. Fifteen years later President Hindenburg declared marshal law following the Reichstag fire, which neither historians nor criminologists have ever fully explained. With his decree Hindenburg withdrew the rights guaranteed by the Weimar constitution and gave Hitler the green light to persecute his political opponents.

The Reichstag was destroyed by aerial bombing in the last weeks of World War II. Two red army soldiers raised a Soviet flag on what was left of it on April 30, 1945, giving poignant testimony to the ruin of German self-confidence. Despite its reconstruction in the sixties, the Reichstag remained unused—a situation that aptly symbolized the state of a divided Germany. Following the reunification of Germany, the first joint session of the democratically elected German parliament took place at the Reichstag on January 17, 1991. The historic moment evokes the fervent wish of former Berlin Mayor Heinrich Alertz: "We were terribly good at being the capital of war," he said. "We could now become the capital of peace. Utopia? How could we exist in this city without

Wilhelm I laying the cornerstone for the Reichstag
on June 9, 1884

utopias?" The Reichstag could embody this wish.

Following its wrapping by the artist duo Christo and Jeanne-Claude, the Reichstag was reconstructed according to the design of the British architect Norman Foster. But Berlin's critics again raised their voice, labeling Foster's dome a "decapitated dud." But not even the harshest criticism can diminish the hope for a peaceful future.

The Reichstag, as it is today after revamping by
Lord Norman Foster: The symbol of a transparent
democracy, dreaming of a united Europe

Shepherd to the Clouds
The Eiffel Tower in Paris

France; 1887–1889
Architect: Gustave Eiffel

"We, writers, sculptors, architects and painters, passionate lovers of the (until now) unspoiled beauty of Paris, in the name of the preservation of good taste, and in the name of the culture and the history of France which is being threatened, rise up in protest against the construction of the useless and monstrous Eiffel Tower.
Will the city of Paris continue to participate in ventures with the baroque and commercial ideas of an engineer in order to betray its own honor beyond all hope of redemption?"

Protest of an artist, *Le Temps*, February 14, 1887

It was bitterly cold on January 28, 1887 when the foundation stone for the Eiffel Tower was laid. But the controversy over the sense or nonsense of the project reached fever pitch, and the tempers in Paris were fraying. The planned iron construction was criticized as "monstrous," dubbed the "giraffe cage," "ugly skeleton" and "tragic floor lamp" which presided over the loss of good taste like "a lighthouse overlooking the sinking of a ship." Many saw the clever construction as a "humiliation to Notre Dame," a "tragic break from the rules of classicism" and "an unprecedented crime against the art of architecture."

To such criticism Gustave Eiffel, the creator of the structure destined to become the true symbol of Paris, responded, "I believe that the tower will possess its own kind of beauty. Does not the balance of its power correspond to the laws of harmony? And is not the functionality of the design the primary principle of architecture?" It was not, in fact, Eiffel's idea to construct a gigantic steel scaffold on the Field of Mars in Paris in the first place. It came from the French government.

In 1886 the Ministry of Trade and Industry had launched a competition for "the construction of a new world wonder," which would be "a tower made of iron, 900-feet high and 375-feet broad." They wanted a spectacular attraction that would impressively symbolize technical progress and the industrial development of the century at the World Fair which would take place in Paris on the 100th anniversary of the French Revolution. The winning design chosen from the seven hundred that were submitted was that of the engineer and bridge builder Gustave Eiffel. But government officials did not trust his calculations, and when a mathematics professor prophesied that the tower would collapse as soon as it

reached a height of 660 feet, the project was jeopardized. Eiffel was only allowed to build the tower after he promised to put up his own fortune as a guarantee in the event of its collapse.

The predicted catastrophe did not occur. It took three hundred workers twenty-six months to build the 985-foot-high tower. It is made of 15,000 steel parts and contains exactly 1,050,846 rivets. In heavy storms it swings about four inches, and it is still standing more than one hundred years after it was built, although it was only meant to last for twenty years.

When the Eiffel Tower was officially opened on March 31, 1889, the initial criticism turned to celebration. It was the tallest building in the world at that time. Full of pride, Eiffel declared: "France is the only country in the world whose flag waves from a 985-foot-high pole." Tens of thousands applauded his words. Visitors to the World Fair were appropriately impressed by Eiffel's masterpiece of technology and the tower brought him universal respect and fame.

The iron giant, from which the first transatlantic wireless message was sent in 1916, advanced to the position of the "Grande Dame of the Nation" and became the focus of apparently never-ending popular festivities. Zeppelins and double-deckers circled its tip, trapeze artists and entertainers climbed its scaffolding, and those unafraid of heights leapt from its platforms with parachutes and unfurled umbrellas. Pranksters even forced horses and elephants into its elevators. Only the novelist Guy de Maupassant remained unimpressed by the monster. Every day he dined in the expensive and excellent restaurant on the first level of the Eiffel Tower because "it is the only place in Paris where you can't see the damned thing."

It took 300 workers 26 months
to complete the tower

The Eiffel Tower as a symbol of French technology and industry: entrance to the World Exhibition in 1889

One of the new wonders of the world, a technical and artistic triumph

A Cathedral of Commerce
Moscow and its GUM Department Store

Russia; 1888–1894
Architect: Alexander Nikaranorowitsch Pomeranzen

"There is no way around it—the GUM is overwhelming. The department store has corridors, galleries, bridges, cellars, halls and small temples that make it comparable to the fantastic architecture of Piranesi."

Wolfgang Koeppen, *To Russia and Elsewhere*, 1973

Moscow's great historian Ivan Sabelin noted that cities of historical importance do not develop anywhere at random. Their existence is independent of divine providence or the whims of rulers. The significant factor is trade, and most great cities grew up along ancient trade routes and rivers used for the transportation of goods. Moscow, which has been a center of trade throughout its history, is no exception. Located at the juncture of waterways connecting the Baltic and the Black Seas, the city has dominated movements between East and West throughout its history. Russian rulers were quick to take advantage of its strategic position.

The first historical reference to Moscow comes from a letter written by Prince George in 1147. "Come to me my brother, to Moscow and remain with me," he wrote. George, known as "the Long Fingered," for his insatiable appetite for acquiring territory is credited with the founding of Moscow. In reality it was probably already a lively market town where commerce blossomed, and George merely took advantage of the favorable circumstances to make Moscow the base of his princely power.

Such cities need an occasional influx of wealth to spur their growth. Prince Ivan, appropriately dubbed "the Sack of Gold," provided just that for Moscow. Charged with collecting tribute for the Tartar invaders, Ivan taxed his people and added another 10% for himself. Under his rule Moscow became the most important city in eastern Europe. The city grew in splendor and attracted merchants from all over the world. It became the trade center for silk from China, glass from Venice, jewels from Byzantium, and wood carvings from Scandinavia.

A seventeenth-century traveler described the market in his day: "It has a religious section, known as the 'god market' where pictures of

the saints are bought and sold…. It is full of merchants—men and women, slaves and ne're-do-wells—throughout the day." In the nineteenth century, the GUM department store replaced the colorful market that had stood to the east of present-day Red Square, along a street named Trader's Row for its stalls and shops.

The gigantic structure with its glass roof and facade, inspired by Russian fairy tales, has borrowed from the oriental charm of the old market. Its area of some seventy thousand square feet has five parallel passages connected by bridges and walkways. It resembles an Arabian bazaar and contains 150 shops. GUM is more a shopping center than a department store in the strictest sense of the word. The three-story consumer paradise has been described as a "labyrinthine caravansary" and a "fantastic crystal palace." Its transparent roof filters light, plunging the interior into "jungle-like shade."

At the height of the Communist era, spending money at GUM was sometimes as difficult and time-consuming as earning it. "There are processions, queues without end or apparent beginning, inching along and stretching through the halls, foyers and staircases. This is clearly a socialistic society. Most of the shoppers read while they line-up for goods. But I was never able to determine what they were queuing up to buy," wrote Wolfgang Koeppen. Others have described GUM as a "shopping cathedral."

"This department store with its glass domes, gurgling fountains and its cast-iron staircases," wrote novelist Geno Hartlaub, "resembles a multiple-naved basilica." The shops have crystal chandeliers, mirrored walls and stuccoed ceilings—a place where every customer could feel like a king.

View from the main entrance of the GUM department store of Red Square and the Kremlin walls

"A labyrinthine caravansary" and a
"fantastic crystal palace" at the same time

Allah in Africa
The Djenné Mosque

Mali; 1907–1909

"Those who don't get there in the early hours of the morning, find no space to pray—the crowd becomes enormous when the black worshippers don their white clothing on Fridays and set out to honor their great creator god."

From a report written by El Omari, date unknown

The kings of Mali were famous for their legendary wealth

Ramadan was always celebrated with unbelievable splendor in Mali. But that says as little about the faith of the people as a chronicler's tale of children being chained to make them learn the Koran. In their day to day life, the citizens of Mali did not take the religious rules of Islam all that seriously. It was even possible, given the local cuisine's reliance on a certain kind of meat deemed "unclean," to occasionally overlook the inconvenient laws forbidding it. The commandment to refrain from marrying more than four wives was also frequently circumvented. But what upset fervent Muslims most was the fact that the Koran had not completely succeeded in suppressing Mali's ancient form of spirit worship. Even at the royal court, where the kings of Mali had converted to Islam as early as the thirteenth century, mysterious magicians wearing bird masks practiced their animistic rites. The palace also kept two rams whose duty it was to protect the ruler, his family and his advisors from the "evil eye."

Despite such lapses, Djenné, a city in the fertile alluvial plane of the Niger, became a center of Islamic learning in the Middle Ages. The route of the great caravans led from the desert in the north to the jungles in the south. Caravans from Morocco and Algeria crossed the Sahara and made their way through Mali transporting gold, ivory, rubber, slaves, and ostrich feathers. They also brought the religion of Mohammed and were responsible for the cultural exchange that raised Djenné to the most important city in ancient Mali after Timbuktu.

In the Middle Ages Mali was the largest kingdom in Africa, stretching from the shores of the Atlantic to the border of modern Nigeria and from the edge of the jungle in the south to the oasis of central Sahara in the north. The trade brought fabled riches to Djenné. Schools were founded and learned scholars from other countries were invited to teach. The intellectual discourse in the city made Djenné famous throughout the Islamic world. Crowds of educated Muslims traveled to the city—in the words of an ancient scripture—"in order to broaden their perspectives." The spiritual center of Djenné was its Great Mosque.

The original mosque, dating to the fourteenth century, was destroyed by radical Muslims who were disturbed that the mud structure did not conform to the traditional Islamic architectural ideas. The old Mosque was organic in form, following the local tradition of utilizing mud and clay—the only building materials available in plentiful supply. To the radical Muslims it represented the animist beliefs of the population and was razed in the 1830s. Seventy years later the

verdict was reversed and a new mosque resembling the style of the old was built. With its facade some 450-feet wide and its three towers, each more than thirty-feet high, the new mosque is now the largest mud building in the world. The beams, made of palm wood, stick out of the walls like spikes and help stabilize the building in its continuous battle against the elements.

During the rainy season, the torrential downpours erode the walls, making renovation during the dry season a dire necessity. The Mosque of Djenné has another uniquely African feature—

Every year the clay on the external walls has to be patched

instead of the traditional half-moon symbol of Islam, the towers are crowned with ostrich eggs. In the animistic religion that still persists, they represent fertility and guard against evil spirits.

The Djenné Mosque, religious center of the former
Kingdom of Mali

When the Body Turns All Red
The Gellert Spa in Budapest

Budapest, Hungary; 1914–1918
Architects: A. Sebestyèn, A. Hegedüs and I. Stark

"When someone is struck by the French disease, there is no better cure than the water from Gellert Hill. One should stay in the bath until the body turns all red. Afterwards one should wrap towels around himself to keep warm."

From an account written by the seventeenth-century globetrotter Evilya Tschelebi

Bishop Gellert of Csanád, the first Christian missionary in Hungary, died a violent death at the hands of unscrupulous murderers who showed no mercy. They stuffed him into a barrel, pounded countless nails into its sides and dropped him from the top of a hill near Buda into the blue waters of the Danube. His martyrdom was tragic for two reasons. First, because the Bishop was a virtuous man whom King Stephan, the first Christian king of Hungary, had brought to his kingdom on the Danube to be his personal advisor and to convert heathens. The second reason is associated with the place where Gellert died. It is an historical irony that the foot of the hill is the source of a spring, used since Roman times as spa, renowned for its life-restoring powers.

The ancient spa at Gellert Hill, named in honor of its martyr, taps ten of the one-hundred-and-fifty hot mineral springs that bubble out of the ground. The 45° water contains calcium, magnesium and hydrogen-carbonate. It is slightly chloride and sulfurous, and its healing power is especially effective in cases of rheumatic or arthritic diseases. Little wonder that limping Roman legionnaires, on their way to a conquest in the eastern reaches of the empire, found it their fountain of youth and stayed behind to found the provincial capital Aquincum, better known by its modern name, Budapest.

Day after day, seventy million liters of hot water flowed into the ancient baths, giving rise to an unprecedented blossoming of antique bath culture. Within a few years more than twenty thermal baths had been built in the new capital. In the Middle Ages, the roman baths fell into disuse and the hot springs of Gellert Hill served only the revelers of Walpurgis night, better known as the Witches' Sabbath. In the thirteenth century a hospital was built on the site where the Gellert spa stands today. During the Ottoman occupation the spa, renamed *Aatschik Llidsche*, again became known for its healing powers and the traveler Evliya Tschelebi, cited above, made it more famous through his writings.

After the Turkish invaders were driven out of Hungary, mud baths came back into vogue. The Gellert baths, with their rich tradition, reached their zenith at the beginning of the twentieth century. While World War I raged in the rest of Europe, Hungarians built an Art Nouveau palace on the site where Bishop Gellert's barrel had landed and rolled over one last time before sinking into the river.

The main facade of the majestic building presides over the Buda side of the Danube. Behind the curving complex with its low domes, an open air recreational area with its central pool, fountains and statues evokes court gardens of a bygone era. Lavish display also reigns within, where a vaulted ceiling, reminiscent of the Crystal Palace in London, spans the swimming pool. Rows of columns support wrought-iron balconies. Steam baths, saunas and massage rooms are artfully decorated with daring oriental-patterned tiles and precious mosaics. Its worldly splendor has made the Gellert spa Hungary's most important architectural achievement. The building also contains a hotel, a clinic for the treatment of rheumatic disorders and other therapeutic facilities. Even when feeling unwell, a visit to the Gellert spa can help a speedy recovery.

The splendor of the Orient in the baths on the Danube

To be pampered like a king:
the magnificent baths in Budapest

The Center for Anthroposophy: Rudolf Steiner's Goetheanum

Dornach, Switzerland; 1924–1928
Architect: Rudolf Steiner

"Concrete forms are going to have to be completely different, and certain things will need to be done, on the one hand, to master the brittle material of concrete so that the eye of the human soul can perceive it artistically. On the other, it will be necessary to create certain apparently decorative elements in an artistic, painterly, sculptural fashion, yet evolving from the concrete material itself. Thus concrete will finally be made to reveal artistic qualities. I would like to ask you to consider this seminal idea as the one from which the Goetheanum will actually develop."

Taken from Rudolf Steiner's lecture to members of the Anthroposophical Society on December 31, 1923

On New Year's Day in 1923 Rudolf Steiner, the founder of anthroposophy, was faced with the ruins of his life's work: during the previous night, unidentified arsonists had set fire to the Goetheanum on the Dornach hill near Basle. The impressive wooden building with its two domes, the "primal house" according to Steiner's teachings, representing the "cave of the mother's body" to shelter anyone "seeking the spiritual," no longer existed. Steiner had been so proud of the building he had designed.

The esoteric, who was not only occupied with the transmigration of souls and spiritual cosmology, but who also inquired into the occult roots of Christianity and the European intellectual tradition, had founded a center for his teachings by building the Goetheanum. He intended it as "a place where people meet to acquire transcendent knowledge." For Steiner understood anthroposophy as the ability of the individual, whose perception has been trained, to gradually understand the essence of the spiritual in mankind and the world. In his opinion this was "a basic requirement for human freedom, which can be applied in various ways."

Deeply convinced of the importance of a holistic view of man and all human activity, Steiner applied his teachings to various domains of practical life: he not only founded Waldorf pedagogy and organic farming, but also gave decisive impulses to medical professionals and theologians. In addition, he worked as an architect, because the "anthroposophically oriented humanities are not merely theoretical but active in all areas, and are capable of developing an architectural style of their own." In this area, however, he oriented himself on Goethe. To

Steiner, who had worked on the Weimar edition of Goethe's works from 1883 to 1897, and was particularly fascinated by Goethe's writings on natural science, architecture was not the result of rational thought but the projection of a contemplative awareness. He was thus applying Goethe's concept of the metamorphosis of plants: "nature's inner creation of form" was what he had tried to incorporate in the first Goetheanum burnt down in 1922.

In the second Goetheanum, for which he was again in charge of the planning, Steiner stayed with Goethe's concept even though this time the building material was reinforced concrete. He was aware of the problems: "Everything that has been achieved in concrete construction to date is not really a basis for what is to develop here," he said. Using a plasticine model, he searched for a valid form, whereby it was important that the building be as functional as possible. It had to contain studios, lecture halls, and, of course, a large auditorium for plays and concerts. The result was a building that Steiner did not live to see completed. In terms of artistic quality, the Goetheanum is among the most important buildings ever made of reinforced concrete. It has been called "one of the grandest architectural and sculptural inventions of the twentieth century." As the international center of the Anthroposophical Society today, it is also the home of the Freie Hochschule für Geisteswissenschaften (Free University of Humanities and Liberal Arts) founded in 1924.

Rudolf Steiner with a model of the first Goetheanum

"Every door offers something friendly and welcoming,"
the second Goetheanum

The boiler house

Engulfed in flames: the first building
burned down on New Year's Eve, 1922/23

Cubes and Flat Roofs
The Quintessence of Functionalism: the Bauhaus in Dessau

Dessau, Germany; 1925–1926
Architects: Walter Gropius and Adolf Meyer

"Separated from the railroad tracks by a crowded group of small, gabled houses in this provincial town are two gigantic, brilliant-white blocks rising above their green surroundings: one upright, the other placed transversely to it. A few red balcony doors and large glass windows break up the surface, otherwise the whole thing is bare and smooth, and can by no means be categorized as a house. Instead, it looks as if someone wanted to demonstrate—using a clear exhibition model—what 32,000 square yards of building space look like."

Taken from Rudolf Arnheim, "Das Bauhaus in Dessau," in *Die Weltbühne*, 1927

Weimar was the birthplace of the Bauhaus. For it was there that the architect Walter Gropius formulated his credo in 1919: "We will only arrive at one goal if art and craftsmanship permeate each other once again." Craftsmanship and industry, according to Gropius, need the "vital infusion of artistic creative power;" on the other hand, an artist is dependent upon the principles of craftsmanship if he wishes to have complete control over his materials.

It was this conviction that inspired Walter Gropius to found a state art school, the "Bauhaus." The courses of study on offer included bookbinding, stage design, printing, painting on glass, wood and stone sculpture, metalworking, carpentry, pottery, mural-painting and weaving, and at a later stage also incorporated architecture and photography.

The unconventional teaching methods attracted attention throughout Europe. Each subject was taught by two teachers working together. Alongside a "master of form," who included the painters Lyonel Feininger, Paul Klee, Oskar Schlemmer, and Wassily Kandinsky—a "master craftsman" was on hand in every studio. The students, who were called "apprentices," had to take general and master-grade examinations recognized by the craftsman's guild. Above all, the feeling for form stressed by all teachers at the Bauhaus was considered revolutionary. The beauty of an object was not a decisive criterion, but rather its application: "Modern man needs housing to suit himself and his time, which is equipped with all of the up-to-date things for everyday life." These things, for example chairs, should first and foremost "fulfill their functions practically," be durable, and inexpensive. This philosophy inevitably led to the creation of unusual designs which broke with tradition. These ideas gained

wide acceptance; the Bauhaus had a decisive influence not only on the design of living environments in the twentieth century, but also on architecture and industrial design. Nevertheless there was some resistance on a national level. In December 1919 Walter Gropius wrote: "The stupid narrow-mindedness of the Weimar government has thrown down the gauntlet to us and is trying to excite opposition."

The fear that the school's budget could be torn apart by the state parliament was to become a reality in 1924. The Thuringian government withdrew all its funding. The Bauhaus then relocated to Dessau, a town governed by Social Democrats who were willing to support Bauhaus ideas. Within a very short period, a new school had been built in a field on the edge of the town—an epoch-making structure which included teaching and workshop wings, a theater, a cafeteria, a gymnasium, and twenty-eight studio apartments with roof gardens for students. The glass facade which encloses the

Functional and practical: the Bauhaus staircase in Dessau

152

Unity of art and technology, the Bauhaus in Dessau

workshop wing like a curtain was considered spectacular and a similar sensation was caused by the two-story bridge-like structure built over a road housing the school's administrative offices and Walter Gropius' private architecture studio.

The move brought some changes: the twofold study plan was abandoned, and the apprentices were simply called "students." But in one area everything stayed the same as before: the free spirit and communist leanings of those at the Bauhaus soon proved to be a thorn in the side of increasingly powerful right-wing partisans in Dessau. In 1932 the town government decided to dissolve the Bauhaus.

The final relocation to Berlin and the attempts by the last director of the school, Ludwig Mies van der Rohe, to carry on privately with the Bauhaus were without success. In 1933, after renewed attacks and faced by a hopeless political situation, the "Bauhäusler," gave up the fight once and for all.

The Bauhaus, founded by Gropius, where art and craftsmanship were interdependent

King Kong's Jungle Gym
The Empire State Building in New York

New York City, USA; 1929–1931
Architects: Shreve, William Lamb & Harmon

"The Empire State Building is the tallest building in the city and claims to be the eighth wonder of the world. All of humanity crowds into the elevators for a ride up to heaven. Signposts flash by like vast storm fronts. Confusing writing. Security guards guide the traffic. It's as busy as a large train station."

Wolfgang Koeppen, *New York*, 1961

King Kong on the Empire State Building

The Waldorf Astoria, arguably the most exclusive and most expensive hotel in New York, once stood between Fifth Avenue and 34th Street. But in 1929 the bulldozers closed in. The stylish, up-market hostelry moved to Park Avenue, and the old, decaying walls were torn down to make way for another building which would also become a legend.

Within only twelve months and forty-five days, the Empire State Building climbed into the sky and held the record as the world's tallest building for almost half a century. 1,150 feet is the distance between street-level and the ceiling of the highest of the 103 floors. And if you count the flagpole at the top—where, according to someone's bold idea, zeppelins would be able to land (this proved to be impossible due to strong gusts of wind)—it would even come to 1,345 feet. One of the men who commissioned the project confronted the chief architect at the start of the planning phase. As the story goes, he held up a pencil like a miniature skyscraper and asked, "Bill, how high can you build something like this without it falling over?" The architect's sixteenth attempt at a suitable design finally brought the solution.

Since then, other, even higher skyscrapers have been built, and the Empire State Building has had to surrender its place in the Guinness Book of World Records. But it can never be robbed of its significance as a symbol of an unshakable belief in the future. The project's investors, among others the automotive giant General Motors, pushed ahead with their plan even when the New York Stock Exchange crash seemed imminent—the cornerstone of the Empire State Building being laid just three weeks before Black Friday. Despite the economic crisis, construction work progressed at an enormous speed. 3,400 workers, fourteen of whom would be killed in accidents, managed to add on a new story every day, thus setting a new world record which would not be broken for years. The amount of materials used also

caused a sensation: 60,000 tons of steel were riveted and 10 million bricks cemented together, 6,500 windows installed and 2,500 miles of telephone cable laid. When the skyscraper was inaugurated in 1931 and the building expenses amounted to only forty-one million dollars instead of the estimated fifty million, it seemed as if the impossible had been achieved.

The Empire State Building could be seen as a symbol of the American renaissance. Its sleek elegance also brought rave reviews: "I could lie down on the sidewalk and stare at it forever," said the French architect Le Corbusier on his first visit to the Empire State Building. However, a slightly bitter aftertaste remained. Because of the economic depression, the majority of the office space remained unused for many years, which is why some mockingly spoke of the "Empty State Building." The young American film industry helped to distract attention from this calamity. To the horror of fearful young ladies, King Kong clung to the facade of the Empire State Building, making the skyscraper famous at last. When an American Air Force bomber crashed into the 79th floor in heavy fog on July 28, 1945, the building passed its first ordeal by fire. Although the building, in which 16,000 people work today, gave a couple of feet as a result of the impact, it still remained standing. The catastrophe happened on a Saturday morning and as a result the number of victims was not as high as it may otherwise have been. However, twelve people died in the flames and wreckage—far fewer than the number of people who would commit suicide every year by jumping off one of the two outdoor viewing platforms. In order to overcome the shadow of death, the managers added lights to the building. The thirty top floors are lit up from nightfall until midnight with different colors, depending on the occasion. And so, on national holidays, the Empire State Building is immersed in the red, white, and blue of the American flag.

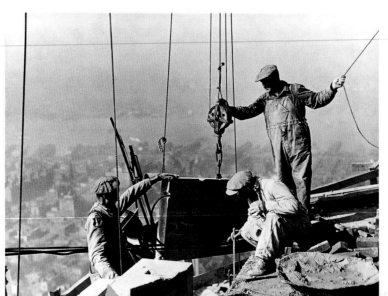

Death defying— construction workers near the top of the skyscraper

"I could lie down on the sidewalk and stare at it forever" (Le Corbusier on the Empire State Building)

San Francisco and its Landmark
The Golden Gate Bridge

San Francisco, USA; 1933–1937
Architect: Joseph B. Strauss

"All day long a thick bank of fog hung over the bay, while from time to time showers of rain fell out at sea. But at the end of the day the unexpected happened: the sun set in the west and bathed the bay and the shores in rosy evening light. And over the channel the bridge was a black silhouette against the sun."

John Haase, San Francisco, 1983

A technical masterpiece, the bridge's elasticity can absorb a thirty-foot sway

"I love San Francisco," the American writer William Saroyan professed. Because San Francisco is a town of writers, every city block is a short story, every hill a novel, and every house a poem. But he also loves the town because it is on a peninsula, a place "surrounded by wonderfully wide expanses of water, soaked in a cooling mist which lets the symphony of the foghorns echo in everyone's memory."

Without a doubt, its location, on a promontory between the Pacific Ocean and the San Francisco Bay, gives the city its special charm. Its harbor is one of the most important in the American west. And the bay is still full of life: tugboats, tankers, cruise ships, and sailboats plow through the blue waters which surround San Francisco, "the Baghdad on the bay," on three sides.

It's not surprising that a bridge is the landmark of this city on the water. The Golden Gate Bridge spans the only gap in the barrier of the coastal mountains, the only channel leading from the Pacific Ocean to the San Francisco Bay— the "Golden Gate." For almost three hundred years, the narrow strait behind impenetrable banks of fog played hide-and-seek with the Spanish conquistadores. Once discovered, it quickly became a doorway for the onrush of gold diggers—the gate to the treasures of California.

The fortified settlement, which the Spanish established in 1776 in the shadow of a mission of Franciscan monks south of the Golden Gate, grew rapidly following the discovery of gold. San Francisco became the metropolis of the American west. The city grew beyond its borders—extending towards the north, in the direction of the Golden Gate. Finally it reached the water, and in the nineteenth century ferries used to carry passengers over to Marin County on the other side of the Golden Gate. Due to

the continually increasing shuttle traffic, it was decided that a bridge should be built.

Building started in 1933—and provided work for thousands of unemployed who had lost their jobs during the Great Depression. It was clear that this would be a delicate undertaking. Because of the enormous amounts of water which squeeze through the Golden Gate with the turning tides, swirling into treacherous whirlpools, for a long time it was believed that building a bridge at that point would be an impossible task. In order to solve this problem, retaining walls had to be constructed on the ocean floor before the foundations of the two 680-foot-high piers which hold up the bridge could be laid. Four years later, when the 1.5-mile-long Golden Gate Bridge was inaugurated, a technical masterpiece made of 20,000 tons of steel and over 60,000 miles of cable, it was the largest suspension bridge in the world. Some 3,800 feet separate its two piers—a distance far greater than that of any other construction at the time. The six-lane highway runs more than 200 feet above the water's surface. Despite the fact that its height may vary according to the temperature and the volume of traffic, the bridge is not high enough for some ships to fit under it. The aircraft carrier "Enterprise" had to wait for low tide before it could try passing under the bridge.

The strong winds which sometimes whistle through the Golden Gate cause fewer difficulties than were expected; the design of the structure enables the bridge to sway some thirty feet without any danger. It has thus been able to withstand hurricanes, tidal waves, and earthquakes. The Golden Gate Bridge has never had to be closed except after road accidents, or on days such as its fiftieth anniversary when—like on the day of its inauguration—it was turned into a pedestrian bridge for twenty-four hours.

In 1935 construction started during the Great Depression and provided work for thousands

At its inauguration in 1937 the Golden Gate Bridge in San Francisco was the largest suspension bridge in the world

The House Built over the Waterfall
Frank Lloyd Wright and Fallingwater

Bear Run, Pennsylvania, USA; 1936–1937
Architect: Frank Lloyd Wright

"The architectural beauty of the house remains as fresh as the untouched nature that surrounds it. As a residence Fallingwater had served us well—although it is more than that. It is a work of art beyond common rules of elegance. Here is an ancient human dream made reality. Architecture and landscape joined into one—just as any of us would like to be joined to nature. It is a miracle that one dare not possess alone."

Edgar Kaufmann, Jr., *Fallingwater*, 1994

The reporter did not sink down on his knees but showed the greatest reverence. At an interview with Frank Lloyd Wright, he said he knew that before him stood the most famous architect of his time. The remark elicited an explosion from Wright who corrected the reporter, pointing out that he was the most famous architect of *all* time. Editors did well to remember this remark. Frank Lloyd Wright's formidable self-confidence was legendary.

Even before he was born in 1867 in Wisconsin, his mother had determined he would become an architect when he grew up. In order to inspire him, she decorated his room with engravings of English cathedrals. The seed bore fruit. Refusing to be discouraged by private tragedy (which finally made him the subject of an opera) Frank Lloyd Wright continued on his course despite many disappointments.

His use of lavish ornament in the 1920s led his critics to accuse him of having overslept the arrival of the new spirit of the times. The more poisonous of them dubbed him, "the most important American architect of the nineteenth century."

He refused to admit defeat and persevered, even though success was slow in coming. He finally managed to synchronize his personal sense of aesthetics with the spirit of the age. By the time he had built Fallingwater he was in his seventies and acclaimed as the "Grand Old Man" of American architecture. It was a role he played with passion and arrogance.

Fallingwater, the weekend residence of the Kaufmann family, was built directly over a waterfall on the Bear Run stream in the woods of western Pennsylvania. It was indeed a stroke

of genius. Frank Lloyd Wright convinced the Kaufmanns to build their house over the falls rather than with a view of them, as they had requested. "I want you to live with the waterfall, not merely to watch it," wrote Wright to Edgar Kaufmann.

At first Kaufmann hesitated, causing Wright to feel insulted and exclaim, "If you don't trust me—then to the hell with the whole thing!" Kaufmann gave in and Wright let his fantasy have free reign.

He designed the house with three levels that followed the natural projections in the rock. The stones upon which the family had lounged in the sun now formed the floor of the living room. The rocks that had flanked the waterfall now framed the fireplace. A long flight of stairs connected the various levels and brought the living room directly to the stream. The house has been received by critics in very different ways. Comments range from criticism, claiming it is "a self-glorifying structure that wants to dominate nature without consideration for it." Others proclaim it to be a "precedent-breaking experiment in organic architecture." Although opinions vary, Fallingwater remains the most famous residence of modern architecture.

Many architects who make their pilgrimage to Fallingwater have declared it a milestone in the history of architecture. But it suffers the same fate that threatens he leaning tower of Pisa. The house is leaning because Wright supposedly ordered it built with reinforced concrete that contained too little steel. Now the question being posed is whether Fallingwater may indeed one day fall into the water.

View of the living room

Living with the waterfall

The steps lead down directly
to the river

159

I Breathed Life into Concrete
The Pilgrimage Church Notre Dame du Haut near Ronchamp

Ronchamp, France; design after 1950, construction 1953–1955
Architect: Le Corbusier (Charles Édouard Jeanneret-Gris)

"Your Excellency. In building this chapel I sought to create a place of silence, of prayer, of peace and inner joy. This attempt found your blessing. And we adhered to our mathematical formulas which are the creator of infinite space. I hand over to you a church of concrete. It was built, perhaps with daring, certainly with courage. I hope that you and all who climb this hill will respond positively to what we have accomplished."

Taken from Le Corbusier's letter to the bishop, June 25, 1955

Plan dated 1951

Perhaps the ancient Druids had offered sacrifices to Celtic gods at this place. It is quite likely because for centuries a Christian church has crowned the hill top near Ronchamp, between Belfort and Dijon, and such churches were usually built on the foundations of earlier pagan temples. The first record of pilgrims on their way to the church of Notre Dame du Haut dates from 1271. And the stream of worshippers continues to this day.

The original church, rebuilt and expanded many times, was destroyed in 1913 during a World War I bombing raid. It was finally rebuilt in 1936 but the scaffolding had barely come down when World War II broke out. The strategic hill of Ronchamp was again hotly contested, and the new church was totally destroyed by artillery fire.

Plans for the rebuilding of the church began at the end of the 1940s. The commission went to Charles Édouard Jeanneret-Gris, better known as Le Corbusier, the renowned revolutionary architect whose Paris office was the cradle of modern architecture. Le Corbusier visited Ronchamp, sketched the ruins and set to work. "Ronchamp serves no other function but the celebration of the mass, one of the oldest institutions of mankind. A powerful personality was also present at the planning—namely the landscape, stretching to the four points of the compass. And it was the landscape that dictated the design."

Reinforced concrete, which requires fewer weight-bearing interior walls or supports made the free form plan of the building possible. Le Corbusier designed a church which was "directed like a word to an audience." The neighboring hills are mirrored in the dynamic lines of the facade. The soaring roof lines echo nature. The architect was also inspired by a seashell he found on a beach in Long Island.

The east wall, which curves inward, is covered by an overhanging roof providing space for an outdoor altar and a place flooded by the morning light where mass can be held under the open sky. The interior is plunged into a mystical shadow. But light also plays an important role, being the only form of decoration. The light enters through narrow crenels and endows the concrete with new life, making it sparkle like a diamond. The colored glass panes reflect light onto the walls, imparting shimmering designs like the sparkle of Christmas decorations. The light removes every vestige of heaviness from the construction. The roof, which is separated from the walls by a thin band of light appears to float above the structure. The two-ton portal

appears light and transparent because of the two slits of light on either side of it.

The center of attention is the old statue of the Virgin, rescued from the original church, which pilgrims have honored since the eighteenth century. Le Corbusier placed the statue in a window so that its silhouette rises up against the blue sky and indicates the way to heaven.

The design was a stroke of genius that has greatly influenced contemporary church architecture. Many critics were overwhelmed, praising Le Corbusier by saying: "Had he built nothing but the chapel of Ronchamp, he would still remain one of the greatest creators of beauty in our century."

The pilgrimage church Notre Dame du Haut—its seashell-inspired design and its soaring lines have been termed a stroke of genius

The main entrance to the church

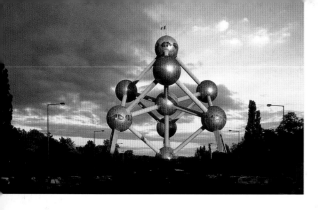

The Symbol of World Exposition
The Atomium

Brussels, Belgium; 1954–1958
Architect: André Waterkeyn

"Of course the millions who visit 'Brussels 1958' will experience this World Exhibition in a million different ways. What can a show conceived for the masses mean for the individual? Certainly if he finds something that is successful, he will feel pride in the contribution with which his country has enriched this epoch, but also gratitude for those things that he must thank others for—things which he only now has the opportunity to get to know."

Based on Theodor Heuss, *Ein Wort zur Fragestellung*, 1958

The Atomium has been described as "the most astounding structure on earth." It is certainly unusual—in fact it is an imagined cube standing on one of its corners so that its diagonals are in a vertical position. The whole thing represents an iron crystal lattice magnified 165 billion times.

The nine spheres, each of which has a diameter of nearly sixty feet, represent the nine atoms of the structure—and the nine-foot-thick tubes between them symbolize the bonding power which holds the crystal together. All in all the gigantic construction of steel and light metal—which was actually almost scrapped soon after it was built—is more than three hundred feet tall.

The idea for it came from André Waterkeyn, the director of the Association of Metalworking Industries in Belgium at that time. Once the decision was made to hold the 1958 World Exposition in Brussels, the organizers tried to find a suitable symbol—a symbolic structure to reflect the chosen theme "Progress and Man" and to be constructed on the exhibition grounds in the north of the city. Waterkeyn proposed his enormously enlarged iron crystal. This response not only produced looks of astonishment but also harsh words.

But the proposal hadn't just come off the top of his head; mining in Belgium had been the major catalyst for the industrial development of Belgium when the country began to draw upon its iron ore resources. This sector of the economy still plays a crucial role today. Iron, steel and other metals are among Belgium's most important exports.

At that time discussions about the atom—the basis of all sciences dealing with the composition of matter—dominated public debate. Of course people were aware of the dangers involved in the use of atomic power, Hiroshima had shocked them deeply. But precisely for this reason, discussions were all the more heated about how atomic power could be put to use for the good of mankind. With great idealism they planned the first atomic power stations and envisioned the glorious future of this new technology.

The Atomium, which was constructed as an emblem of the atomic age, and which illustrates the relationships between normally invisible atoms by showing something infinitely small depicted in a monumental form, reflects this belief in progress. It was built to demonstrate the optimism of Belgian industry in the most recent discoveries of modern research, hoping for a better future. However, the Atomium is not only a symbolic object—it also has an interior which can be visited. Six of the nine aluminum spheres, each of which weighs two hundred tons and is divided into two floors, are open to visitors. The uppermost sphere contains a restaurant with a panoramic view of the entire city. In the spheres below there are several rooms for events with up to two hundred seats, and exhibition spaces for exhibitions on man and medical research. The spheres can be reached by escalators in the connecting tubes and by the central elevator which, with a speed of fifteen feet per second, was originally claimed to be the fastest elevator in the world. By paying 350,000 Belgian francs the Atomium

The Atomium's spheres are connected by escalators and a central elevator

can even be hired for an evening—certainly an unusual venue for that special event.

The Atomium in Brussels is a representation of an iron crystal that has been magnified 165 billion times

The Atomium towering over the model "Mini Europe" in Bruparck, Brussels

A Temple to the Spirit, a Monument!
The Solomon R. Guggenheim Museum in New York

USA; planned, 1946; built 1956–1959
Architect: Frank Lloyd Wright; extension constructed
1988–1992 by architects C. Gwathmey and R. Siegel

"I have been busy at the boards—
putting down some of the thoughts
concerning a museum that were in my
mind while looking for a site. I think
we have said too little about the building to each other and too much about
the site....
When I have satisfied myself with the
preliminary exploration, I'll bring it
down to New York before going West
and we can have anguish and fun over it.
The whole thing will either throw you
off your guard entirely or be just about
what you have been dreaming about."

From a letter by Frank Lloyd Wright to Hilla Rebay, Solomon
R. Guggenheim's consultant on the arts, January 20, 1944
© The Frank Lloyd Wright Memorial Foundation, published
by the Southern Illinois University Press

Solomon R. Guggenheim was born with a silver spoon in his mouth. His father, who came from Switzerland, emigrated to the United States of America in 1847 and managed, within the shortest period of time, to put together a gigantic industrial empire with worldwide holdings in tin, copper and silver mines, which formed the basis for the family's legendary wealth. Following his father's death, Solomon's eldest brother Daniel took over the family firm and further expanded it, earning the Guggenheims more money than ensuing generations could possibly spend.

Solomon, who was not only the beneficiary of inherited wealth but who also felt responsible

for the future of the firm, invested his part of the fortune—much as his niece Peggy would do later—in establishing a foundation for promoting abstract art. When he founded the "Museum of Non-Objective Painting" in 1937, the rapidly growing collection was still without a permanent home. It wasn't until June, 1943 that America's star architect Frank Lloyd Wright, who was already seventy-six years old, received a handwritten letter, practically begging him to design a museum for the collection that in the meanwhile contained works by Cézanne, Ernst, Modigliani, and Picasso. The letter came from Baroness Hilla Rebay von Ehrenwiesen, Solomon R. Guggenheim's consultant on the arts.

The architect Frank Lloyd Wright, Baroness Hilla Rebay von
Ehrenwiesen, and Solomon R. Guggenheim with a model of
the Guggenheim Museum

"I feel," she wrote, "that each of these great masterpieces should be organized into space and you, so it seems to me, would test the possibilities to do so. I want a temple to the spirit, a monument!" Although an appropriate site was soon found in the heart of Manhattan—directly on Central Park, at the corner of Fifth Avenue and 89th Street—the plans for the museum would have to wait a long time to be realized. World War II was raging in Europe, and no one could know how it would end.

Only in 1956 when America's economy emerged from its post war slump, would the foundation stone for the museum be laid. Frank Lloyd Wright's plans were considered revolutionary. Several building contractors thought the plans too risky to attempt and were afraid to accept the contract. Solomon R. Guggenheim wanted an unconventional building, and Frank Lloyd Wright designed it for him in the form of a gigantic spiral made of reinforced concrete, containing a funnel-shaped space. A broad, spiral ramp leads past the paintings, winding gradually upward from the ground floor to the majestic glass dome. The design was deemed technically impossible until contractor George Cohen decided to take the risk.

Enthusiasts view the building as a stroke of genius. Less generous critics make fun of the structure, dubbing it—depending on their mood—"the coffee grinder," "salad bowl" or "washing machine." The founder and his architect could not be effected by such criticism. Neither Solomon R. Guggenheim nor Frank Lloyd Wright lived to see the grand opening of their museum on October 21, 1959.

Where Milk and Honey Flow
Brazil's Parliament Building in the Jungle

Brasilia, Brazil; 1957–1960
Architect: Oscar Niemeyer

"The project was to build the capital of the country! It was not about simply building a city, rather the task was to find a solution utilizing the concepts of modern city planning that matched the chosen location, conformed to the program underlined in the competition and was able to provide the atmosphere of culture, civilization and monumental size that a city of this type required."

Oscar Niemeyer, *Self-introduction, Critique, Work,* 1957

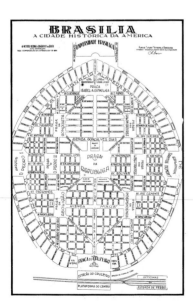

The first design for the new Brazilian capital, 1930

The idea of the perfect city goes back to ancient times. The Egyptians tried to create one around 3000 B.C. when they built Memphis, a capital that did not develop or evolve, but one that was designed from the word go. Since then the world has known fifty such capitals, all laid out where cities had never been before. In this respect Brasilia, the capital of the world's fifth largest country, which also rose out of the earth in one fell swoop, is not unique.

The plan for a new capital originated in the twentieth century. Brazil's first capital, Salvador de Bahia, a port city founded by the Portuguese was Brazil's capital until 1763 when it was moved to Rio de Janeiro. As early as 1822 when Brazil declared its independence from Portugal, the question of a new capital was being discussed. The new capital was to be in the interior in order to provide access to the rich natural resources in central Brazil and to promote the cultural development of this sparsely populated region.

The realization of the dream took somewhat longer even though Father Don Bosco, an Italian priest who became a popular hero in Brazil, had a vision in 1883 in which he saw a large city appear in South America between 15° and 20° latitude before the year 2000. In Don Bosco's vision the city "flowed with milk and honey."

The first constitution of the Republic of Brazil, written in 1891, provided for an area of some 7,000 square miles in the central plain to be set aside for a future capital. For more than half a century nothing would come of this optimistic provision. The plan for a new capital would have to wait until 1956 when Juscelino Kubishek de Oliveira, who was then President of Brazil, took steps to turn it into reality.

The architect Lucio Costa won the competition to plan a new city. He appointed Oscar Niemeyer as technical director of the project. A short time later a modern city of half a million inhabitants rose out of the jungle. Its plan resembled a giant airplane. Within three years residential areas, a neighborhood of villas, embassies, churches, schools and kindergartens were built. The city had its own university, sport center, botanical garden, zoo, airport, cemetery and yacht club.

This "City of the Future" was meant to help solve Brazil's economic problems. The central feature of the new capital, built at an altitude of 3,000 feet above sea level, was the "Place of Three Powers," where the executive, legislative and judicial branches of government were based. The most notable building in this city where "milk and honey" do not flow, is the parliament.

In keeping with the airplane analogy of the city's layout, the parliament building with its two half-domes, one of which is turned upward, evokes images of flying saucers. Some critics have compared the adjacent H-shaped skyscraper containing the offices of the representatives and senators to a rocket launching ramp. Although many have praised Brasilia for its "precedent-breaking futuristic architecture," less charitable critics see the reference to the traditional dome as a "pretentious half-measure." Asked if his creation, with its rounded forms could be styled as "feminine architecture," Oscar Niemeyer answered, "No. It is the architecture of an architect who loves women."

"Precedent-breaking futuristic architecture"—
the Parliament Building in Brasilia

Billowing Concrete Sails
The Sydney Opera House

Sydney, Australia; 1959–1973
Architect: Jørn Utzon

"There she stands, like Santa Maria della Salute in the Venetian lagoon—a perfect symbol linking the city with the ocean and yet contemporary in appearance. And it continues to remind us of different epochs in history when great buildings were erected, not just to fulfill a useful purpose, but to praise the Lord and to reflect the glory of princely patrons."

John Martin Douglas Pringle on the Sydney Opera House

Originally, or so the story goes, the peninsula belonged to an Aborigine called Bennelong. Then the first Australian sheep and cattle herds grazed here—so that the English prisoners and their guards, who had come to this country, would not have to do without the lambs wool or milk for their five-o-clock tea that they were used to. Later a fortress was built on this place in an effort to defy the much-feared Russian invasion. When it didn't come, the fort was transformed into a streetcar depot. Today the Sydney Opera House stands on this site. The mockery that was directed at the unconventional structure at Bennelong Point has almost satirical character: the building reminded some of "copulating white turtles" or "veiled nuns in a panic." It was said to look "like something that is crawling out of the ocean with nothing good in mind," like "an albino plant, whose roots are bursting out from too small a pot." One determined opponent to the design openly said what most people were thinking: she certified the architect Jørn Utzon as having "lousy taste." The Danish architect was only 38 years old when, in 1957, he participated in an architectural competition for an opera house in Sydney, entering a pile of sketches and promptly winning first prize. Until then he had only known the building site from photographs. And, according to members of the jury, his first design was hardly more than "a few splendid line drawings." But the revolutionary, tiered roof, which today is the symbol of an entire continent, could already be recognized in its initial stages. The opera house, which links the harbor with the city, stands proudly as a cultural flagship sailing into the 21st century. Its billowing sails, however, are not made of canvas, but of solid concrete. Since no roofs of this kind existed, it was not possible to make a realistic estimate of construction costs beforehand—something that almost steered the project onto the rocks. Instead of the seven million Australian dollars originally estimated, the costs soon exceeded more than a hundred million; the planned construction time of five years was finally extended to fourteen years. But then again, the opera house's statistics alone are awe inspiring: the roof weighs 158,000 tons and is covered with more than one million fungus-resistant Swedish tiles that never have to be cleaned! Underneath these towering masses are more than one thousand rooms, including a gigantic concert hall with 2,700 seats and one of the world's largest organs. But there is a sadder note to add: after the architect had been put under so much pressure by the exploding costs, he threw in the towel in 1966 (seven years before the opening by Queen Elizabeth II), leaving both country and construction site behind and swearing never to return to the fifth continent. A number of his original details were then scrapped. As a result, the building is perfect for rock concerts, movie performances, conventions and chamber orchestras, but for staging classical operas it is not suitable.

Monumentality and movement:
Sydney's harbor and Opera House

The Opera House's interior
features the architect's fine
decorative sensibility

Floating Architecture
The Olympic Park in Munich

Munich, Germany; 1968–1972
Architects: Günther Behnisch with Frei Otto

"We are grateful to the Olympic Committee and consider their awarding the XXth Olympic Games to Munich a sign of confidence in a new Germany. We were all very pleased at hearing the news. No other occasion could provide a better opportunity for us to show a modern Germany to the world."

Hans Dietrich Genscher, Minister of the Interior of West Germany, 1972

In 1971, one year before the Olympic games began, the entire city seemed to have gone mad. Everyone seemed to want to get involved. "Olympic Waldi" was presented as the mascot for the Olympic games; the German President dropped in to check on how construction was progressing, Prince Philip, the Royal Consort, came to inspect the still unfinished equestrian facilities, and tickets went on sale. Despite the fact that not one row of seats was in place, more than four million tickets were sent out to 124 countries.

In 1966 the German government awarded Munich a subsidy to construct facilities for the XXth Olympic games. In only six years the arenas, stadium, tracks and other facilities for competitive sporting events would have to be constructed, along with press offices and housing for the athletes. Everything would have to be built from scratch and be finished in time for the international event.

The games aroused high expectations. These games—the first to take place on German soil since the end of World War II—were meant to differ fundamentally from the strictly organized events of the 1936 Olympic games in Berlin, which the National Socialists used to divert attention away from their preparations for war. Munich was to prove to the world that post-war Germany stood for democracy and freedom.

The general wish was to have a good time inspired by a setting with a soaring, imaginative architecture. They hoped the games could be held in a "green belt area" with short distances between venues. The organizers settled on the Oberwiesenfeld, a seventy acre site about two miles north of the city center. The land had served as the Bavarian capital's first commercial airport and later as a military parade ground. First of all, munitions experts were called in to

remove ammunition and unexploded bombs left over from World War II. Only then could construction begin. A work force of more than 8,000 toiled under the direction of 550 architects and engineers. Although the complex they created is not even thirty years old, it has already been listed as a site of special architectural interest.

One reason for such high regard is the unusual construction of the tent-like roof that rises above Munich's Olympic Park. It covers an area of 225,000 square feet which spreads over part of the track and field stadium and covers the entire swimming pool and multipurpose arena. The advanced technology of the construction was greatly admired by many critics from around the world, and is still admired today.

Twelve gigantic slanted steel pillars support a steel cable net fitted with 8,300 panes of fireproof smoked Plexiglas. The similarity to a tent is intentional. It is meant to symbolize the nomadic nature of the games that always change venues. At the same time the flowing skyline of the Olympic tent blends naturally and elegantly into the landscape of the park with its man-made hills.

The roof, reflecting sunlight or glowing with artificial light from within, is spectacularly beautiful and symbolizes the temporary nature of sports contests which absorb our attention today, only to move elsewhere tomorrow. Practical considerations also played a role in the choice of the transparent roof. Television cameras for color broadcasting, still in its early development at that time, needed a great deal of light, which was no problem with this light-diffusing material. At the same time the Plexiglas provided shade for spectators and athletes and remained cool even in the heat of the competition.

Poster for the XXth Olympic Games, Munich, 1972

Light, flowing and transparent: the tent-like
roof of Munich's Olympic Park symbolizes
the nomadic nature of the games

The flowing form of the roof is echoed in
the surrounding man-made landscape

Pulling in the Crowds
The Centre Pompidou in Paris

Paris, France; 1972–1977
Architects: Renzo Piano and Richard Rogers

"Disneyland is successful because it cheers people up. It's about the same with the Centre Pompidou. The building is popular because people like to go there. There is absolutely no obligation but people come anyway. That's why we have to assume that the building fulfills a genuine need. Otherwise the Parisians could of course just stay in bed or watch T.V."

Richard Rogers interviewed by Alexander Fils, January, 1980

Beaubourg prior to the construction of the Centre Pompidou in Paris; to the right of the picture are the old market halls

All supporting structures are on the outside of the building; here the caterpillar-like construction housing the escalators

As always, the opponents were the first to get all worked up. The city wanted to build a "useless, gigantic toy," they said, a "refinery," a "monstrous machine." No less than seven court cases were filed in the hopes of blocking the project. But Justitia was on the architects' side. The National Art and Culture Center Georges Pompidou, "Centre Pompidou" for short, couldn't be hindered through litigation. After its opening, it became a hit with the public. Today the center is visited by over six million people per year—which is why the managers have now moved some of the offices to other premises in order to make more space available.

Le Corbusier had already dreamed of building a "museum of unlimited ideas" here in Beaubourg, one of the oldest neighborhoods in Paris. An empty space near the market halls seemed suitable. Tuberculosis had raged violently here at the turn of the century and, as a result, many of the old, dilapidated houses had been torn down. What remained was an enormous gap which was used as a parking lot—hardly an example of successful urban planning. Finally President Georges Pompidou, a lover of literature and a passionate art collector, took the initiative.

In 1971 he announced an international competition with the goal of "erecting a cultural center on the plateau Beaubourg." 687 architects from fifty countries participated. The jury decided in favor of a design by two unknown architects who not only seemed surprisingly young, but—to the horror of nationalists—weren't even French. Renzo Piano and Richard Rogers had convinced the judges because of the flexibility of their design—an important criterion for the future. "The organization of the office landscape can be changed in a matter of minutes, the elements of the exhibition rooms

can be completely dismantled within an hour, and the fire barriers within a day. Everything can be moved."

The cultural center needed exactly this freedom to rearrange the space, as Georges Pompidou explained: "It is my wish that the building should accommodate a great center for painting and sculpture, but also special facilities for music and, beside that, a record collection, a cinema, and an experimental theater as well as a public library."

The audacious steel and glass construction designed by Piano and Rogers, in which all supporting structures are placed on the outside to allow complete freedom to arrange the rooms on the inside, makes the building come alive. The center has become an aesthetic playground where it is possible to stage contemporary operas as well as experimental dance shows, video performances, and temporary exhibitions on its five floors which are suspended from steel girders. Individual departments, however, have their own defined spaces. The National Museum of Modern Art, the library, the Center for Industrial Design, the cinematheque, the language laboratory, the Institute for the Research and Development of Contemporary Music, and the children's workshop—all of these institutions have their permanent place in the Centre Pompidou. But they don't simply exist next to each other; they interact. The spirit of the house is interdisciplinary. In an exemplary pedagogical experiment at the Centre Pompidou, they are establishing a forum for exchanges between different branches of the arts and for promoting dialogue by building communication bridges to broaden horizons and be fun. When announcing its decision in favor of the design by Piano and Rogers, the jury simply added: "Our times love exuberant lifestyles," and this is certainly reflected in the Centre Pompidou.

The Centre Pompidou—an aesthetic playground that has transformed Beaubourg

A Monument to the *Joie de Vivre*
Niki de Saint Phalle's Tarot Garden

Capalbio, Tuscany, Italy; 1979–1996
Designed by the artist Niki de Saint Phalle

"If life is a game of cards, we were born without knowing the rules. And yet we have to play along. Is Tarot just a card game, or does it hide a deeper meaning? I am convinced that these cards contain an important message—a philosophy for life."

Niki de Saint Phalle, on her *Giardino dei Tarocchi*, 1987

The sculpture "Moderation"

The Pope's nose resembles a cucumber, moderation dances on one leg and the devil is a woman. Niki de Saint Phalle was always good for surprises. In the sixties she fired a gun at pictures made of plaster, to which bags of paint were attached. The violent happening was a public sensation but the press was indignant. The critics were also unkind to her work, "Altars" in which crucifixes and holy figures, as seen through the eyes of Niki de Saint Phalle, consorted in scandalous synthesis with machine pistols, naked youths and winged monsters.

The art establishment only accepted Saint Phalle once she had ended her aggressive, stubborn, regimented, narrow-minded phase and "formally calmed down." Her "Nanas"—fat, brightly painted female figures evoking ancient fertility goddesses—ruined her health (the polyester used in their creation releases toxic fumes when mixed) but finally brought her fame and acceptance. But she wanted to achieve something even greater. For the Museum of Modern Art in Stockholm she created a giant *Nana* which could be entered through the vagina and contained a bar, book shop, aquarium, movie theater and love nest. The giant work convinced her that a sculpture garden was to be her crowning achievement.

The publisher of the daily newspaper *La Repubblica*, a friend of the artist, put a plot of unused land at her disposal. The land in Capalbio, in the furthest reaches of Tuscany, had formerly been a quarry and was now filled with olive trees. Like a princely medieval builder she gathered artists and artisans from the entire world around her. Prominent among them was her husband, painter and sculptor Jean Tinguely, whose kinetic junk sculptures made him famous. The artists went to work and soon a fantastic park grew out of the bare earth. The critics hailed it as an "art world wonder" which "bubbled over with joy, possessed a zest for liveliness—a work of genius, free and fresh. The very thought of it released feelings of well-being, and the effect of it was like an overdose of optimism."

The bizarre figures, some of which are as big as houses, are made of reinforced concrete, surfaced with bits of broken tile and glass, which reflect the sunlight thousand-fold and plunge the visitor into the magic sphere of Tarot. The sculptures in the garden of Capalbio represent the twenty-two trump cards of the Tarot game. Among them are "Death," "Power," and the "Wheel of Fate," which represent, respectively, human themes such as life and death, loneliness and love, arrogance and justice.

The origin of Tarot, Europe's oldest card game, is veiled in mystery. It is known that emperors and popes used Tarot to foretell their fate. The priests of ancient Egypt were once believed to have created the symbols in order to pass on their esoteric knowledge. In fact, tarot symbols are borrowed from various cultures, religions and historical periods. Numerology, cabbala, gnosticism, and Christianity merge with the belief in ancient gods and animistic spirit cults, with sagas, legends and historical fact. The fascinating Tarot world of allegory and

"The Devil"

riddle is palpable in the Garden of Capalbio. But it is doubtful that it answers all questions about the meaning of life—the symbol of man in the garden of Tarot is "The Fool."

"The Mistress" and
the "Wheel of Fortune"

"The Fool" in the magical
world of the Tarot Garden

175

An Overture to Art
The Louvre Pyramid

Paris, France; 1983–1993
Architect: I. M. Pei

"The form of the pyramid is quite a bit older than all of the Egyptian examples. Besides, in Egypt they are made of stone and are heavy, a work for the dead. My pyramid, on the other hand, is light, is life."

I. M. Pei, 1991

Construction work continued for generations at the Louvre, the former royal palace at the heart of Paris. In the early Middle Ages, a kennel for wolfhounds called the "Lupara" most probably stood here, which is thought to have later given the castle its name. In 1190, Philip Augustus had the fort expanded as a bulwark with a defensive tower from which an iron chain was attached to the opposite side of the Seine in order to control ship traffic on the river. Several centuries later the drafty fortress stood empty. The rulers preferred to live in the magnificent castles of the Loire valley.

The building regained popularity only once King François I had the Louvre transformed into a splendid palace after the fortress had lost its

The Louvre—depicted in the Duc de Berry's Book of Hours *Les très riches Heures*, 1413–1416

military importance. Even Louis XIV, who moved the royal residence from Paris to Versailles, had a new wing built onto the Louvre which, however, remained a ruin for a long time and was only completed when Napoleon moved in. Nonetheless, it certainly seems that at least every second French ruler tried to renovate, build onto, remodel, or expand the Louvre.

The last in this series was François Mitterrand. He was not a crowned head, of course, but president of the republic. He ordered that the centuries-old tradition of building onto the Louvre with modern forms and materials must be continued. A glass pyramid was to be built in the historic quadrangle which opens westward towards the Tuileries. Vehement protest erupted. Those opposed to the project claimed

that the pyramid would block the view of the time-honored facades and hoped that Mitterrand would be out of office before the project could be realized. Their wish was not to be granted. Mitterrand remained president and work on the pyramid forged ahead. But the pyramid is only the externally visible part of a general reconstruction which made the Louvre the largest museum in the world while retaining all of the splendor of its exterior.

Half of the palace with its important art collections was already opened to the public in 1793. After the 6,000 administrators in the finance ministry had moved out of their wing and into a new building on the outskirts of the city, a total of nearly 200,000 square feet —double the amount of exhibition space— became available. The "Grand Louvre," as the expanded museum is called today, has 198 rooms in which thousands of exquisite objects as well as unique works of art such as the *Venus de Milo* or the *Mona Lisa* are presented to a public of millions. The seventy-five-foot-high glass pyramid marks the entrance to the treasury of world art. Under its 803 panes of glass, which are held in place by a network of steel girders and cables, the earth opens up to reveal a wide, light-flooded reception area (below the level of the courtyard and accessible via escalators), a free-standing spiral staircase, and a cylindrical elevator. Here in the center of the Louvre complex are the cash registers, shops, an auditorium, a cafeteria, a first-class restaurant, and an area for temporary exhibitions. Most importantly, from this point corridors lead in all directions towards the above-ground areas of the Louvre. "What a view up and out!" architecture critics enthused about the pyramid's filigree transparency, and praised the bold design as the "brave continuation of history into the next millennium."

The planners of the pyramid had only forgotten one thing: glass gets dirty. In the meantime, though, they have found a remedy for this nuisance. A specially developed cleaning machine now goes over the pyramid once a week to ensure a clear view of the skies.

I. M. Pei's glass pyramid marks the new entrance
to the expanded "Grand Louvre"

Mountains of Metal
The Guggenheim Museum in Bilbao

Spain; 1993–1997
Architect: Frank O. Gehry

"The bizarre forms of the Guggenheim Museum in Bilbao are visible from afar. The titanium surface of the spectacular building radiates throughout the colorless cityscape and exerts a magical attraction. Up close one observes facades that seem to be in the process of disintegration and lead all former meaning to an absurd conclusion.
A fish? A ship? A flower whose petals are dropping? Or perhaps, a giant octopus?"

Ulrike Wiebrecht, "The word Bilbao has gotten a new meaning," from the *Süddeutsche Zeitung*, April 20, 1999

Until recently Bilbao was a blank spot on the tourist map. And for good reason. Uncontrolled expansion begun under Franco's rule had completely altered the architectural profile of the 1,200-year old city in northern Spain. The River Narvión, formerly filled with fish, had turned into an evil-smelling sewer. Those who had to do business in the city could only find consolation in the exquisite Basque cuisine and try to forget the miserable surroundings. "Bilbao is gray," according to a contemporary account. "Gray is the color of its business streets through which the traffic rushes. Gray is the river that winds lifelessly through this industrial metropolis. And gray is the color of the state owned apartment blocks that stretch all the way to the mountains."

Financial ruin quickly followed on the heels of aesthetic desolation. Hundreds of companies fled the economically depressed region which was also torn by social conflicts and subject to growing violence. The steel industry collapsed; property values plunged. Bilbao was, without doubt, one of the ugliest cities in Spain. Following the floods of 1983, when the entire city lay submerged under the muddy toxic slime of industrially polluted water, the end appeared to have finally arrived.

Then Frank Gehry, an American architect of Canadian origin arrived. In the 1970s he had started his career by designing inexpensive furniture for department stores and had gone on to become one of the foremost architects in the world. The Basque government desperately needed his talents to stage its comeback. In addition to a modern underground public transportation system and a new airport, designed by other architects, the Basque leaders decided they needed a spectacular new art museum. Gehry was consulted following agreement with the Solomon R. Guggenheim Foundation to build a new branch of the museum in Bilbao.

The museum's storage areas were bursting with art that its various buildings could not accommodate.

Gehry designed a sparkling art cathedral, which within a very short time became a symbol of the Basque economic and spiritual renaissance. "What Frank Gehry designed, with the help of the computer 'Catia,' in terms of form and pre-fabrication will, within a few years, symbolize the power of architecture at the expense of other arts," gushed the international press. In fact the radiant new museum altered

The Guggenheim in Bilbao: not only renowned for its stunning architecture but also for its collections and exhibitions

the face of the Basque city as no bomb or building had ever done before. It was built on a cleared parcel of industrial land which was a part of the harbor area, between the river and the new section of the city. The building has been universally praised for the way it fits into a landscape dominated by the river, bridges and railway facilities. "Whatever Gehry may have inflicted upon the art entrusted to his care in the interior space, the exterior, with its craggy surfaces fits perfectly into the cityscape. He dealt easily with whatever stood in his way in this industrial terrain, subordinating it to his needs and amalgamating it into his triumph."

The hopes focused on the new museum have been fully realized. When it opened on November 1, 1997 more than 7,000 visitors

were recorded—breaking all attendance records in the history of Spanish museums. International airlines still run special flights to accommodate passenger demand and hotels have been forced to expand. Thousands of tourists line up each day in front of the shining titanium clad museum.

With its dynamic design and contrasting materials, the Guggenheim Museum has brought a new dimension to the cityscape of Bilbao

Vertical City
The Millennium Tower:
Looking Toward the Future

Designed for the Bay of Tokyo, Japan; 1989
Architect: Norman Foster

"Those in political power must commit themselves to finding solutions to the problems of ecology, the depletion of natural resources, the uncontrollable population explosion that is pushing cities beyond their boundaries. We need to develop a commercial model that meets the complex needs of human settlements."

Lord Foster, on his Millennium Tower project, 1992

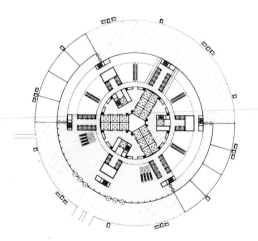

The waters of the biblical deluge had risen up to poor Noah's neck, and King Nimrod, his great grandson, didn't want to risk a similar fate. In the event God chose to unleash a second apocalyptic flood to punish mankind, Nimrod wanted to be on the safe side, so he ordered a tower to be built in Babylon. The tower was to be high enough that "the waters of the flood would never reach its pinnacle," according to the ancient chronicler Josephus Flavius. God felt the king was trying to get the upper hand. According to the Book of Genesis, he descended from heaven to examine the

construction and concluded: "This is just the beginning of your undertaking. Nothing that you plan will now seem impossible."

The rest of the story is well known. Angered by man's presumption, God punished the Babylonians by mixing up their language so that no one understood what the other was saying and everyone spoke at the same time. Work on the tower ceased due to the lack of communication and the gigantic Tower of Babel became the most famous construction ruin in history. Whether British star architect Norman Foster studied the biblical scenario of the building of the tower, is not known. Clearly, he was undeterred by Nimrod's disaster and planned a project that would cast the Tower of Babel in its shade. If the earthquake-proof Millennium Tower were to be built on the artificial island in the Bay of Tokyo, the 2,500-foot-

high skyscraper would be twice as tall as the Sears Tower in Chicago.

Foster's plan to accommodate 50,000 people would provide an area of three million square feet of residential and commercial space. The 170-story building, surrounded by the sea, would be a vertical city with its own schools, libraries, sports facilities, theaters, hospitals, police and fire stations. The tower would be divided into seven zones with restaurants and viewing platforms on the upper two levels. Radio and television antennas along with wind and solar collectors for the power supply would also be fitted.

The main portion of the Millennium Tower, with a diameter of 350 feet at its base, would be divided into five equally high zones, providing several thousand apartments and offices. The huge halls separating them could be used to establish city neighborhood centers. The plans include an embankment and harbor at the foot of the tower, visually bridging its vertical dimension with the horizontal vastness of the ocean surrounding it.

All this is still far in the future. But feasibility studies, commissioned by the Japanese Obayashi concern, have already begun. The reason behind the project is that the population of Tokyo is exploding. No other city is expanding as rapidly as the Japanese capital; nowhere is the price of real estate so high. At the same time land crucial to agricultural use limits the city's sprawl into the neighboring countryside.

The first designs—which seemed to lean heavily on science fiction—appeared in the eighties when the Japanese economy was booming and its commercial triumphs made it appear invincible. The technology needed for the construction of such a building is theoretically available. The question that remains is whether such projects, despite their palm gardens, petting zoos, fountains and reflecting pools with daylight, would ever be a realistic and acceptable alternative to present day housing problems.

Models, drawings, and plans of the projected skyscraper which, with its 170 stories, is almost twice the height of the Sears Tower

Appendix

Suggested Reading

The Enigma of Stonehenge

— Atkinson, R. J. C., *Stonehenge*, London 1987

— Balfour, Michael, *Stonehenge and its Mysteries*, London 1979

— Bender, Barbara, *Stonehenge: Making Space*, Oxford/New York 1998

— Burl, Aubrey, *Great Stone Circles: Fables, Fictions, Facts*, New Haven 1999

— North, John David, *Stonehenge: Neolithic Man and the Cosmos*, London 1996

The Secrets of the Cheops Pyramid

— Bazhaw, W. O., *The Search for Cheops and his Treasures*, Bellingham 1988

— Kadare, Ismail, *The Pyramid*, New York 1998

— Piazzi Smyth, Charles, *Life and Work at the Great Pyramid*, London 1867

— Piazzi Smyth, Charles, *Our Inheritance in the Great Pyramid*, London 1864

The Cliff Temple of Abu Simbel

— Hägg, T. (ed.), *Nubian Culture Past and Present, Main Papers Presented at the Sixth International Conference for Nubian Studies in Uppsala, August 11–16, 1986*, Stockholm 1987

— MacQuitty, William, *Abu Simbel*, New York 1965

— Shinnie, P. L., *Ancient Nubia*, London/New York 1996

— *Temples and Tombs of Ancient Nubia*, Published by UNESCO, London/Paris 1987

Persepolis and the New Year's Festival

— Fergusson, James, *The Palaces of Nineveh and Persepolis Restored*, Delhi 1981

— *Persepolis and Ancient Iran*, Chicago 1976

— Wheeler, Mortimer, *Flames over Persepolis*, London 1968

— Wilber, Donald Newton, *Persepolis: The Archaeology of Parsa, Seat of the Persian Kings*, Princeton 1989

Olympia and the Games of Old

— Buchanan, David, *Greek Athletics*, London 1976

— Golden, Mark, *Sport and Society in Ancient Greece*, Cambridge/New York 1998

— Harris, Harold Arthur, *Greek Athletes and Athletics*, Westport, Connecticut 1979

— Swaddling, Judith, *The Ancient Olympic Games*, London 1980

The Acropolis in Athens

— Hopper, Robert John, *The Acropolis*, London 1971

— Hurwit, Jeffrey M., *The Athenian Acropolis*, Cambridge/New York 1999

— Rhodes, Robin Francis, *Architecture and Meaning of the Athenian Acropolis*, Cambridge/New York 1995

— Woodford, S., *The Parthenon*, Cambridge, Mass. 1980

The Theater of Epidaurus

— Burmeister, Enno, *Theater in Attika und auf der Peleppones*, Munich 1996

— Ovid, *Ars amatoria*, ed. by A. S. Hollis, Oxford/New York 1989

— Tomlinson, R. A., *Epidauros*, London/New York 1983

The Mysterious Past of Teotihuacán

— Berlo, Janet (ed.), *Art, Ideology, and the City of Teotihuacan*, Washington, DC 1992

— Hassig, Ross, *War and Society in Ancient Mesoamerica*, Berkeley 1992

— Pasztory, Esther, *Teotihuacan: An Experiment in Living*, Norman, Oklahoma 1997

— *Teotihuacan: Art from the City of the Gods*, New York/San Francisco 1994

The Drama of Masada

— Ben-Yehuda, Nachman, *The Masada Myth*, Madison, Wisconsin 1995

— Josephus, Flavius, *The Jewish War*, translated by G. A. Williamson, Harmondsworth/New York 1981

— Rosenthal, Monroe, *Wars of the Jews*, New York 1990

— *The Story of Masada: Discoveries from the Excavations*, Provo, Utah 1997

The Cliff City of Petra

— Hammond, Philip C., *The Temple of the Winged Lions: Petra, Jordan*, Fountain Hills, Arizona 1996

— Hutchings, Noah W., *Petra in History and Prophecy*, Oklahoma City 1991

— Maqsood, Rosalyn, *Petra*, Reading 1994

— McKenzie, Judith, *The Architecture of Petra*, Oxford/New York 1990

The Pont du Gard

— Evans, Harry B., *Water Distribution in Ancient Rome*, Ann Arbor, Michigan 1994

— Hodge, A. Trevor, *Roman Aqueducts and Water Supply*, London 1992

— *The Pont du Gard: Water and the Roman Town*, Paris 1992

— Rousseau, Jean-Jacques, *Les Confessions*, edited by J. Voisine, Paris 1964

Gladiators at the Colosseum

— Futrell, Alison, *Blood in the Arena: The Spectacle of Roman Power*, Austin 1997

— Kyle, Donald G., *Spectacle of Death in Ancient Rome*, London/New York 1998

— Luciano, Roberto, *The Colosseum: Architecture, History, and Entertainment in the Flavian Amphitheatre*, Novara 1990

— Nardo, Don, *The Roman Colosseum*, San Diego 1998

— Wiedemann, Thomas, *Emperors and Gladiators*, London/New York 1992

Shrine of the Planet Gods: The Pantheon

— MacDonald, William Lloyd, *The Pantheon: Design, Meaning, and Progeny*, London 1976

— Salvadori, Renzo, *An Architect's Guide to Rome*, London/Boston 1990

— Woodward, Christopher, *Rome*, Manchester/New York 1995

The Baths of Caracalla

— Fagan, Garrett G., *Bathing in Public in the Roman World*, Ann Arbor, Michigan 1999

— Lombardi, Leonardo, *Le Terme di Caracalla*, Rome 1995

— Seneca, Lucius Annaeus, *Ad Lucilium epistulae morales*, 2 volumes, ed. by L. D. Reynolds, reprint from 1965, Oxford 1985/86

— Yegul, Fikret K., *Baths and Bathing in Classical Antiquity*, New York/Cambridge 1992

Hagia Sophia — A Shrine to God's Wisdom

— Browning, Robert, *Justinian and Theodora*, New York 1987

— Evans, J. A. S., *The Age of Justinian*, London/New York 1996

— Moorhead, John, *Justinian*, London/New York 1994

— Schneider, Alfons Maria, *Hagia Sophia zu Konstantinopel*, Berlin 1938

The Church of the Nativity in Bethlehem

— Freeman-Grenville, G. S. P., *The Basilica of the Nativity in Bethlehem*, Jerusalem 1994
— Kroll, Gerhard, *Auf den Spuren Jesu*, Leipzig 1970[4]
— Weigand, Edmund, *Geburtskirche von Betlehem*, Leipzig 1911

The Pilgrimage to Mecca

— De Gaury, Gerald, *Rulers of Mecca*, New York 1980
— Ibrahlm, Mahmood, *Merchant Capital and Islam*, Austin 1990
— Peters, F. E., *Mecca: A Literary History of the Muslim Holy Land*, Princeton 1994
— Rutter, Eldon, *The Holy Cities of Arabia*, London/New York 1930
— Stewart, Desmond, *Mecca*, New York 1980

Sacred to Three World Religions: The Dome of the Rock

— Kroyanker, David, *Jerusalem Architecture*, New York 1994
— Nolli, Gianfranco, *Grabeskirche und Felsendom in Jerusalem*, Herrsching 1989
— Pringle, Denys, *Secular Buildings in the Crusader Kingdom of Jerusalem*, Cambridge/New York 1997

The Former Imperial City of Nara and the Hall of the Great Buddha

— Alex, William, *Japanese Architecture*, London 1968
— Holmes, Burton, *Japan, the Country*, Philadelphia 1998
— Holmes, Burton, *The Cities of Japan*, Philadelphia 1997

The Mezquita of Córdoba

— Allee, Alban, *Andalusia: Two Steps from Paradise*, London 1974
— Garaudy, Roger, *Córdoba/Calahorra, Puente entre Oriente y Occidente*, Cordoba 1998
— Goodwin, Godfrey, *Islamic Spain*, San Francisco 1990
— Totton, Robin, *Andalusia*, Wiltshire 1991

The Palatine Chapel, Aachen and the Holy Roman Empire

— Braunfels, Wolfgang, *Die Welt der Karolinger und ihre Kunst*, Munich 1968
— Collins, Roger, *Charlemagne*, Toronto 1998

— Conant, Kenneth John, *Carolingian and Romanesque Architecture*, Harmondsworth/Baltimore 1973
— Macdonald, Fiona, *The World in the Time of Charlemagne*, Parsippany, New Jersey 1998

The Hradčany in Prague

— Hucek, Miroslav, *The Castle of Prague and its Treasures*, London 1994
— Schwarzenberg, Charles, *The Prague Castle and its Treasures*, New York 1994
— Seibt, Ferdinand, *Karl IV*, Munich 1985

The Pilgrimage to Santiago de Compostela

— Frey, Nancy Louise, *Pilgrim Stories: On and off the Road to Santiago*, Berkeley 1998
— *The Pilgrimage to Compostela in the Middle Ages*, New York 1996
— Selby, Bettina, *Pilgrim's Road: A Journey to Santiago de Compostela*, Boston 1994
— Spaccarelli, Thomas Dean, *A Medieval Pilgrim's Companion*, Chapel Hill, North Carolina 1998
— Tate, Robert Brian, *The Pilgrim Route to Santiago*, Oxford 1987

The Tower of London

— Abbott, Geoffrey, *Tortures of the Tower of London*, Newton Abbott 1986
— Ainsworth, William Harrison, *Tower of London*, London 1920
— Mears, Kenneth J., *The Tower of London: 900 Years of English History*, Oxford 1988
— Parnell, Geoffrey, *The Tower of London: Past and Present*, Stroud, Gloucestershire 1998

Mont-Saint-Michel

— Bely, Lucien, *Wonderful Mont Saint-Michel*, Rennes 1986
— De Stroumillo, Elisabeth, *The Tastes of Travel: Normandy*, London 1979
— Whelpton, Barabara Crocker, *History, People, and Places in Normandy*, Bourne End 1975

The Seat of the English Monarchy

— De-la-Noy, Michael, *Windsor Castle: Past and Present*, London 1990
— Hibbert, Christopher, *The Court at Windsor: A Domestic History*, London 1977
— Mackworth-Young, Robin, *The History and Treasures of Windsor Castle*, New York 1982

— Robinson, John Martin, *Royal Palaces: Windsor Castle*, London 1996
— Shakespeare, William, *Merry Wives of Windsor*, New York 1901

Cluny: The Most Magnificent Abbey Church

— Rosenwein, Barbara H., *To Be the Neighbor of Saint Peter: The Social Meaning of Cluny's Property*, Ithaca, New York 1989
— Tellenbach, Gerd, *The Third Church at Cluny, in: Medieval Studies in Memory of Kingsley Porter II*, Cambridge 1937
— Virey, J., *L'Abbaye de Cluny*, Paris 1950

The Temple Complex of Angkor Wat

— Dagens, Bruno, *Angkor, Heart of an Asian Empire*, New York 1995
— Dumarcay, Jacques, *The Site of Angkor*, New York 1998
— Freeman, Michael, *Angkor: The Hidden Glories*, Boston 1990
— Giteau, Madeleine, *The Civilization of Angkor*, New York 1976
— Riboud, Marc, *Angkor, the Serenity of Buddhism*, New York 1993

Simplicity as the Ideal in Fontenay Abbey

— Bazin, Jean-François and Marie-Claude Pascal, *Die Abtei Fontenay*, Rennes 1992
— Dinzelbacher, Peter, *Bernhard von Clairvaux*, Darmstadt 1998
— Pasquereau, Pierre, *Fontenay*, Lucon 1993

The Leaning Tower of Pisa

— Berti, Graziella, *Pisa*, Firenze 1997
— Mallinson, Arnold, *The Leaning Tower, or, Out of the Perpendicular*, Oxford 1982
— Twain, Mark, *A Tramp Abroad*, New York 1997

The Cathedral of Chartres

— Burckhardt, Titus, *Chartres and the Birth of the Cathedral*, Bloomington, Indiana 1996
— Favier, Jean, *The World of Chartres*, New York 1990
— James, John, *The Masons of Chartres*, Sydney/New York 1990
— Simson, Otto Georg von, *The Gothic Cathedral*, Princeton 1988

Death-Defying: The Cliff Dwellings of Mesa Verde

— Chapin, Frederick H., *The Land of the Cliff-Dwellers*, Tuscon, Arizona 1988

— Ferguson, William M., *The Anasazi of Mesa Verde and the Four Corners*, Niwot, Colorado 1996

— Fewkes, Jesse Walter, *Mesa Verde Ancient Architecture*, Albuquerque, New Mexico 1999

— Flint, Richard, *A Field Guide to Mesa Verde Architecture*, Villanueva, New Mexico 1991

— Hawkes, Jacquetta (ed.), *The World of the Past*, 2 volumes, New York 1963

Emperor Frederick II and Castel del Monte

— Abulafia, David, *Frederick II: A Medieval Emperor*, New York 1992

— Götze, Heinrich, *Castel del Monte: Geometric Marvel of the Middle Ages*, Munich/New York 1998

— Willemsen, C. A., *Castel del Monte*, Frankfurt am Main 1982

Fortress and Monastery in One: The Malbork

— Boockmann, Hartmut, *Die Marienburg im 19. Jahrhundert*, Berlin 1992

— Jablonski, Krysztof and Mariusz Mierzwinski, *Die Marienburg*, Warsaw 1993

— Sienkiewicz, Henryk, *The Teutonic Knights*, New York 1993

Venice, Its Wealth, and the Doge's Palace

— Concina, Ennio, *A History of Venetian Architecture*, Cambridge/New York 1998

— Hale, J. R., *Renaissance Venice*, London 1974

— Hibbert, Christopher, *Venice, the Biography of a City*, London 1988

— Huse, Norbert, *The Art of Renaissance Venice*, Chicago 1990

— Zorzi, Alvise, *Venetian Palaces*, New York 1989

The Alhambra and Poor Boabdil

— Fernandez Puertas, Antonio, *The Alhambra*, London 1997

— Grabas, Oleg, *The Alhambra*, Sebastopol, California 1992

— Hewson, David, *Granada and Eastern Andalucia*, London 1990

— Irving, Washington, *The Alhambra*, Boston 1983

The Great Wall of China: The Longest Structure in the World

— Debaine-Francfort, Corinne, *The Search for Ancient China*, New York 1999

— Loewe, Michael and Edward L. Shaughnessy (eds.), *The Cambridge History of Ancient China*, Cambridge/New York 1999

— Schwartz, Daniel, *The Great Wall of China*, London/New York 1990

— Waldron, Arthur, *The Great Wall of China: From History to Myth*, Cambridge/New York 1990

Florence and Its Cathedral Dome

— Giovannetti, Bruno, *Architect's Guide to Florence*, Oxford/Boston 1994

— Henderson, John, *Piety and Charity in Late Medieval Florence*, Oxford/New York 1994

— Kreytenberg, Gert, *Dom von Florenz*, Berlin 1974

Machu Picchu

— Bingham, Alfred M., *Explorer of Machu Picchu: Portrait of Hiram Bingham*, Chestnut Hill, Mass. 1999

— Bingham, Hiram, *Lost City of the Incas: The Story of Machu Picchu and its Builders*, Westport, Conn. 1981

— Hemming, John, *Machu Picchu*, New York 1981

The Medieval Hospital Hôtel-Dieu in Beaune

— Flanagan, Sabine, *Hildegard of Bingen, 1098–1179: A Visionary Life*, London/New York 1998

— Gunn, Peter, *Burgundy: Landscape with Figures*, London 1976

— Speaight, Robert, *The Companion Guide to Burgundy*, Woodbridge/Rochester, New York 1996

Oxford University: One of the Intellectual Centers of England

— Halliday, Tony, *Oxford*, Boston 1997

— *Interventions in Historic Centres: The Buildings of Magdalen College, Oxford*, London 1993

— *Oxford Yesterday and Today*, Stroud 1997

— Tyack, Geoffrey, *Oxford: An Architectural History Guide*, Oxford/New York 1998

Moscow and the Kremlin

— Ascher, Abraham, *The Kremlin*, New York 1972

— Burian, Jiri, *The Kremlin of Moscow*, London 1977

— Duncan, David Douglas, *Great Treasures of the Kremlin*, New York 1979

— Rodimtseva, Irina Aleksandrovna, *The Kremlin and its Treasures*, New York 1987

Rome and St Peter's Cathedral

— Blunt, Anthony, *Guide to Baroque Rome*, London/New York 1982

— Di Federico, Frank R., *The Mosaics of Saint Peter's*, University Park, Pennsylvania 1983

— Jung-Iglessis, E. M., *St Peter's*, Florence/New York 1980

— Rice, Louise, *The Altars and Altarpieces of New St Peter's: Outfitting the Basilica*, Cambridge/New York 1997

The Château of Chambord in the Loire Valley

— Binney, Marcus, *Chateaux of the Loire*, San Francisco 1992

— Eperon, Arthur, *The Loire Valley*, Lincolnwood, Illinois 1994

— Hibbert, Christopher, *Chateaux of the Loire*, New York 1972

— Pozzoli, Milena Ercole, *Castles of the Loire*, New York 1997

King Philip II of Spain and El Escorial

— Kamen, Henry Arthur Francis, *Philip of Spain*, New Haven, Conn. 1997

— Kubler, George, *Building the Escorial*, Princeton, New Jersey 1982

— Parker, Geoffrey, *Philip II*, Chicago 1995

— Williamson-Serra, Herbert William, *The Eighth Wonder of the World: The Monastery of El Escorial and the Prince's Lodge*, Madrid/New York 1953

The Country Residence "La Rotonda," near Vicenza

— Boucher, Bruce, *Andrea Palladio: The Architect in his Time*, New York 1998

— Constant, Caroline, *The Palladio Guide*, New York 1993

— Parissien, Steve, *Palladian Style*, London 1994

— Puppi, Lionello, *Andrea Palladio: The Complete Works*, New York 1986

— Wolf, Reinhart, *Villas of the Veneto*, New York 1988

Il Gesù, the Jesuit Church in Rome

— Brodrick, James, *Saint Ignatius Loyola: The Pilgrim Years, 1491–1538*, San Francisco 1988

— Brodrick, James, *The Origin of the Jesuits*, Chicago 1997

— *Ignatius of Loyola: Personal Writings*,
London/New York 1996

— Tellecha Idigoras, Jose Ignacio, *Ignatius of Loyola:
The Pilgrim Saint*, Chicago 1994

A Dream in Marble: The Taj Mahal

— Havell, E. B., *Indian Architecture*, London 1927

— Lall, J. S., *Taj Mahal and the Saga of the Great
Mogals*, Delhi 1994

— Non, Jean-Louis, *Taj Mahal*, New York 1993

Taj Mahal: The Illuminated Tomb,
Cambridge/Seattle 1989

The Winter Palace of the Dalai Lama

— Alexander, Andre, *The Old City of Lhasa*, Berlin
1998

— Brignoli, Frank J., *Lhasa, Tibet's Forbidden City*,
Hong Kong 1987

— David-Neel, Alexandra, *My Journey to Lhasa*,
Boston 1993

— Guise, Anthony (ed.), *The Potala of Tibet*, London
1988

The Royal Palace of Versailles

— Babelon, Jean Pierre, *Versailles: Absolutism and
Harmony*, New York 1998

— Lablande, Pierre-André, *The Gardens of Versailles*,
London 1995

— Mitford, Nancy, *The Sun King*,
London/New York 1994

— Sturdy, David J., *Louis XIV*, New York 1998

— Walter, G., *Louis XIV's Versailles*, London 1986

Final Resting Place of Heroes: St Paul's
Cathedral in London

— Hart, Vaughan, *St Paul's Cathedral*, London 1995

— Gray, Donald D., *Christopher Wren and St Paul's
Cathedral*, Minneapolis 1982

— Porter, Darwin and Danforth Prince, *London*,
New York 1998

— Yale, Pat, *London*, Hawthorn 1998

The Imperial Palace in Peking

— Beguin, Gilles, *The Forbidden City: Center of
Imperial China*, New York 1997

— Holdsworth, May, *The Forbidden City*, New York
1998

— *Palaces of the Forbidden City*, New York 1984

— Polo, Marco, *The Travels of Marco Polo*, New York
1993

The Spanish Steps in Rome

— Elling, Christian, *Rome: The Biography of its
Architecture from Bernini to Thorvaldsen*,
Tübingen 1975

— Fokker, Timon Henricus, *Roman Baroque Art. The
History of a Style*, New York 1972

— Magnuson, Torgil, *Rome in the Age of Bernini*, 2
volumes, Stockholm/Atlantic Highlands, New
Jersey 1982–1986

Prince Eugene and the Upper Belvedere in
Vienna

— Kraft, Maria, *The Imperial Vienna*, Vienna 1990

— Kraus, Wolfgang, *The Palaces of Vienna*, New York
1993

— McKay, Derek, *Prince Eugene of Savoy*, London
1977

— Steiner, Dietmar, *Architecture in Vienna*, Vienna
1990

Dominikus Zimmermann and the Wies Church

— Bauer, Hermann, *Johann Baptist und Dominikus
Zimmermann*, Regensburg 1985

— Harries, Karsten, *The Bavarian Rococo Church*,
New Haven, Conn. 1983

— Hitchcock, Henry Russell, *German Rococo:
The Zimmermann Brothers*, London 1968

— Schnell, Hugo, *Die Wies, Wallfahrtskirche zum
Gegeißelten Heiland*, Munich/Zurich 1979

The Wise Man of Monticello

— Jefferson, Thomas: *Life and Selected Writings of
Thomas Jefferson*, New York 1944

— Lautman, Robert C., *Thomas Jefferson's
Monticello*, New York 1997

— McLaughlin, Jack, *Jefferson and Monticello: The
Biography of a Builder*, New York 1988

— Padover, Saul Kussiel, *Thomas Jefferson and the
Foundations of American Freedom*, Princeton, New
Jersey 1965

— Stein, Susan, *The Worlds of Thomas Jefferson at
Monticello*, New York 1993

The Capitol in Washington, D.C.

— Bowling, Kenneth R., *Creating the Federal City,
1774–1800*, Washington, DC 1994

— Bushong, William, *Uncle Sam's Architects: Builders
of the Capitol*, Washington, DC 1994

— Maroon, Fred J., *The United States Capitol*, New
York 1993

— *The United States Capitol: Designing and
Decorating a National Icon*, Athens, Ohio 1999

Napoleon and the Arc de Triomphe de l'Etoile

— Chandler, David G. (ed.), *On the Napoleonic Wars*,
London 1999

— Dufraisse, Roger, *Napoleon*, New York 1992

— Luvaas, Jay (ed.), *Napoleon on the Art of War*,
New York 1999

— Remarque, Erich Maria, *Arc of Triumph*,
New York 1998

The Houses of Parliament

— Boyne, Sir Harry, *The Houses of Parliament*,
London 1981

— Fell, Bryan H., *The Houses of Parliament*,
London 1994

— Woolf, Virginia, *The London Scene*,
New York 1982

The Old Symbol of a New City: Trinity Church

— Beauvoir, Simone de, *America Day by Day*,
Berkeley 1999

— Gambee, Robert, *Wall Street: Financial Capital*,
New York 1999

— Geisst, Charles R., *Wall Street: A History*, New York
1997

— Janowitz, Tama, *Slaves of New York*, New York 1986

— Merriam, Dena, *Trinity: A Church, a Parish, a
People*, New York 1996

Neuschwanstein Castle and Its Tragic King

— Burg, Katerina von, *Ludwig II of Bavaria: The Man
and the Mystery*, Windsor 1989

— King, Greg, *The Mad King: The Life and Times of
Ludwig II of Bavaria*, Secaucus, New Jersey 1996

— McIntosh, Christopher, *The Swan King, Ludwig II
of Bavaria*, London 1982

— Sailer, Anton, *Castles, Mystery, and Music:
The Legend of Ludwig II*, Munich 1983

The Royal Greenhouses of Laeken

— Blyth, Derek, *Brussels*, London 1993

— Goedleven, Edgard, *The Royal Greenhouses of
Laeken*, Tielt/Brussels 1989

— McDonald, George, *Brussels*, London/Boston 1997

The Statue of Liberty

— Bartholdi, Frederic Auguste, *The Statue of Liberty Enlightening the World*, New York 1984

— Blumberg, Barabara, *Celebrating the Immigrant: An Administrative History of the Statue of Liberty National Monument*, Boston 1985

— Dolkart, Andrew, *Guide to New York City Landmarks*, Washington, DC 1998

— Goodman, Roger B., *The Statue of Liberty and Ellis Island*, Union, New Jersey 1990

— Hayden, Richard Seth, *Restoring the Statue of Liberty*, New York 1986

The Burgtheater in Vienna

— Häussermann, Ernst, *Wiener Burgtheater*, Vienna 1975

— Link, Dorothea, *The National Court Theatre in Mozart's Vienna*, Oxford 1998

— Steiner, Dietmar, *Architecture in Vienna*, Vienna 1990

— Yates, W. E., *Schnitzler, Hofmannsthal, and the Austrian Theatre*, New Haven, Conn. 1992

Gaudí and the Sagrada Familia

— Bassegoda Nonell, Juan, *Antonio Gaudí*, New York 1998

— Burry, Mark, *Expiatory Church of the Sagrada Familia*, London 1993

— Collins, George Roseborough, *The Designs and Drawings of Antonio Gaudí*, Princeton 1983

— Fahr-Becker, Gabriele, *Antoni Gaudí: Architecture in Barcelona*, Woodbury, New York 1985

— Permanyer, L., *Gaudí of Barcelona*, New York 1997

The Berlin Reichstag

— Christo: *The Reichstag and Urban Projects*, Munich/New York 1993

— Foster, Norman, *Rebuilding the Reichstag*, Woodstock, New York 1999

— Tucker, James, *Blaze of Riot*, London 1979

The Eiffel Tower in Paris

— *Architectural Guide to the Eiffel Tower*, Monticello, Illinois 1981

— Harriss, Joseph, *The Eiffel Tower: Symbol of an Age*, London 1976

— Loyrette, Henri, *Gustave Eiffel*, New York 1985

— Sagan, Françoise, *The Eiffel Tower: A Centenary Celebration, 1889–1989*, New York 1989

Moscow and its GUM Department Store

— Anisimov, A.V., *Architectural Guide to Moscow*, Amsterdam 1992

— Murrell, Kathleen Berton, *Moscow: an Architectural History*, London/New York 1990

— Rice, Christopher, *Moscow*, New York 1998

The Djenné Mosque

— Ajayi, J. F. A. and M. Crowder (eds.), *History of West Africa*, 2 volumes, Harlow 1987

— Lamb, David, *The Africans*, New York 1987

— Lynch, Hollis (ed.), *Black Africa*, New York 1973

— Zoghby, Samir M., *Islam in Sub-Saharan Africa*, Washington, DC 1978

The Gellert Spa in Budapest

— Enyedi, Gyorgy, *Budapest, a Central European Capital*, London/New York 1992

— Sarhozi, Matyas, *Budapest*, Oxford/Santa Barbara, California 1997

— Vorga, Domohos, *Budapest*, Woodstock, New York 1985

The Center for Anthroposophy: Rudolph Steiner's Goetheanum

— Bayes, Kenneth, *Living Architecture*, Edinburgh 1994

— *In Partnership with Nature*, Wyoming 1981

— Steiner, Rudolf, *Der Baugedanke des Goetheanum*, Dornach 1932

The Quintessence of Functionalism: the Bauhaus in Dessau

— Forgacs, Eva, *The Bauhaus Idea and Bauhaus Politics*, Budapest/New York 1995

— Hochman, Elaine S., *Bauhaus: Crucible of Modernism*, New York 1997

— Kentgens-Craig, Margret, *The Bauhaus and America*, Cambridge, Mass. 1999

— Sharp, Dennis, *Bauhaus, Dessau: Walter Gropius*, London 1993

The Empire State Building in New York

— Langer, Freddy, *Lewis W. Hine: The Empire State Building*, Munich/London/New York 1998

— Landau, Sarah Bradford, *Rise of the New York Skyscraper, 1865–1913*, New Haven, Conn. 1996

— Reynolds, Donald M., *The Architecture of New York City*, New York 1994

— Tauranac, John, *The Empire State Building: The Making of a Landmark*, New York 1996

The Golden Gate Bridge

— Dillon, Richard H., *High Steel: Building the Bridges across San Francisco Bay*, Millbrae, California 1979

— McGrew, Patrick, *Landmarks of San Francisco*, New York 1991

— Van der Zee, John, *The Gate: The True Story of the Design and Construction of the Golden Gate Bridge*, New York 1986

Frank Lloyd Wright and Fallingwater

— Costantino, Maria, *The Life and Works of Frank Lloyd Wright*, Philadelphia 1998

— Kaufmann, Edward, jr., *Fallingwater. A Frank Lloyd Wright Country House*, New York 1986

— Mc Carter, Robert, *Fallingwater—Frank Lloyd Wright*, London 1994

— Treiber, Daniel, *Frank Lloyd Wright*, London/New York 1995

The Pilgrimage Church Notre Dame du Haut near Ronchamp

— Brooks, H. Allen, *Le Corbusier's Formative Years*, Chicago 1997

— Burri, Rene, *Le Corbusier: Moments in the Life of a Great Architect*, Basel/Boston 1999

— Gans, Deborah, *The Le Corbusier Guide*, New York 1998

— Stoller, Ezra, *The Chapel at Ronchamp*, New York 1999

The Atomium

— Blyth, Derek, *Brussels*, London 1993

— McDonald, George, *Brussels*, London/Boston 1997

The Solomon R. Guggenheim Museum in New York

— Barnett, Vivian Endicott, *Hundred Works by Modern Masters from the Guggenheim Museum*, New York 1984

— Krens, Thomas: *Masterpieces from the Guggenheim*, New York 1991

— Wright, Frank Lloyd, *Frank Lloyd Wright, the Guggenheim Correspondence*, Fresno, California 1986

Brazil's Parliament Building in the Jungle

— Braga, Andrea de Costa, *Guia de urbansimo: arquitetura e arte de Brasilia*, Brasilia 1997

— Holston, James, *The Modernist City: An Anthropological Critique of Brasilia*, Chicago 1989

— Shoumatoff, Alex, *The Capital of Hope: Brasilia and its People*, New York 1990

The Sydney Opera House

— Beaume, M., *The Sydney Opera House Affair*, Melbourne 1968

— Drew, Philip, *Sydney Opera House: Jorn Utzon*, London 1995

— Hubble, Ava, *More than an Opera House*, Sydney/New York 1983

— Sykes, Jill, *Sydney Opera House from the outside in*, Pymble, Australia 1993

The Olympic Park in Munich

— Beust, Joachim, *Munich*, Boston 1993

— Dheus, Egon, *Olympiastadt München*, Stuttgart 1972

— Knight, Theodore, *The Olympic Games*, San Diego 1991

The Centre Pompidou in Paris

— Bragstad, Jeremiah O., *Pompidou Center*, Paris 1983

— Bordaz, Robert, *Le Centre Pompidou: une nouvelle culture*, Paris 1977

— Silver, Nathan, *The Making of Beaubourg: A Building Biography of the Centre Pompidou*, Cambridge, Mass. 1994

Niki de Saint Phalle's Tarot Garden

— Mock, Jean Yves, *Niki de Saint-Phalle: exposition retrospective*, Paris 1980

— Saint-Phalle, Niki de, *Il Giardino dei Tarocchi*, Bern 1997

— Saint-Phalle, Niki de, *Niki de Saint-Phalle, Insider, Outsider*, La Jolla, California 1998

The Louvre Pyramid

— Archimbaud, Nicholas d', *Louvre: Portrait of a Museum*, New York 1998

— Bres-Bautier, Genevieve, *The Architecture of the Louvre*, London 1995

— Cannell, Michael T., *I. M. Pei: Mandarin of Modernism*, New York 1995

— Gleininger, Andrea, *Paris: Contemporary Architecture*, Munich/New York 1997

— Wiseman, Carter, *I. M. Pei: A Profile in American Architecture*, New York 1990

The Guggenheim Museum in Bilbao

— Bruggen, Coosje van, *Frank O'Gehry: Guggenheim Museum Bilbao*, New York 1997

— Friedman, Mildred (ed.), *Gehry Talks: Architecture and Process*, New York 1999

— *Museo Guggenheim Bilbao: estudio de viabilidad*, Bilbao 1992

The Millennium Tower: Looking Toward the Future

— Foster, Norman, *Norman Foster Sketch Book*, Basel/Boston 1993

— Pawley, Martin, *Norman Foster: A Global Architecture*, New York 1999

— Treiber, Daniel, *Norman Foster*, London/New York 1995

Photo Credits

Numbers refer to page numbers of illustrations

Every effort has been made by the Publisher to acknowledge all sources and copyright holders. In the event of any copyright holder being inadvertently omitted, please contact the Publisher directly.

Abbé René Bolle-Reddat, Ronchamp: 161 (bottom)

Aga Khan Visual Archives, MIT (Photo: Labelle Prussin, 1983): 146 (center)

all over: Brooke, Marcus 56 (top), 57 (top) and p. 5, 90 (top), 123 (top); Grosskopf, Rainer 129 (top); Häusler, Nicole 64 (top); Hoenig, Tom 124 (top); Hollweck, Ferdinand 106 (top), 112 (top), 170 (top); JBE Photo 61 (2), 64 (top), 65 (top and p. 5), 65 (bottom left), 139 (top); Link 104 (bottom); Löhr, Dieter 47 (top) and p. 4; Müller, Ralf 151 (top); Schinner, Dieter 116 (top), 117 (top); Scholz, Werner 105 (top, bottom right); Strigl, Egmont 72 (top), 73 (top); Tölle, Frank 128 (top) and p. 6; Voss, Heinrich 126 (top)

Archiv für Kunst und Geschichte, Berlin: 120 (right), 123 (bottom), 126 (bottom), 127 (bottom)

Artothek/Blauel, Joachim: 21 (bottom)

Artway Editions: 62 (top)

Bavaria/The Telegraph: 42/43

Beron, Alfred: 52 (bottom left)

Bildarchiv Monheim, Meerbusch: 10/11 (top), 70 (bottom)

Bildarchiv Preußischer Kulturbesitz, Berlin: 122 (right), 140 (center)

Bilderberg/Games, Werner: 160 (top); Zuder, Samuel 136 (bottom)

'Castel del Monte', Heinz Götze, Munich · London · New York, 1998, p. 138: 44 (bottom left)

Cattin, Eric: 66 (top, bottom), 67 (top)

Champollion, Hervé: 12/13, 19 (bottom, center), 21 (top), 22 (top) and p. 4, 22/23, 70 (top), 89 (top, bottom) and p. 5, 161 (top)

Contur, Cologne/Reinhard Görner: 141 (top)

'Mummies: Life after Death in Ancient Egypt', Renate Germer, Munich · New York 1997, p. 106: 12 (bottom left)

Davies, Richard: 180/181

Deutsches Museum, Munich 30 (bottom)

'Die Götter des Himalaya', Munich 1989, p. 8: 106 (bottom)

'Die Marienburg im 19. Jahrhundert', Hartmut Boockmann, Frankfurt am Main 1982, ill. 50: 77 (bottom right)

'Durch den Kreml', Moscow 1970, p. 246: 92 (bottom)

© English Heritage Photo Library: 10 (bottom left)

Frei, Franz Marc: 33 (bottom), 52 (top), 53 (bottom left), 58 (top) and p. 5, 71, 73 (bottom), 114 (top), 115 (bottom), 149 (bottom), 154 (top) and p.7, 164 (center) and p. 7, 165, 171 (bottom), 177 (top) and p. 7, 178 (center)

Frikha, Abdelaziz: 42 (top)

Garff, Michael, Bethel/CT: 134 (top)

Germanisches Nationalmuseum, Nuremberg: 77 (bottom left)

Gilbert, Dennis/View 141: (bottom)

Girard, v.: 20 (top) and p. 4

Goetheanum © Verlag am Goetheanum, Dornach: 151 (bottom left)

Götze, Heinz: 74/75 (3)

Greenhaus, Ben, Courtesy of the Solomon R. Guggenheim Museum, New York: 164 (bottom)

Hackenberg, Rainer 46 (top, bottom), 47 (bottom)

Hammel, Lisa, Annet van der Voort: 53 (bottom right)

Hartmann, Herbert: 35 (bottom), 69, 84 (top), 115 (top), 118 (top), 119 (top), 125 (bottom), 143 (top), 173 (bottom right), 177 (center)

Heald, David, ©The Solomon R. Guggenheim Foundation, New York: 164 (top)

Herfurth, Dietrich: 102 (top) and p. 5, 103 (bottom right)

Hucek, Miroslav, Barbara Hucková: 52 (bottom)

Courtesy of the Thomas Jefferson Memorial Foundation Inc.: 121 (bottom)

Kaplan, Peter: 154 (bottom)

Kiedrowski, Rainer: 13 (bottom), 15 (top), 51 (top, bottom), 59 (top), 60 (top), 79 (2), 104 (top) and p. 6, 120 (top), 171 (top) and p. 7

Kienberger, Klaus and Wilhelm: 119 (bottom)

'L'Art de l'Ingenieur', Paris 1998, p. 163: 142 (bottom)

Laif, Cologne: Brunner, Ralf 135 (bottom); Gaultier 138 (bottom); Gebhard, Peter 135 (top) and p. 6; Gonzalez, Miquel 25 (2), 127 (top); Hahn, Paul 67 (bottom), 137 (top), 162/163 (4) and p. 7; Huber, Gernot 98 (top), 99 (bottom), 148 (bottom) and p. 7, 149 (top); Krause, Axel 14 (top, center), 83 (bottom); Krinitz, Hartmut 125 (top), 176 (top); Linke, Manfred 97 (left, bottom), 166/167, 167 (bottom); Moleres, Fernando 178 (bottom), 179 (top) and p. 7; Neumann, Anna 80 (top), 81 (right), 148 (top); Piepenburg, C. 156 (bottom); Richardson, Fidel 179 (bottom); Specht, Heiko 59 (bottom); Tavernier 172 (bottom right); Ebert, Thomas 173 (top); Turemis, Mürat 107 (2); Zanettini, F. 34 (top) and p. 4, 36 (top), 94 (top), 126 (center)

Länderpress, Mainz: 45 (bottom)

Liese, Knut: 38/39 (3), 48 (top, bottom), 109 (center, bottom), 139 (bottom), 173 (bottom left)

Look, Munich: Dressler, Hauke 168 (bottom); Galli, Max 37 (bottom), 68 (top) and p. 5; Greune, Jan 26 (top) and p. 4, 27 (top), 28 (center), 40 (top, bottom), 41 (top), 44 (bottom right), 45 (top) and p. 4; Heeb, Christian 96 (top), 111 (top and p. 6), 111 (bottom), 121 (top), 122 (top) and p. 4, 129 (bottom), 136 (top), 155, 157 (bottom); Johaentges, Karl 113 (top), 177 (bottom); Kreder, Katja, 146 (top), 147 (2); Martini, Rainer 24 (top), 138 (top) and p. 6, 142 (top) and p. 6, 156 (top), 157 (top) and p. 7; Naundorf, Cathleen 166 (top); Pompe, Ingolf 10 (top) and p. 4; Richter, Jürgen 31 (top), 85 (top and p. 5), 85 (bottom), 99 (top), 178 (top); Seer, Ulli 130 (top), 168 (top), 169 (top); Werner, Florian 131 (right) and p. 6; Wiesmeier, Uli 92 (top); Wothe, Konrad 57 (bottom), 82 (top), 113 (bottom)

Mangold, Guido: 48/49, 132 (top), 132/133 and p. 6, 133 (bottom)

Meisel, Rudi: 140 (top)

'Merian' 4, 1990, p. 41: 68 (bottom)

Mesa Verde, National Parc Museum: 72 (bottom) and p. 5

Neumeister, Werner: 27 (bottom left), 41 (bottom left, right), 50 (top), 53 (top), 54 (bottom), 55, 81 (bottom), 86 (top), 91 (2), 93 (2), 94 (bottom), 95 (top) and p. 5, 97 (top right), 100/101 (2), 103 (top, bottom left), 109 (top), 130 (right), 131 (left), 143 (bottom), 144 (top) and p. 7, 145 (2), 150 (top), 151 (bottom right), 152 (bottom), 152 (top), 153 (bottom), 161 (center), 172 (top)

'Olympia und seine Bauten', Mallwitz A., Munich 1972: 18 (bottom), 19 (top)

'Otl Aicher zum 75. Geburtstag', exhibition catalogue Hochschule für Gestaltung, Ulm, Stadthaus Ulm, 1998, p. 44: 170 (bottom)

'Passagen', Johann Friedrich Geist, Munich 1982, ill. 160: 144 (bottom)

Picture Press: 156 (bottom)

Reichold, Klaus: 174/175 (5)

Richner, Werner: 63 (top, bottom)

Riestra, Pablo de la: 76 (bottom)

Photo Rietmann, © Verlag am Goetheanum, Dornach: 150 (bottom)

Rocheleau, Paul, Photographer, Canaan, Richmond/MA: 158/159 (4) and p. 7

Süddeutscher Verlag Bilderdienst, Munich: 140 (bottom)

Thiele, Klaus: 12 (top left), 44 (top) and p. 4, 54 (top), 76 (top), 77 (top), 152/153

Thiem, Eberhard/Lotos Film: 24 (bottom), 26 (bottom), 32 (bottom), 37 (top)

Thomas, Martin: 3, 18 (top), 30 (top) and p. 4, 32 (top), 33 (top), 35 (top), 82/83 and p. 5, 87 (top), 95 (bottom), 110 (top)

Tiziou, Michel: 88 (top)

Veaux, Amélie, La Licorne Bleue. 21150 Flavigny: 62 (bottom)

Weber, Michael: 160 (bottom) and p. 4, 17, 28 (top), 29 (top)

'Weltgeschichte der Architektur, Rom', Stuttgart 1987: 34 (bottom)

Werner, Heike: 15 (bottom), 27 (bottom right), 31 (bottom), 65 (bottom right)

WFVV: 117 (bottom) and p. 6

ZEFA/Photo Researcher: 10 (bottom right)

Guardi, Franceso, *View of the Doge's Palace and the Promenade*, 1770, London, National Gallery: 78 (top)

After Pierre Patel, *The Castle around 1668*, Museum Versailles, AKG: 108 (top)

Front cover: Eiffel Tower, photo: Herbert Hartmann

from top to bottom: Sydney Opera House, photo:
Clemens Emmler/Laif; Neuschwanstein castle, photo:
Florian Werner/Look; Parthenon, Athens, photo: Hervé
Champollion; Taj Mahal, Agra, photo: Werner Scholz/all over;
Pyramids, Giza, photo: Hervé Champollion; Colosseum,
Rome, photo: Martin Thomas

Back cover: Statue of Liberty, New York, photo:
Peter Gebhard/Laif

Frontispiece: The Great Wall of China, photo: Martin Thomas

Photo credits: see page 190

Library of Congress Catalog Card Number: 99-65365

© Prestel Verlag, Munich · London· New York, 1999

© of works illustrated by the architects, their heirs or
assigns, with the exception of works by: Niki de Saint-Phalle,
Frank Lloyd Wright by VG Bild-Kunst, Bonn 1999;
Le Corbusier by FLC/VG Bild-Kunst, Bonn 1999.

Prestel Verlag

Mandlstrasse 26 · 80802 Munich
Tel. (089) 381709-0, Fax (089) 381709-35;

16 West 22nd Street · New York, NY 10010
Tel. (212) 627-8199, Fax (212) 627-9866;

4 Bloomsbury Place · London WC1A 2QA
Tel. (0171) 323 5004, Fax (0171) 636 8004

Prestel books are available worldwide.
Please contact your nearest bookseller
or write to any of the above adresses for
details concerning your local distributor.

Translated from the German by Jacqueline Guigui-Stolberg
and Mariana Schroeder

Edited by Christopher Wynne

Production coordination by Claudia Hellmann

Designed and Typeset by WIGEL

Cover design by Iris von Hoesslin

Lithography by ReproLine, Munich

Printed and bound by Passavia Druckservice, Passau

Printed in Germany
Paper: Galerie Art Silk 150g/m² by Schneidersöhne

ISBN 3-7913-2150-1 (English edition)
ISBN 3-7913-2181-1 (German edition)